BUCKEYE
REFLECTIONS

LEGENDARY MOMENTS FROM
OHIO STATE FOOTBALL

Jack Park and Maureen Zappala

Introduction by Archie, Ray and Duncan Griffin
Foreword by Luke Fickell, Ryan Miller and Mike Vrabel

Production director and interior design: Gary Hoffman
Technical editor: Jeff Rapp
Readability editor: Jane Park
Cover design: Denise Hollerich
Illustrations: Tom Hayes
Picture of Griffin brothers on back cover: Jim Davidson
Picture of Vrable, Fickell and Miller on back cover: Ryan Miller
SAN: 297-6730

Publisher's Cataloging-in-Publication data

Names: Park, Jack L., author. | Zappala, Maureen, author. | Griffin, Archie, contributor. |
Griffin, Duncan, contributor. | Griffin, Raymond, contributor. | Vrabel, Mike, contributor. |
Fickell, Luke, contributor. | Miller, Ryan, 1974-, contributor.
Title: Buckeye reflections : legendary moments from Ohio State football / by Jack Park
and Maureen Zappala ; Introduction by Archie, Duncan and Ray Griffin ; Foreword by
Mike Vrabel, Luke Fickell and Ryan Miller.
Description: Columbus, OH: Lexington Press, 2017.
Identifiers: ISBN 978-1-881462-31-6
Subjects: LCSH Ohio State University—Football—History. | Ohio State Buckeyes
(Football team)—History. | BISAC SPORTS & RECREATION / Football
Classification: LCC GV958.O35 .Z37 B83 2017 | DDC 796.332/63/0977157—dc23

Lexington Press
2439 Andover Road * Columbus, Ohio 43221
Printed in the United States of America

Maureen Zappala Dedication

I dedicate my efforts in co-writing this book to the memory of my parents, Ann and Jack Burns. They cultivated in me three things: A love of sports (I grew up loving the New York Mets, Jets, Nets and Knicks), a love of books (like my Dad, I'm a voracious reader) and a love of learning (college was always the goal). It was their unwavering belief that I could be whatever I wanted to be that propelled me on a path to pursue, first engineering, and now writing and speaking. Mom and Dad, it's been a wild ride. If you could see me now, I hope you'd be proud.

Jack Park Dedication

My wonderful parents, Amelia and Emmett Park, were avid Ohio State fans who got me hooked on the Buckeyes at a very young age. They taught me the value of hard work, dedication to excellence, caring for others, and friendships. Over the years they helped me understand that football is a splendid metaphor for things in life that are far more important than football itself — our country, our fellow Americans, our customers and clients, and most of all our families and friends. Thank you, Mom and Dad. I was most fortunate to have you as parents.

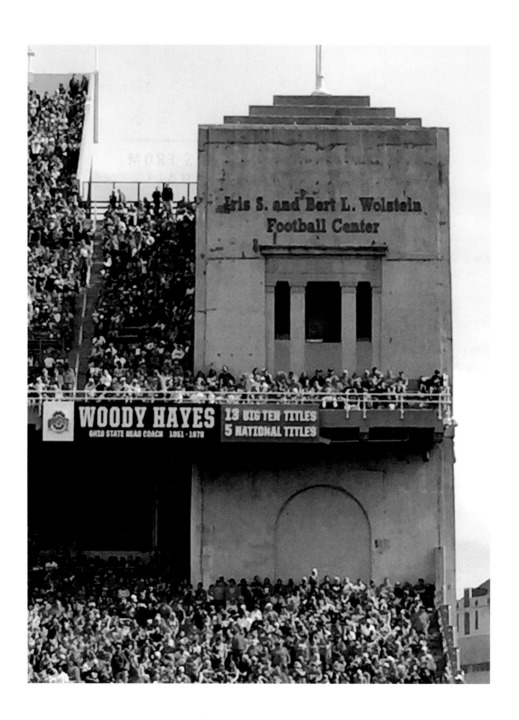

BUCKEYE
REFLECTIONS

LEGENDARY MOMENTS FROM OHIO STATE FOOTBALL

Contents

Archie Griffin
Ray Griffin
Duncan Griffin

"It was a joy to play football at Ohio State with my brothers."

We three experienced that joy, as we reflect back to our years on the gridiron during a heyday of Ohio State football. From 1972 through 1978, one or more of us were privileged to wear the Scarlet and Gray. We all played on Big 10 Championship teams, we were awarded a total of 12 football letters, and we are very grateful for our Ohio State football experiences. Without it, we would not be the men we are today. Ohio State helped build a life buoyed by the three-fold foundation of **family, football**, and **future**.

Growing up in Columbus, we were a very athletic **family** of 10 — seven brothers, a sister, and two wonderful parents. Sports was the fiber of our family. All seven brothers played college football, and our sister excelled in track and field. For the three of us, going to Ohio State allowed our parents to watch us without having to split their loyalty or travel a great distance. When a coach from Nebraska tried to recruit one of us, our dad told him, "I like to watch my boys play football, and if

From left: Archie, Ray and Duncan Griffin *Courtesy Ohio State University Photo Archives*

they're at Ohio State, we get the chance to do it more often." We're glad it worked out. Playing together on the same team was fun, challenging and inspiring. We wanted to make each other proud.

Football at Ohio State is a rich and exciting world that vibrates with energy and pride. We were part of a legacy of outstanding players, amazing statistics and impressive seasons. During our combined seven seasons, Ohio State captured six Big Ten titles. Our seven year record was 65-14-3. It was our privilege to play under the leadership of Woody Hayes, one of college football's all-time finest coaches. He was the architect of some incredible teams, and he recruited great players with varied backgrounds who came together and made it happen. Coach Hayes was a terrific coach, but an even better person. He was wise and funny, and he would dig into his own pocket to help others. We may not have always agreed with him, but we always respected his opinion and knew he always had our best interests at heart.

Coach Hayes loved his players, and he taught us his philosophy of "Paying Forward." We learned that "You can seldom pay back the good that someone has done for you, but you can always pay forward by helping someone else or being involved in your community." That inspired many of his players to get involved with paying forward, and today many continue to be very active with charitable organizations. Coach Hayes had a powerful impact on us. The Archie and Bonita Griffin Foundation and the Archie Griffin Scholarship Fund are direct results of Woody's influence to pay it forward. Others gave *us* scholarships — we want to pass it on and pay it forward.

Ohio State carved out an amazing **future** for us, one that we are so grateful to live. The opportunities that opened up as a result of our years at Ohio State were spectacular! We each received college degrees, two of us played professional football, and we all three moved on to rewarding careers. We knew that football was a means to an end, not just an end in itself. It taught us how to get back up after falling down — again and again. We learned to stand up for what was right, go after what we wanted, and build great relationships along the way. We experienced how to play as a team and get along with others from different backgrounds. We gained confidence and we crystallized our priorities.

Everyone has a story, and The Ohio State University is a huge part of ours. We were blessed to be born to fantastic parents, have wonderful siblings, and be raised in the shadow of Ohio Stadium. We are so grateful to have been in the right place at the right time, to play with incredibly talented teammates, and be part of a most successful period in Ohio State football.

We know you will enjoy reading and reminiscing through *Buckeye Reflections*. Maureen and Jack have shared many little known happenings from all periods of our great tradition. It will stir your Buckeye pride as you learn about many of the events that have helped made Ohio State one of our nation's most extraordinary universities. Go Bucks!

Luke Fickell
Ryan Miller
Mike Vrabel

Second and Seven Foundation

When facing a tough decision, most people struggle with making the right choice. What if, instead, they focused on making the choice right? When we were being recruited by Coach John Cooper to play at Ohio State, we realized the gravity of the decision we were facing. Picking a college team was going to be a major turning point in our lives, and we felt the pressure to make a right choice.

At most schools, the head coach met with us one-on-one to present a scholarship offer and ask for our reaction. Ohio State's John Cooper was different. At a 1992 luncheon attended by many Ohio State recruits, Cooper stood up and said "Everything happens for a reason. Every one of you in this room is here for a reason. I believe the reason is to win the Rose Bowl, and continue the pride of Ohio State football." It was a powerful moment and we felt his excitement.

Cooper said, "We've got the best high school football players in the Midwest sitting here in this room. Korey Stringer, you're the best offensive lineman in the history of Ohio high school football. Stand up, and show everyone how big you are. Now, can you look me in the eye right now and tell me you want to be a Buckeye? Because I need you!" Korey says with fiery passion, "Coach, I'M COMING TO OHIO STATE!" The recruits begin cheering!

From left: Luke Fickell, Ryan Miller and Mike Vrabel. *Courtesy Ohio State University Photo Archives*

Cooper then said, "Luke Fickell, you stand up! You grew up in the shadows of Ohio Stadium. Can you tell me you're going to be a Buckeye and play here?" Fickell says yes and we all cheer. One by one, Cooper asks each of us if we're going to be a Buckeye, and everyone is saying yes! It was electric! Mike Vrabel had the same experience in 1993.

The decision to attend Ohio State was a game changer for each of us. We didn't know if it was the right decision, although it did feel right in the moment, but we were committed to making the decision right. It worked out very well. We had a great run at Ohio State, and it put us on the path to fabulous things later on in our lives.

Buckeye Reflections is a collection of stories of people who ran a path that includes a connection with The Ohio State University. Many of them may not have known if they were making a right choice, but they went on to make the choice right. Whatever path they chose became the path they ran. That's how you do life. When we started our non-profit organization, The 2nd and 7 Foundation, where we read and donate books to 2nd grade kids all over the country, we tell them that same thing. Whatever your path, you can choose to make your path right. We believe that our motto "Tackle Illiteracy" is one way to make the path right.

Coach Jim Tressel once said that the No.1 fundamental that he looked for in a football player was their ability to run. He said, "If you can't run, you simply can't play at the collegiate level. Plain and simple." He's an avid reader, and he added "The No.1 fundamental in life is reading. If you can't read, life is going to be an uphill battle at best. Plain and simple." He echoes our commitment to reading, and shares with us a rich connection to The Ohio State University.

We're very honored to write the Foreword for *Buckeye Reflections*. We've known Jack Park, the master Ohio State storyteller for many years, and we are huge fans of his work. Our new friend Maureen Zappala is a talented and spirited woman who, though a Notre Dame graduate, has become a Buckeye fan after living in Ohio for over 34 years. We hope that reading these stories will strengthen your own rich connection to Ohio State, and see how your path…the path you run…is the path you've made right. Go Bucks!

Acknowledgements

Buckeye Reflections has been a team effort. We are genuinely grateful for the guidance and support of so many people who offered their expertise, advice and time to craft this unique book that celebrates the distinguished tradition of Ohio State football.

Deep gratitude goes to long-time friend and business associate Gary Hoffman, who did the interior design. Gary's ideas are always appreciated and his work is simply the best.

Jack and Maureen prior to the 2016 Ohio State-Michigan game. *Courtesy Gary Housteau*

We were privileged to have the involvement and support of Archie, Ray and Duncan Griffin who contributed the Introduction, and Luke Fickell, Ryan Miller and Mike Vrabel who provided the Foreword. These Buckeye greats kindly spent many hours with us, sharing cherished insights from both their playing careers and their lives after Ohio State football. We highly appreciate their contributions and encouragement.

We extend a genuine thank you to Coach Urban Meyer and Coach Jim Tressel for their valued time spent with us sharing their beliefs and experiences. Ohio State Associate Director of Athletics for Communications Jerry Emig, and his talented staff, contributed valuable historical information, without which we could not have written some of the stories in this book.

We so appreciate the excellent creative work of our cover designer, Denise Hollerich. Photographer Jim Davidson provided many superb action shots from games he has covered over the past 15 years. A special thank you goes to Gary Housteau for the photograph used with this Acknowledgements section.

Many thanks to Jeff Rapp for his technical editing and Jane Park for her readability editing — both were excellent. The late Tom Hayes furnished 12 superb hand-drawn illustrations for some of the earlier stories, which were later colorized by Phojoe Photo. Jennifer Riemenschneider of Sheridan Books and Pam Nuffer of Publishers Storage & Shipping offered valuable guidance and insight during the publishing process.

We are deeply indebted to Michelle Drobik from The Ohio State University Photo Archives for her assistance with selecting many of the photographs and program cover images. We appreciate permission from Rick Van Brimmer, Assistant Vice President for Business Advancement, Trademark & Affinity Management to use selected photographs from the Brockway Collection at the Ohio State University Photo Archives.

We value the permission granted by *The Columbus Dispatch* to use selected headlines and illustrations from past publications. We offer a special thank you to Diana Hill from *The Columbus Dispatch* Managing Editors' offices. We also appreciation permission granted by *The South Bend Tribune, The Akron Beacon Journal,* and the now defunct *Ohio State Journal* and *The Columbus Citizen.* These visuals bring life to many of the stories.

Jack is most grateful for the opportunity to provide football commentaries on Sports Radio 97.1 The Fan over the last 39 seasons. Recently he was worked most closely with Dave Van Stone, Jay Taylor, Anthony Rothman, Skip Mosic, Bob Taylor, Emily Everett, Bobby Carpenter, Beanie Wells, Lori Schmidt, Jerry Rudzinski, and Dee Miller. Many of the stories which follow originated from material he developed for these commentaries.

Maureen is deeply thankful for the encouragement and support from all of her family, friends and professional peers (including two mastermind groups) who endured her endless retellings of stories and hours plucking away at the computer to bring this project to fruition.

We appreciate all the fine people who shared their stories and photographs with us. They include John U. Bacon, Andy Bemer, John Crawford, Mike Coyle, Dr. Paul Droste, T.J. Downing, Frank Ellwood, Brian Fogle, Shelley Graf, Andy Groom, Bill Gue, George Kauffman, Buckeyeman Larry Lokai, Bruce Madej, Jerry Marlowe, Shelley Meyer, Butch Moore, Linda Mrukowski, Dennis Parks, Dr. Jerry Pausch, Big Nut Jon Peters, Bruce Peterson, John Porentas, Beth Siracuse, Gene Smith, Lindsey Tinsley, Emily (Moor) Williams, and Trevor Zahara.

Lastly, the authors want to acknowledge each other, even though that sounds a bit unconventional. What started as a random conversation between two people who didn't know each other very well has developed into a deep respect, rich admiration and wonderful friendship. Meshing two skills sets, two perspectives and two backgrounds has made this ride a joy from start to finish.

Jack Park *Maureen M. Zappala*

SITE OF THE FIRST
OHIO STATE FOOTBALL GAME

On the morning of May 3, 1890, Ohio Wesleyan University and The Ohio State University met at this location for a football game. It was the first game in Ohio State football history. Ohio Wesleyan had invited the newly organized team to a contest as part of OWU's May Day Weekend. The OSU team traveled here in horse drawn wagons leaving Columbus at daybreak and returning by evening. The playing field was in the flat plain to the north of this marker. It was bounded by the hill on one side and the steep-sided Delaware Run on the other. The spectators sat on the hillside to watch. Ohio Wesleyan granted special permission for coeds to be in attendance. The field was later moved to a new location behind Edwards Gymnasium because the ball frequently ended up in the creek. Ohio State won the first game over Ohio Wesleyan 20-14.

THE KROGER COMPANY
NATIONAL CITY BANK
DEDICATED MAY 3, 2008

CHAPTER ONE

1890-1912

The Early Going

Today's rich and splendid Ohio State football tradition stands in dramatic contrast with its humble beginning. While Ohio Stadium crowds of 108,000 fans and millions of national television spectators now scrutinize all aspects of the Buckeyes, early games were played before small, casual groups who were learning about this new sport of "foot ball."

What we know and love as football today most likely traces its roots to the ancient Roman game of "harpastum," a raucous, mob-like, exhausting contest where two teams competed to keep a small ball on their own half of a field by any means possible. Points were awarded when a team succeeded in throwing, running or kicking the ball past a line on the field of play.

While the game is mentioned in some ancient literature, there is very little information about the game's structure, strategy or rules — although it appears that the game resembled rugby. Similar mob-like games emerged in China in the third century, as well as other countries including Australia, Japan, Italy, Ireland and England as late as the 12th century. However, the games were considered violent and dangerous, and were banned in Europe for hundreds of years.

In the early 1800s, some schools in England were developing similar team games that involved kicking and running balls toward opposing goal lines. From school to school, the games differed slightly with variations in rules and structure, and eventually two distinct sports emerged: rugby and association football (soccer). The two sports crossed the Atlantic and a rugby-like game caught on in American colleges.

Sports historians generally agree that Nov. 6, 1869, is the birth date of football in the United States when Rutgers and Princeton, two East Coast universities, met for the first intercollegiate football game. In those early games, there were 25 players to a team and the sport still more closely resembled rugby than modern football. The scoring standard was simple: kick the ball through a set of upright goal posts that were 25 feet apart to get one point.

The Ohio State University, originally titled The Ohio Agricultural and Mechanical College, opened on September 17, 1873. Baseball, already a popular sport in the United States, was the first recreational sport at the school, and many intramural baseball games were played in the late-1870s and 1880s. In 1878, the school officially was renamed The Ohio State University.

Unorganized football was played by male students in the 1880s. These "jolly games" were played with homemade footballs in the early evenings on a large athletic field near the old North Dorm on the west side of Neil Avenue near Eleventh Avenue, directly across from where Oxley Hall and Mack Hall now stand. By this time in New England, the rules of the game were solidified and standardized, largely due to the efforts of a Yale football player named Walter Camp.

Camp was influential in establishing such norms as the line of scrimmage, the snap of the ball from center to quarterback, scoring standards (which emphasized kicking over running or passing), and the number of players per side (11). A kicked goal was worth four points, a touchdown four, and a safety two.

Players wore no protective gear, and the game still resembled rugby with a scrum-like group huddle formation pushing against the opposing team on each play. Forward passing wasn't part of the game, but drop-kicking was a frequent strategy of game play. However, these rules and standards developed in New England had not yet made their way to Columbus, so the early games were very unstructured.

After several years of this informal play, Ohio State student George N. Cole, class of 1891, helped organize Ohio State's first official football team. Cole purchased a rules book and a "real football" from the Spalding Athletic Supply Company, and arranged for his friend Alexander S. Lilley to coach the team. Lilley lived on East Main Street in Columbus and rode an Indian pony to campus for practices. The students did not realize a football was oblong in shape, having played with a more spherical rugby-like ball, and there was some concern that it had been shipped in error.

Informal baseball and football games were played during the early years near the old North Dorm. *Courtesy Ohio State University Photo Archives*

Ohio State's first game was a 20-14 victory at Ohio Wesleyan University in Delaware on Saturday, May 3, 1890. Quarterback Joseph Large scored OSU's first touchdown. The Buckeyes played three more games in November, losing all three — 64-0 at home to Wooster, 14-0 at Denison, and 18-10 at home to Kenyon on Thanksgiving Day.

By the close of the 1800s, football had spread rapidly to colleges in the United States, and some 250 sported teams. It is interesting to note that while football caught on as a favorite activity, many school administrators were opposed to the sport. The game was still rough, despite regulations and refereeing, and universities were not in favor of something that so distracted students from their academics.

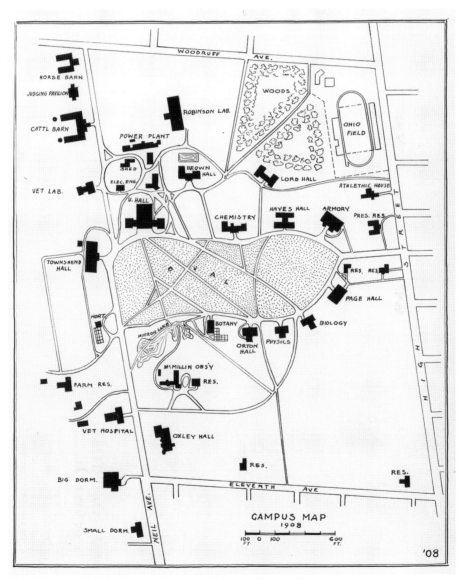

Ohio State Campus 1908. *Courtesy Ohio State University Photo Archives*

In the book *"The American College and University: A History,"* author Frederick Rudolph writes, "... administrators initially were not eager, generally speaking, to embrace such contests that they viewed as inappropriate distractions from serious scholarly work." Indicative of the administrative outrage at such elaborate contests was the telegram sent by President Andrew White of Cornell University to officials at the University of Michigan in 1873, when he learned that student teams from the two institutions were planning to meet in Cleveland for a football game: "I will not permit 30 men to travel four hundred miles merely to agitate a bag of wind." So, many school programs in these early years were led by students and alumni, often without support, control or involvement by the school administration.

Ohio State played home games during the early years in several locations including Recreation Park at the intersection of South High and Whittier Streets, Goodale Park on West Goodale Street, and on campus at the aforementioned North Athletic Field. In 1898, a new 500-seat capacity playing field was developed at the southwest corner of North High Street and Woodruff Avenue. Unofficially called both University Field and Ohio Field, it was the first on-campus home to both football and track events. It was officially named Ohio Field in 1908. The seating capacity was periodically increased, and in 1910 it could hold 14,000 fans. The University's enrollment was steadily increasing, and by 1912 the student population was nearly 4,000. The campus itself was blossoming as more than three dozen buildings dotted the landscape.

Ohio State fielded its first football team in 1890. At left is coach Alexander S. Lilley. *Courtesy Ohio State University Photo Archives*

The Buckeyes' 23-year record from 1890 through 1912 was 126-72-17 (62.6%). During this period, Ohio State had 11 different head coaches, with five staying just one season. For 22 of those 23 years, the last game of the season was on Thanksgiving Day, with Kenyon College being the opponent 12 times. All of those final games of the season were played in Columbus except for an 11-6 victory at Cincinnati on Thanksgiving of 1911.

Ohio State defeated Denison 8-4 in 1891 at Recreation Park, near the corner of South High and Whittier Streets in Columbus. *Courtesy Ohio State University Photo Archives*

Michigan defeated Ohio State 21-0 in 1901 at University Field. Basketball games were played at the old Armory, shown in the background. *Courtesy Ohio State University Photo Archives*

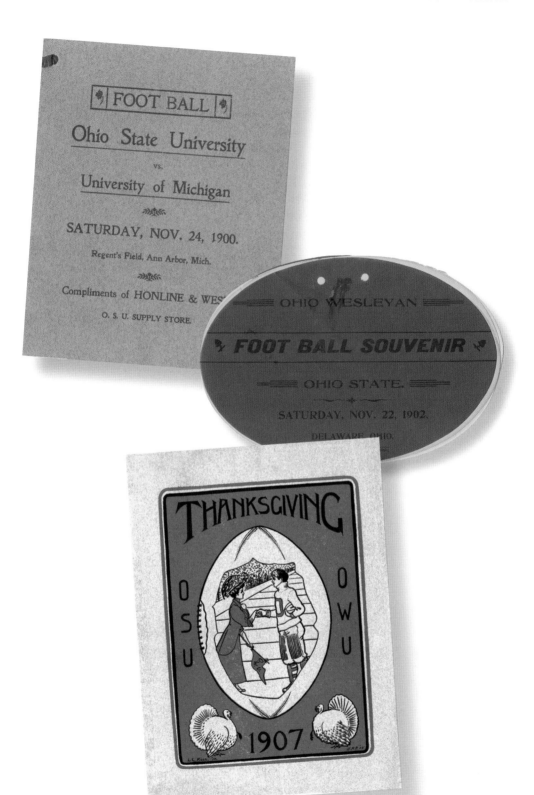

First School Colors

The Ohio State University library website includes a wonderful story of how scarlet and gray were chosen as the Ohio State colors. But some of the intersecting stories from other colleges make the Ohio State story even more interesting.

In 1866, a Princeton freshman named George Ward noticed that other schools had an identifying color scheme, but Princeton did not. He and some classmates wanted a way of distinguishing themselves from other schools. Princeton's oldest building is Nassau Hall, named to honor King William III of the House of Nassau. William III was also called The Prince of Orange, so Ward suggested orange as the school color.

It took more than a year before the rest of the student body embraced the idea, and in 1867 the Princeton baseball team sported badges of orange ribbon printed with black ink. This was the first time the orange and black color combination was used by the school in an athletic contest. Princeton officially adopted the colors in 1868.

In 1869, Rutgers wanted to use orange as its school color for a similar reason as Princeton. Rutgers University was established by the Dutch Reformed church, which has history that is traced to the same William III of the House of Nassau/Orange. However, students suggested scarlet because, in their opinion, it was a more striking color. Probably more importantly, red ribbon and fabric were easier to obtain than orange. Interestingly, the first intercollegiate football game was played between Rutgers and Princeton on Nov. 6, 1869. Rutgers wore scarlet turbans and scarfs. It is assumed that Princeton wore its orange and black colors.

Fast forward a few years to Columbus, Ohio, where school colors were a topic of conversation at Ohio State. In 1878, 12 years before Ohio State fielded its first football team, a committee of three students put considerable effort into color selection. They went to a dry-goods store and from the array of colorful ribbons, chose orange and black as the school colors because they looked good together. However, they soon learned that Princeton had already chosen orange and black,

GREAT GAME REMEMBERED
Ohio State 26 - Kenyon 10
November 24, 1892 - Columbus, Ohio

A Thanksgiving Day gathering of 1,200 cheered the Buckeyes to their first victory over Kenyon, after losing to the Lords during their first two seasons of football. The Buckeyes used the "Ryder wedge" formation to successfully gain yardage throughout the game. Ohio State finished with a record of 5-3 to garner its first winning season.

The game was scheduled for Thanksgiving morning, but the Kenyon team chose to attend a Wednesday dance in Gambier rather than travel to Columbus that evening. The season-ending contest was postponed to the afternoon to accommodate the visitors, causing many disturbed Ohio State fans to adjust their Thanksgiving dinners.

so they instead chose scarlet and gray. An excerpt from the OSU library page reads: "Alice Townshend, one of the members on the committee, reported that the colors did not signify anything. Instead, the committee wanted to choose something that was a nice combination and had not been used by any other college." Apparently they were unaware that Rutgers was unofficially using scarlet.

Regardless of the history of the color choices, it can't be denied that the combination of "scarlet and gray" elicits fierce loyalty and impassioned devotion from all dedicated Ohio State fans.

Ohio State and the Heisman Launch

Ohio State was defeated 40-0 at Oberlin on Oct. 15, 1892, in the season opener for both schools. Later that fall on November 7, Oberlin overwhelmed Ohio State 50-0 in Columbus. Oberlin was directed by John W. Heisman, 23, who was in his very first season as a college football coach. The Yeomen finished the 1892 season at 7-0, outscoring their opponents 262-30.

This was the very beginning of Heisman's highly successful 32-year coaching career at eight different colleges and universities, with a career record of 186-70-18 (71.2%). He became one of the game's greatest innovators, and the coveted Heisman Trophy is named in his honor.

Heisman was born at 2825 Bridge Avenue in Cleveland, Ohio, on Oct. 23, 1869. He grew up in Titusville, Pa., where he played high school football and was

salutatorian of his graduating class. Heisman played college football at both Brown University and the University of Pennsylvania. He died of pneumonia at age 66 in New York City on Oct. 3, 1936. Heisman and his wife, Edith, are buried in her hometown of Rhinelander, Wisconsin.

Oberlin's team trainer in 1892 was a pre-med student named Clarence Hemingway. He later earned his medical degree from Rush Medical College, established a medical practice in Oak Park, Ill., and became father to future author Earnest Hemingway.

Bush Boosts The Buckeyes

Samuel P. Bush, grandfather of President George H.W. Bush and great-grandfather of President George W. Bush, was an Ohio State volunteer

Oberlin Coach John W. Heisman in 1892. *Courtesy Oberlin College Athletic Communications*

assistant coach in 1892 under Coach Jack Ryder. It was the Buckeyes' third year of football, and their very first winning season with a record of 5-3.

The Bush family has always had a very strong sports tradition. In 1884, Samuel Bush graduated from Stevens Institute of Technology in Hoboken, N.J., where he played on one of the very first college football teams. After graduating from Stevens, Bush began working in the rail industry and was transferred to Columbus in 1891. He moved to Milwaukee in 1899, then returned to Columbus in 1901 to work at The Buckeye Malleable Iron & Coupler Company. In 1908, Bush became president of the company, which had been renamed Buckeye Steel Castings Company. He held that position until 1927.

Bush was a successful industrialist, civic leader, and avid sports enthusiast who had a tremendous impact not only on the nation's business environment, but on central Ohio cultural and athletic history. He organized the first amateur baseball league in Columbus, helped develop the Scioto Country Club golf course, was the first president of the Ohio Manufacturers Association, and co-founded the Columbus Academy.

Samuel P. Bush died in 1948 at age 84, and is buried at Green Lawn Cemetery in Columbus.

GREAT GAME REMEMBERED
Ohio State 6 - Oberlin 0
October 28, 1899 - Oberlin, Ohio

After losing its first six games to Oberlin and being outscored 200-10, Ohio State finally gained its first victory over the Yeomen. Delbert Sayers, left tackle and Buckeye captain, sprinted 25 yards for the game's only score after recovering an Oberlin fumble early in the first half. A special train carried 327 faithful Ohio State students to Oberlin to support their team. Heavy rain throughout the day forced the game to be played in a quagmire of mud.

Super Spy

In the fall of 1893, a newly enrolled Ohio State student practiced with the Buckeye football team just long enough to learn the plays, then disappeared. He was recognized a few weeks later as a member of the Kenyon College team when Ohio State played at Kenyon on Oct. 28. Kenyon romped over Ohio State, 42-6, handing the Buckeyes their biggest loss of the season. A month later, on Thanksgiving Day, Kenyon again defeated Ohio State by a score of 10-8. Years later, when reminiscing about the first game and the lopsided score, Ohio State quarterback Charles Wood recalled that "Kenyon just seemed to have all of our signals down pat."

That player was never identified. Ohio State finished the season with a 4-5 record. Perhaps it could have been 6-3 if this mystery man had stayed with Ohio State.

Football at the Fair

The Ohio State Board of Agriculture scheduled two Ohio State football games for the 1894 Ohio State Fair in Columbus. The major intention was to introduce football to those who were not familiar with the sport and had likely never attended a game.

Akron defeated Ohio State 12-6 on Saturday, Sept. 15, and Wittenberg defeated Ohio State 6-0 on Monday, Sept. 17.

Ohio State – Otterbein and the Presidency

The Ohio State-Otterbein game of Oct. 17, 1896, was played in Canton, Ohio, home of former Ohio Governor William McKinley who was running for President. The game was scheduled for 2:30 p.m., but was postponed until 3:45 p.m., because the train bringing many fans from Columbus was delayed. By mutual consent, the game was called because of darkness with six minutes remaining.

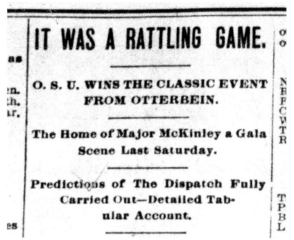

Courtesy The Columbus Dispatch, Oct. 19, 1896

Bringing this game to Canton as part of his presidential effort might have been good luck for the famous "front porch" campaigner. Ohio State beat Otterbein 12-0, and McKinley defeated William Jennings Bryan by just under 600,000 votes for the Presidency.

Whose Side Are You On?

Marietta College played at Ohio State on Oct. 22, 1898. It was Judge C. M. Showalter's second season as Marietta coach and his first game against Ohio State.

As was typical in the early days of college football, the Marietta Pioneers' traveling squad consisted of only 12 players — 11 starters and one substitute. Midway through the second half two Marietta players were injured and unable to continue play. With only one backup, and not wanting to forfeit the game, Showalter asked Ohio State Coach Jack Ryder if Marietta could "borrow" one of the Buckeyes' players to finish the game.

Ryder somewhat reluctantly agreed, and signaled to his bench for a Buckeye substitute to join the Marietta squad. The player assigned to the Pioneers is believed to have been halfback Bob Hager. On his very first carry, Hagar sprinted 67 yards around end for a Marietta touchdown. Ohio State (and probably everyone in attendance) was totally stunned! Marietta held on and secured its first victory over the Buckeyes in Columbus, 10-0.

The following year, Ohio State piled up over 300 yards in a 28-0 win over Wittenberg. Hagar had another stupendous game with 153 yards on 28 carries. Thankfully, Mr. Hagar contributed them to his own team, Ohio State.

And Coach Ryder? He never again loaned a player to an opposing team!

Courtesy Tom Hayes

First Come, First Serve

The Cincinnati Bearcats were scheduled to play Ohio State in Columbus on Saturday, Oct. 19, 1901. On Thursday, Oct. 17, just two days before the scheduled game, Cincinnati canceled and provided no reason for the abrupt decision.

Ohio State sprang into action to find another opponent. Telegrams were sent quickly to Denison, Heidelberg, Marietta, Mt. Union and Wooster, offering a game against the Buckeyes in Columbus to any school that might have an open date. Marietta accepted Ohio State's invitation and traveled to Columbus, where the Buckeyes defeated the Pioneers, 24-0.

Can you imagine this happening today? Football schedules are not only set years in advance, it's unthinkable that a school would cancel a game just two days before kickoff. Furthermore, the chances of scheduling a comparably-skilled and well-prepared opponent with two day's notice is beyond remote!

Courtesy The Columbus Dispatch, Oct. 18, 1901

Remembering John Sigrist

Ohio State defeated Western Reserve 6-5 in Columbus on Saturday, Oct. 26, 1901. It was the Buckeyes' very first single-point victory. The triumph was greatly overshadowed by heartbreaking news: Center John Sigrist sustained severe neck injuries and died two days later at Grant Hospital. Sigrist is the only Ohio State player ever to die from a football injury.

The university canceled Tuesday's classes and funeral services that morning were held in the chapel in University Hall. The entire football team attended, along with hundreds of students. Mourners formed two long lines down High Street as the casket was moved to Union Station for transport back to Sigrist's hometown of Congress, a small village north of Wooster in Wayne County, where he was laid to rest. The Columbus Dispatch said of the funeral, "Gloom was heavy upon all."

Ohio State President William Oxley Thompson canceled the following Saturday's game against Ohio Wesleyan, and it was never rescheduled. A segment of the students and faculty were in support of eliminating the sport because of its brutality, and the Ohio State Athletic Board allowed the players to decide if the sport should be continued.

On Wednesday, Oct. 29, the majority of the players endorsed the continuation of football, and no other games were canceled. Right tackle Charles Sigrist, brother of the deceased, spoke strongly in defense of continuing the sport. His support was a key factor in the team's decision.

Never Again!

Ohio State's 86-0 loss at Michigan on Oct. 25, 1902, is the highest margin of defeat in all of Ohio State football — and it could have been worse. Michigan scored 15 touchdowns when touchdowns counted five points. Using today's scoring with touchdowns counting six points, the final score would have been

101-0. Because of the lopsided score, the game was simply stopped with 10 minutes remaining in the second half.

The 86 points represent the highest combined score in an Ohio State-Michigan game, even though one team did not score! The second highest total is 83 points in 2013, with Ohio State defeating Michigan, 42-41. The attendance at the 1902 game reached 6,000, including 2,000 Ohio State supporters. At the time, it was the largest crowd to attend a football game at Michigan's Ferry Field.

During this period, Michigan coach Fielding Yost cultivated an impressive team of skilled players who were nicknamed the "Point-A-Minute Teams." During the 1901 and 1902 seasons, Michigan was 22-0 while outscoring its opponents 1,194-12 — at five points a touchdown.

GREAT GAME REMEMBERED
Ohio State 20 - Ohio Wesleyan 9
October 31, 1908 - Columbus, Ohio

Halfback Leslie Wells scored three second-half touchdowns to pace the Buckeye victory. While many Ohio Wesleyan male students traveled to Columbus to support their Battling Bishops, female students were not permitted to attend the game. The Ohio Wesleyan faculty felt "it would not be proper" for co-eds to leave the Delaware campus.

Ohio Wesleyan was coached by Branch Rickey, who later would become President and General Manager of the Brooklyn Dodgers. Rickey would break Major League Baseball's color barrier in 1947 with the signing of Jackie Robinson to a Dodgers contract.

Enough is Enough

Ohio State and Penn State first met on Nov. 16, 1912, in Columbus. The Buckeyes entered the game at 5-1. The Nittany Lions were 6-0 and had outscored their opponents 210-6.

Penn State was clearly the better team and dominated play right from the start. Throughout the afternoon, Ohio State coach John Richards complained to the officials about what he considered "unnecessary rough play." With nine minutes remaining and Penn State leading 37-0, Richards had had enough and pulled his team from the field. When the Buckeyes refused to continue, the officials awarded the Nittany Lions a 1-0 win by forfeit, although both schools have always reported the score as a 37-0 Penn State victory.

After the game was called, an Ohio State student set fire to the Penn State colors on one of the goal posts in view of Dr. E.E. Sparks, President of Penn State University and an Ohio State University alumnus. Several students and alumni immediately apologized to Dr. Sparks, and a formal apology from Ohio State was issued the following week. It would be 44 years before the two schools would again face each other. In 1956, Penn State defeated Ohio State 7-6 in Columbus.

Courtesy Tom Hayes

Refunds for All

College football rules in 1905 specified two 35-minute halves with a 10-minute halftime. The length of either or both halves could be shortened by mutual agreement between the opposing captains.

The Ohio State and Denison captains could not agree upon the length of halves for an Oct. 14, 1905, game at University Field. The Buckeyes wanted 35-minute halves but the Big Red strongly preferred that they be shorter. When mutual agreement could not be reached, the officials ruled in favor of Ohio State (who had won the coin toss) and set the game at two 35-minute halves. Denison refused to play. After a warning and a two-minute wait, the game was forfeited to Ohio State, 2-0. The Denison squad quickly left the playing field and headed home to Granville.

Fans were visibly upset with the entire situation as they stood in line for refunds on their tickets. Ohio State may have won the game, but the Athletic Department definitely lost at the gate. Income from ticket sales totaled $1,078, but the refunds amounted to $1,206, a deficit of $128. Many youngsters had sneaked inside University Field, then stood in line to collect their "refunds."

CHAPTER TWO

1913–1921

Joining the "Big Boys"

Purdue University President James Smart is credited with organizing the collegiate conference known today as the Big Ten. At Smart's invitation, the presidents of seven universities met at the Palmer House Hotel in Chicago on Jan. 11, 1895, to develop a framework of rules to regulate intercollegiate athletics. The universities represented were Purdue, Chicago, Illinois, Michigan, Minnesota, Northwestern, and Wisconsin. Some sources indicate that Wake Forest was also in attendance, but the original list of attendees as recorded in the minutes of this first meeting do not include Wake Forest.

Slightly more than a year later on Feb. 8, 1896, these seven presidents again met at the Palmer House to finalize the organization of a league of schools operating under the rules established the previous year. The new league was named The Intercollegiate Conference of Faculty Representatives and was commonly called The Western Conference.

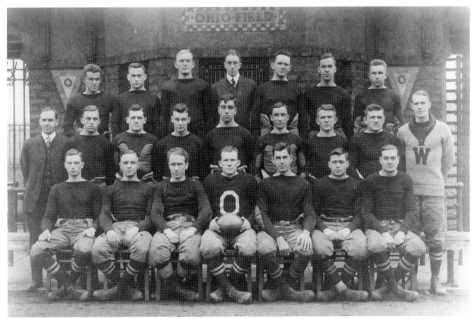

Ohio State's 1913 team was the school's first to compete in the Big Ten. *Courtesy Ohio State University Photo Archives*

Wisconsin won the new league's first football championship in 1896, with an overall record of 7-1-1. The Badger captain was fullback John Richards, who would become Ohio State's head coach in 1912. Indiana and Iowa began play as new members in 1900, bringing the conference membership to nine. Nebraska also petitioned to join, but the request was denied.

A landmark event for the conference was Michigan's overwhelming 49-0 victory over Stanford in the very first Rose Bowl at the end of the 1901 season. The Rose Bowl was intended to be an East-meets-West championship game, but the lopsided score was such an embarrassment that the Tournament of Roses dropped football from its list of activities for the next 14 years.

Michigan was voted out of the league prior to the 1907 season because of non-adherence to new league regulations. The Wolverines were opposed to reducing the number of games to five per season, restricting player eligibility to three seasons, and requiring football coaches to be full-time faculty members. Michigan was admitted back into the conference in 1918.

Ohio State had aspirations of joining this prominent league, even though most of its opponents through 1912 were smaller colleges within the state of Ohio. George W. Rightmire, president of the Athletic Board and a law professor, believed that a more regional schedule would benefit both the university and its athletic programs.

Accompanied by fellow law professor Alonzo Tuttle and Secretary of the Trustees Carl Steeb, Rightmire presented Ohio State's case at a meeting of the members of the Western Conference in Chicago on Jan. 26, 1912. Ohio State's petition was accepted by a vote of the members on April 6, 1912, and the Buckeyes began conference play in 1913.

Ohio State captured its first Big Ten title in 1916 with an overall record of 7-0. *Courtesy Ohio State University Photo Archives*

First Big Ten Title - 1916. *Courtesy The Columbus Dispatch, Nov. 26, 1916*

The hiring of John W. Wilce as head coach brought much needed stability to the football program. Wilce had been a three-sport letterman at the University of Wisconsin, where he was captain of the Badger football team in 1909. His first three OSU teams of 1913-15 finished sixth, fourth, and third, respectively, in the final Big Ten standings.

In 1916, Ohio State accomplished its first perfect record at 7-0, captured its very first Big Ten title, and outscored its seven opponents, 258-29. The Buckeyes were blessed with the splendid play of sophomore Chic Harley, a 5'9", 150-pound halfback who was nearly impossible to tackle in the open field. Harley, a graduate of Columbus East High School, also was an outstanding passer, defender, punter and placekicker.

With a record of 8-0-1, the Buckeyes repeated as conference champions in 1917, outscoring their nine opponents 292-6. By the fall of 1918 with the United States deeply involved in World War I, Harley and most of his teammates were serving in the military. That season, college freshmen became eligible for varsity competition and most Big Ten teams played a shortened schedule that was somewhat unofficial. Ohio State won three non-conference games but lost three league contests to finish the 1918 season at 3-3.

With Harley and most of his teammates back on campus in 1919, Ohio State posted a fine record of 6-1 and outscored its seven opponents 176-12. Illinois handed the Buckeyes a very disappointing homecoming setback, 9-7, in the season's final game. The Fighting Illini scored the only touchdown surrendered by the Buckeyes all season. Harley became Ohio State's first three-time All-American while leading his school to its first two outright Big Ten titles and a three-year record of 21-1-1. He was chosen for the Sphinx Society, an elite senior honorary recognition.

Prior to Harley's arrival on campus, many Columbus high school teams drew larger crowds than Ohio State. Interest in the Buckeyes swelled with the

Second Big Ten Title - 1917. *Courtesy The Columbus Dispatch, Nov. 18, 1917*

play of Harley and his talented teammates, and suddenly old Ohio Field, with a seating capacity of 20,000, was too small to accommodate the crowds. This intense enthusiasm created the momentum to build Ohio Stadium, which opened in 1922.

Ohio State's 1920 team, led by two-time All-American Pete Stinchcomb, captured the school's third outright Big Ten championship with a regular-season mark of 7-0. That season the Buckeyes played in their first Rose Bowl, losing to California 28-0 on Jan. 1, 1921.

After a very respectable record of 5-2 in 1921, good for a second-place Big Ten finish, the curtain came down on old Ohio Field.

It was there where the early Buckeye fans became energized with the development of a football program that obtained a national presence. Ohio State had compiled an impressive nine-year record of 50-12-3 since joining the Big Ten, and the roots of its "great tradition" were now firmly entrenched.

Halfback Chic Harley. *Courtesy Ohio State University Photo Archives*

Senior Tackle

One of Ohio State's oldest traditions, Senior Tackle, was initiated by Coach John Wilce during his first year as head coach in 1913. Senior players take "one last ceremonial hit" at a tackling dummy during the final practice prior to their last game for the Scarlet and Gray. For many years it took place at the close of the final practice prior to the regular season finale against Michigan. More recently it has been held at the last home practice prior to the team departing for its postseason game.

Coach Urban Meyer learned about Senior Tackle as a graduate assistant to Coach Earle Bruce in 1986 and 1987. Meyer has great affection for the annual ceremony. "I've done it every place I've ever been because I learned it here," he stated. "It's one of the great traditions to send off a young man to represent his last practice as a Buckeye."

Senior Tackle is simple and moving. Each senior is recognized individually in front of the entire team by both a teammate and the player's position coach. The senior says a few words of appreciation for his time with the team, then runs speedily and batters the tackling dummy. It is short, sweet and very meaningful!

GREAT GAMES REMEMBERED
Ohio State 7 - Illinois 6
Oct. 21, 1916 - Champaign, Illinois

After four unsuccessful ties, Ohio State finally earned its first triumph over Illinois. With his team trailing 6-0 late in the game on an exceptionally muddy field, halfback Chic Harley passed his team to the Illinois 12. Harley then evaded three tacklers to score the tying touchdown in the game's final minute. After putting on a pair of dry shoes, he calmly kicked the classic conversion for the single-point victory.

Illinois suffered its first home conference setback in four seasons. This was a very key victory that boosted Ohio State to its first Big Ten title and first perfect season at 7-0.

Getting In Was Half The Fun!

The late Reverend Ted Lilley, Ohio State class of 1927, spent many years as a highly-respected Presbyterian minister in Cedar Rapids, Iowa. Lilley grew up in Columbus. His father's cousin was Alexander S. Lilley, Ohio State's first football coach in 1890.

Reverend Lilley fondly remembered how he and his childhood friends devised devious methods of gaining entrance to old Ohio Field at the southwest corner of Woodruff and High Streets to watch their beloved Buckeyes play football. Scaling the fences surrounding the field, known as "fencing," was very popular and probably not particularly difficult.

Ohio Field was nestled in a heavily wooded area. The field was surrounded by a fence which was 8-10 feet tall and some distance from the field. The fence was wooden along the two sides and the back of the field, and wrought iron in the front by the ticket gates. The wooden fence ran through trees behind the grandstand and bleachers, making it relatively easy for youngsters to scale the fence unnoticed.

"Blanketing" was another good routine. The players dressed for the games in the old Athletic House near 16th and High Streets, then ran as a group to Ohio Field with blankets in their hands or worn cape-like over their shoulders. As the players approached the gates, young fans would dart under a blanket and gain entrance with the player.

"Gate-crashing" was a popular method. Timing was vital, and Lilley learned the best time to dash through the gates was near kickoff when impatient fans crowded the turnstiles. Lilley had many cherished memories of watching Buckeye greats Chic Harley, Pete Stinchcomb and many others of that period, but he always remembered that getting into old Ohio Field was half the fun.

First All-American

End Boyd Cherry was Ohio State's first All-American and first All-Big Ten selection in 1914. He was from Newark, Ohio, and also played basketball for the Buckeyes. Cherry graduated from Ohio State in 1915, and later became vice president of the Kinnear Manufacturing Company in Columbus. He passed away at age 77 in 1970. Ohio State completed its 25th season of football in 1914 with a school record of 135-76-18 (62.9%).

Boyd Cherry. *Courtesy Ohio State University Photo Archives*

Most One-Sided Triumph

Ohio State's 128-0 drubbing of perennial antagonist Oberlin College on Oct. 14, 1916, is the highest score and largest margin of victory in school history. An Ohio Field crowd of 3,300 saw Coach John Wilce's team score 19 touchdowns and 14 conversions, while totaling 1,140 yards of total offense. Following is the scoring by quarters:

	1	2	3	4	Total
Oberlin	0	0	0	0	0
Ohio State	33	34	35	26	128

Oberlin was forced to punt 16 times, while the Buckeyes punted only twice. The Ohio State Monthly alumni publication wrote, "The game played with our old friends of Oberlin, and resulting in a score of 128-0, caused a lifting of eyebrows not only in Ohio, but among the conference institutions."

This is the only time Ohio State has scored 100 or more points in a single game.

What Was He Thinking?

One of Ohio State's biggest challenges during its first Big Ten title season of 1916 was powerful Wisconsin, which had defeated the Buckeyes three straight times from 1913-15. On a beautiful Homecoming afternoon, the Ohio Field crowd of 12,500 was (at the time) the largest ever to attend a football game in the state of Ohio, surpassing the previous record of 8,200 for the Ohio State-Michigan game of 1902.

OHIO STATE vs. WISCONSIN, NOV. 4

Both teams entered the Nov. 4 encounter undefeated — Ohio State at 3-0 and Wisconsin at 4-0. The Badgers had outscored their four opponents, 91 to 10. It was Wisconsin's first road game of the season, and coach Paul Withington greatly underestimated Ohio State's potential. Instead of accompanying his squad to Columbus, Withington put assistant Ed Soucy in command, while Withington traveled to Minneapolis to scout the Minnesota-Illinois game, two strong teams the Badgers would face later in November.

Ohio State totally stunned the over-confident Badgers with an astonishing 14-13 victory. Halfback Chic Harley scored all 14 of his team's points with a nifty 27-yard scamper in the second quarter, an 80-yard fourth period punt return and both conversions.

Coach Paul Withington was both shocked and embarrassed when learning of the game's outcome, and never again made such an uncanny coaching decision.

Goal Line Safe and Sound

The 1917 Buckeyes captured their second consecutive outright Big Ten title with a league record of 4-0 and overall mark of 8-0-1. OSU outscored its nine opponents, 292-6. The Scarlet and Gray yielded just two field goals, the first during a 26-3 victory at Indiana and the other while winning 16-3 at Wisconsin. This is the only Ohio State squad to go through a complete season without surrendering a touchdown.

The 1917 co-captains were brothers Harold and Howard Courtney of Columbus, who played the two tackle positions. The Courtneys are the only brothers in school history to serve as captains during the same season.

Serious Interruption

An outbreak of Spanish influenza critically affected many parts of the United States in the fall of 1918. Public gatherings were banned in certain cities and many deaths were caused by the plague.

The Ohio State campus was closed in mid-October and many college football games were cancelled in the Midwest. After defeating Dennison 34-0 on Oct. 12, the Buckeyes could not play their next game until four weeks later — a 56-0 victory over Case on Nov. 9. The Buckeyes finished their shortened season with a record of 3-3.

Heated Competition

Emotions ran high between the opposing coaches during the Ohio State-Wisconsin games of 1917, 1919, and 1920. The Buckeyes' John Wilce played college football at Wisconsin and was captain of the 1909 squad. Wisconsin coach John Richards was the Badger captain in 1896, and had been Ohio State's coach in 1912 with a record of 6-3.

Ohio State won all three contests — 16-3 (1917), 3-0 (1919), and 13-7 (1920).

Remembering Chic Harley

One of the homes of Chic Harley and his family while Harley was a standout football player at Columbus East High School, was a two-story brick home at 689 South Champion Avenue. It was located southeast of downtown Columbus, near the intersection of Champion and Newton Street. The Harley boyhood home is long gone, and the Chic Harley Memorial Garden now occupies the site in honor of the legendary Ohio State halfback.

The Memorial Garden was the creation of the Old Oaks Civic Association and neighborhood leaders. It was dedicated in 2015. The original design was created by Larry Walquist, Jr., professor emeritus of Landscape Architecture at The Ohio State University. Walquist's father had been a member of the Illinois team that defeated the Buckeyes 9-7 in 1919 — Ohio State's only loss during Harley's distinguished college career. The 1,000-pound bronze sculpture of Harley carrying the football was designed by Columbus artist Joan Wobst.

Chic Harley Memorial Garden. *Courtesy Jack Park*

Creative Convoy

After World War I, the United States Army stored some of its military trucks at the Ohio State Fairgrounds close to the OSU campus. Hundreds of creative Ohio State students "borrowed" some of these armed vehicles, then formed a caravan to travel to Illinois for a vital season-ending game against the Fighting Illini on Nov. 20, 1920. The contest also was the very first college "Dad's Day" celebration.

Ohio State had the ball at the Illinois 37 with just four seconds remaining in a scoreless game. As Ohio State quarterback Harry "Hoge" Workman dropped back to pass, Fighting Illini defenders covered Buckeye halfback Pete Stinchcomb (anticipated receiver) like a blanket, leaving end Cyril "Truck" Myers all alone. Workman side-stepped two would-be tacklers and hurled the ball to Myers, who caught it in stride at the 17 and raced untouched into the end zone. The timekeeper's whistle sounded to signal that time had expired as Workman's pass was in the air. Ohio State won 7-0 in dramatic style, and captured outright the Big Ten title with a regular season record of 7-0.

GREAT GAMES REMEMBERED
Ohio State 16 — Wisconsin 3
Nov. 10, 1917 — Madison, Wisconsin

This major victory significantly helped Ohio State capture its second consecutive outright Big Ten championship. The Buckeyes entered the game at 5-0 and Wisconsin was 3-1-1. The Badgers had defeated Minnesota 10-7 the previous Saturday during their very first game at new Camp Randall Stadium.

Wisconsin's attacking defense stymied Ohio State's rushing efforts most of the afternoon, but Chic Harley finally got his team's offense going through the air. With the ball at the Wisconsin 44, Harley passed to Charles "Shifty" Bolen, who carried a tackler across the goal line for Ohio State's first touchdown. Harley later connected with Howard Courtney for 32 yards to the 2, and quarterback Howard Yerges sneaked the final two yards to increase the score to 13-3. Harley's 40-yard fourth-quarter field goal finalized the scoring at 16-3, much to the regret of the nearly 6,000 highly partisan local fans.

Night Shift

Oberlin College pulled a huge upset by humiliating Ohio State 7-6 at old Ohio Field on Oct. 8, 1921. It was the last time the Buckeyes have lost to an opponent from within the state of Ohio. The following morning's *Ohio State Journal* provided the following reaction:

If Mars had dropped from its place in the solar system and bumped into Mother Earth yesterday, it wouldn't have caused any greater surprise in Columbus

*than that kicked up by little Oberlin when it licked Ohio State's football team 7 to
6 in the Buckeyes' own back yard.*

*The real story of what happened is brief. The Buckeye Eleven entered the
contest confident no matter what happened Ohio State would win. Oberlin licked
the Buckeyes in a fair and square manner and deserved the victory. From the
middle of the initial period until the close of the contest Oberlin outplayed Ohio
State in every department of the game.*

The tiny town of Oberlin was overjoyed, as evidenced by quotes from the
Oberlin Review newspaper:

*It's a town gone mad and at midnight there was no sign of returning sanity.
It's the darnedest night in town ... Mothers and fathers may be seen holding their
children in arms and telling them 'To look and to remember' for unto us has come
a victory over Ohio State.*

Coach John Wilce was totally irritated with his team's pitiful performance, and
quickly ordered the players to return to the playing field for a strenuous practice.
Searchlights were brought in and very demanding drills continued into the night.
Vigorous scrimmages continued the following week and apparently had an impact
— Ohio State shut out its next four opponents by a combined score of 76-0.

Courtesy Tom Hayes

"Fighting Illini" Originated In Columbus

Ohio State was an overwhelming favorite against Illinois for the very last game played at old Ohio Field on Nov. 19, 1921. It was homecoming, and the powerful Buckeyes entered the game 4-0 in league play, having shut out all four Big Ten opponents by a combined score of 76-0.

Heavy underdog Illinois had lost all four of its league contests while being outscored 51-8. The Illini had not scored a league touchdown, and were in serious danger of not winning at least one conference game for the first time in 22 seasons.

Illinois accomplished the nearly impossible — shutting out Ohio State 7-0. Illini head coach Bob Zuppke, a master psychologist, used only 11 players the entire afternoon. His game plan contained several new schemes, including a "drop-back pass defense" to guard against the fine passing of Ohio State's "Sonny" Workman. Ohio State head coach John Wilce used 33 players, while attempting to wear down the inspired visitors.

Illinois scored in the second quarter on an extremely unusual play. With the ball at the Ohio State 35-yard line, Illini halfback Don Peden passed to end Dave Wilson. The ball escaped Wilson's grasp and bounced off the chest of Buckeye

GREAT GAMES REMEMBERED
Ohio State 13 — Michigan 3
Oct. 25, 1919 — Ann Arbor, Michigan

Courtesy The Columbus Dispatch, Oct. 26, 1919

This was the 16th clash between these archrivals, and Ohio State had never defeated Michigan. The Wolverines held a decided edge in the series at 13-0-2. Michigan had outscored the Buckeyes 369-21 over the first 15 games.

Both teams entered the game undefeated and unscored upon, Ohio State at 3-0 and Michigan at 2-0. Late in the first period, tackle Iolas Huffman blocked a Wolverine punt, and end Jim Flowers recovered in the end zone for Ohio State's first touchdown. Michigan narrowed the halftime margin to 7-3 with a 37-yard second quarter field goal.

Midway through the third period, halfback Chic Harley raced 42 yards around end for the game's final score. In one of his all-time finest games, Harley punted 11 times for a 42-yard average and intercepted four Wolverine passes. Among the Ferry Field crowd of 25,000 were 5,000 Buckeye fans, who were thrilled to see Ohio State finally defeat Michigan!

defender Cyril "Truck" Myers. Illini captain Laurie Walquist quickly snatched the ball and rambled into the end zone for the game's only touchdown.

The Buckeyes completely dominated the game's statistics, running 72 plays from scrimmage compared with the Illini's 49. Ohio State led in first downs, 14 to 5, and in total offense, 251 yards to 128. OSU had three excellent scoring opportunities deep in Illinois territory, but the scrappy visitors came through with timely defensive plays to preserve the shutout.

Sportswriter Harvey Woodruff covered this game for the Chicago Tribune. Woodruff was so impressed with the inspired play of the Illini that he referred to them in his Sunday column as the "Fighting Illini."

"Illini" is another version of the Indian name Illinois. The area land was so named by the French explorers to honor the indigenous Illiniwek (Algonquins) Indians that populated the area. The expression "Fighting Illini" was first used at the University of Illinois in early 1921, to honor students and alumni who had served in World War I. That year the school used the phrase as part of a capital campaign to raise money for a new football stadium.

When Woodruff used the term "Fighting Illini," the name became more widespread … and the Illinois athletic teams have been known as the "Fighting Illini" ever since the monumental 7-0 upset over Ohio State in 1921.

In 2016, landscape markers were placed on the grounds where old Ohio Field stood at the southwest corner of Woodruff Avenue and North High Street. Locations of a portion of the yard lines are identified.

CHAPTER THREE

1922-1928

Creating Ohio Stadium

The United States was rebounding following World War I. Leisure pursuits and entertainment were becoming a higher priority. Government controls on railroad, shipping and manufacturing that supported the war were lifted, and a robust economy began to develop. Wages increased, optimism was high and the future was bright.

The introduction of the automobile, moving pictures, radio and telephone helped cultivate an entertainment mindset that offered a welcomed respite from the daily grind of work. Interest in sports exploded, and universities began to increase funding for their football programs. Student enrollment at Ohio State during the 1920s grew from 10,000 to more than 15,000, and multiple new campus facilities were added. Ohio State football moved to newly constructed Ohio Stadium in 1922.

Serious efforts to build a new stadium began as early as 1917, following Ohio State's first Big Ten title the previous fall. The Ohio Field space at the corner of Woodruff Avenue and High Street was restricted, and the frontage on High Street was becoming too valuable to be used as an athletic facility.

Ohio State president William Oxley Thompson, an ordained Presbyterian minister, was a visionary who was years ahead of his time. He believed a university could serve people in many more ways than just the conventional classroom, including research and expanded services to all of Ohio. Thompson understood that student life

President William Oxley Thompson statue in front of Ohio State Main Library *Courtesy Jack Park*

Ohio Stadium under construction in 1922. *Courtesy Ohio State University Photo Archives*

was an important part of a college education, and he strongly supported the many benefits a large stadium would generate.

Professor Thomas French was Ohio State's faculty representative to the Big Ten from 1913 until his death in 1944. In 1918, French arranged for Architect Dwight Smith to create a stadium design that eventually would include an upper deck, the first ever football stadium of its kind. Thompson, French, Smith, and Athletic Director L.W. St. John would become the "driving forces" behind the construction of Ohio Stadium.

The Ohio State Board approved the new stadium plan, but would not appropriate any funding for the construction. The Board preferred that all state money be used for advancing academic endeavors. Therefore, the stadium funding would have to be generated from private donations.

French organized a Stadium Executive Committee to plan a campaign for raising $1 million. The committee arranged for alumni volunteers from all 88 Ohio counties to contact Ohio State's 30,000 alumni and other friends of the university for donations. The campaign was kicked off with much fanfare on Oct. 16, 1920, and by Jan. 20, 1921, the $1 million goal had been achieved.

Governor Harry Davis turned the first shovel at the stadium's formal groundbreaking on Aug. 3, 1921, and construction was completed in time for the 1922 season. The stadium construction cost exceeded $1.5 million. Borrowings by the Athletic Board totaled approximately $500,000, and were repaid with future funds generated by the athletic programs.

There was, however, a considerable risk assumed by the Athletic Board. If the loans could not be fully met with proceeds from the athletic events, the Athletic Board members would be personally liable for any unpaid amount. On Nov. 1, 1928, St. John happily announced that "all notes outstanding on the stadium indebtedness had been paid."

Ohio State's first game in Ohio Stadium was a 5-0 victory over Ohio Wesleyan on Oct. 7, 1922. Following a 14-0 victory over Oberlin on Oct. 14, Michigan defeated the Buckeyes 19-0 in the official dedication game Oct. 21 before an estimated crowd of 72,500.

Ohio State had played without a losing record 23 consecutive seasons, from 1899 through 1921. Ironically, that streak was broken at the time of the move to Ohio Stadium, where the Buckeyes suffered losing records each of their first three years — 1922 (3-4), 1923 (3-4-1), and 1924 (2-3-3). OSU's three-year Big Ten record was 3-11-2. It is the only time Ohio State has experienced three consecutive losing seasons. These were the school's only losing records during the 44-year period of 1899 through 1942. Since 1924, the Buckeyes have incurred only six losing campaigns — 1943 (3-6), 1947 (2-6-1), 1959 (3-5-1), 1966 (4-5), 1988 (4-6-1), and 2011 (6-7).

Criticism of Coach John Wilce developed during this period, and there were apparent disagreements between Wilce and some of his assistants. After an improved record of 4-3-1 in 1925, the Buckeyes fielded an excellent 7-1 team in 1926 that outscored its eight opponents 196-43. The lone setback was a single-point homecoming loss to Michigan, 17-16.

Ohio State Coaching Staff 1923 - Dean Trott, Walter Essman, Lloyd Pixley, Grant Ward, Clarance MacDonald, Head Coach John Wilce. *Courtesy Ohio State University Photo Archives*

Dr. Wilce earned his medical degree from Ohio State in 1919. To fulfill his desire for a fulltime medical career, he retired from his head coaching position at the end of the 1928 season. Wilce compiled an impressive 16-year coaching record of 78-33-9, including three Big Ten titles. He was inducted into the College Football Hall of Fame in 1954.

Dr. Wilce entered private medical practice full time in 1929, and also taught many years in the Ohio State College of Medicine. He served as the Director of Ohio State's Student Health Services until his retirement from the university in 1958.

Drum Major Delight

Tubby Essington. *Courtesy Ohio State University Photo Archives*

Ohio State drum major Edwin "Tubby" Essington was the creator of the drum major strut so beloved today. Born in Somerset, Ohio, Essington lead the band from 1920-1922. He was an enormously likable guy who introduced a level of showmanship and style that was a stark contrast to the military precision of previous drum majors. He thoroughly entertained the crowds with his prancing, whistling and baton spinning.

After Ohio State's 7-0 victory at Chicago on Nov. 5, 1921, Essington paraded the band through the streets of Chicago and gained national attention for his lively strutting. When the Buckeyes moved to Ohio Stadium the following season, the game program featured a photo of the band with a caption: "Tubby and his gang, the life of the party." Walter Camp named Essington the "All-American Drum Major" in 1922. His picture appeared on the cover of Collier's magazine.

Initial Broadcast

Ohio State's first game in Ohio Stadium was also the school's first to be broadcast. Radio station WEAO transmitted the play-by-play of the Buckeyes' 5-0 victory over Ohio Wesleyan on Oct. 7, 1922. The audio was conveyed from the Robinson Laboratory at 206 West 18th Ave. on the Ohio State campus. WEAO was an acronym for Willing Energetic Athletic Ohio. The station's call letters were changed to WOSU in 1931.

Eternal Classics

Two of football's all-time most electrifying games were played on Oct. 18, 1924. Illinois dedicated its new Memorial Stadium that afternoon against Michigan. The two had shared the Big Ten title the previous season. Illini halfback Harold "Red" Grange thrilled the packed house of 65,000, taking the opening kickoff 95 yards for the game's first touchdown. During the first 12 minutes of play, Grange added three additional scores with runs of 67, 54 and 44 yards while touching the ball only six times. The Fighting Illini won 39-14 as Grange gained 402 yards and accounted for six touchdowns.

It was the Wolverines' first setback since losing its homecoming game to Ohio State, 14-0, three years earlier in 1921. Michigan had given up just four touchdowns in its previous 20 games. Grange's performance remains one of the most dominating in football history. Illinois finished the 1924 season at 6-1-1; Michigan at 6-2.

At the Polo Grounds in New York City that same afternoon, Notre Dame upset favored Army 13-7 before a capacity crowd of 55,000. Noted sportswriter Grantland Rice was so impressed with the play of Notre Dame's backfield, he described them in his *New York Herald Tribune* column as the "Four Horsemen." Coach Knute Rockne's four senior backfield stars were quarterback Harry Stuhldreher, halfbacks Elmer Layden and Don Miller, and fullback Jim Crowley. All four were later inducted into the College Football Hall of Fame.

Army finished the season with a record of 5-1-2 that included a 12-0 season-ending victory over Navy. Notre Dame captured the 1924 national title with a mark of 10-0 after defeating Stanford 27-10 in the Rose Bowl.

GREAT GAMES REMEMBERED
Ohio State 9 - Columbia 0
Oct. 17, 1925 - Columbus, Ohio

Columbia was the nation's largest university in 1925 with a student enrollment of 15,000. The favored Lions were considered "the strongest team in the East."

Using a very well-balanced and polished rushing and passing attack, Ohio State outplayed the shocked visitors in every phase of the game. The Buckeyes led in first downs 12 to 7, and in total offensive yards, 247 to 156. Halfback Elmer Marek punted 10 times for a fine average of 46.8 yards. This was Ohio State's first major home victory since the opening of Ohio Stadium in 1922.

The following season, Ohio State became the first Big Ten team to play in New York City, upending Columbia 32-7 at the old Polo Grounds before a rain-soaked crowd of 30,000.

Illibuck Initiated

Ohio State's junior men's honorary society, Bucket and Dipper, and its counterpart at Illinois, Atius-Sachem, agreed in the fall of 1925 to initiate a traveling trophy which would rotate to the winner of each year's game. Since the two schools already had played 13 times, both societies agreed upon a live snapping turtle because of its longevity. Snapping turtles can live in captivity from 40-60 years with proper care.

Illinois won the 1925 encounter in Columbus, 14-9. Prior to the 1926 game, Bucket and Dipper purchased a live snapping turtle at a Columbus fish dealer and carried the reptile to Champaign for that season's encounter. Representatives of the two honor societies met at halftime and began the annual ritual of smoking a peace pipe and presenting Illibuck to the previous game's winner. The peace pipe custom was later discontinued.

GREAT GAMES REMEMBERED
Illinois 14 – Ohio State 9
Nov. 21, 1925 – Columbus, Ohio

Courtesy The Ohio State Journal, Nov. 22, 1925

Halfback Harold "Red" Grange, one of football's all-time greats, led Illinois to the thrilling five-point victory during his last collegiate game. The Ohio Stadium attendance of 84,295 was, at the time, the largest to attend a sporting event of any type in this country. Sportswriters from all parts of the nation flocked to Columbus to cover Grange's final appearance. The opposing captains, Grange and Ohio State's Harold "Cookie" Cunningham, both wore jersey #77.

Grange's excellent all-around play was a key factor in the visitors' five-point victory. Early in the game his running set up a 2-yard scoring plunge by fullback Earl Britton, and he completed a 13-yard touchdown toss to end Charles Kessel near halftime.

The Buckeyes were driving late in the fourth period for a potential winning touchdown, but Grange intercepted an Ohio State pass near midfield on the game's final play. It was an appropriate ending to one of the college game's finest careers.

The following day Grange signed an NFL contract with the Chicago Bears to play the remaining six games of the 1925 season. The professional league was struggling at the gate, but Grange's presence immediately increased the Bears' attendance, both home and away.

Sadly, the original turtle died in the spring of 1927 and was replaced by a wooden replica, carved from black walnut wood. Scores of each game are engraved on the turtle's back. A total of 10 replicas have been used to display the outcomes of all 89 games through the 2015 season. Ohio State's record in the series is 64-23-2. Illibuck is the Big Ten Conference's second oldest rotating trophy. The Little Brown Jug, exchanged between Michigan and Minnesota, dates back to 1903.

Bucket and Dipper recognizes outstanding members of Ohio State's junior class, based upon scholarship, leadership, and service. Originally an all men's honorary, the society today is comprised of 30 exceptional men and women undergraduates.

All-Time Tiniest

Ohio State's 13-7 victory over Wilmington College on Nov. 6, 1926, was played before a crowd of 5,482, smallest in Ohio Stadium history. It is a huge contrast to the Ohio Stadium record attendance of 110,045 that watched Ohio State defeat Michigan 29-26 in double overtime on Nov. 26, 2016.

It has been the only game between Ohio State and Wilmington, and the score was much closer than anticipated. The Buckeyes at 5-0 apparently expected to win with ease over the 3-3 Quakers and were looking ahead to the following Saturday's game against undefeated Michigan. Coach John Wilce and assistant Sam Willaman traveled to Ann Arbor to scout the Wolverines against Wisconsin (Michigan won 37-0), leaving assistant Jim Oberlander in Columbus to direct Ohio State against Wilmington.

Ohio State's first team was rested for the upcoming clash against the Wolverines and saw no action against the Quakers. The third team played most of the game, with the second stringers seeing limited action in the first half and final period. Michigan won in Columbus the following weekend, 17-16.

GREAT GAMES REMEMBERED
Ohio State 19 - Michigan 7
Oct. 20, 1928 - Columbus, Ohio

The Buckeyes dominated the Wolverines before a partisan home crowd of 72,439. Quarterback Alan Holman passed 16 yards to Wes Fesler for a first quarter touchdown, and connected with Charles Coffee for a 21-yarder in the final period. Halfback Byron Eby sprinted 21 yards untouched on a "naked reverse" for an OSU touchdown near halftime. The Buckeyes led in first downs, 13-1, and in total offensive yards, 157-50. This was Ohio State's first victory over Michigan at Ohio Stadium after losses in 1922, 1924 and 1926.

College Football's Utmost Prank

The election of Maudine Ormsby as Ohio State's 1926 homecoming queen is one of the most remarkable college shenanigans of all time. Maudine was a pure-bred Holstein cow.

Fraternities and sororities submitted the names of 10 women candidates for queen, and "Miss Ormsby" was sponsored by the College of Agriculture. A more fraudulent election was never held!

Ohio State's enrollment totaled 9,300 students in 1926, yet more than 12,000 ballots were cast. Maudine was declared Queen after the election committee was unable to unravel the ballot-stuffing dilemma.

Maudine rode in the homecoming parade, but university officials refused to let the bovine attend the traditional homecoming dance held at the Crystal Slipper dance hall, located on the north side of Lane Avenue close to where the French Field House now stands.

Had it not been for Maudine, the candidate who would have been queen was Rosalind Morrison Strapp. In fact, she actually won the election but respectfully withdrew from the race once it was clear there was voting fraud. In later years Strapp laughed and joked about the event, agreeing that it truly was her claim to fame. After graduation in 1927, Strapp attended every Ohio State homecoming

Homecoming Queen Maudine Ormsby. *Courtesy Ohio State University Photo Archives*

until her death in 1986. Strapp often joked that her epitaph should read: "But for Maudine, here lies a queen."

The memory of this prank lives today in a very concrete way. The Maudine Cow room in the Ohio Union is decorated in an eye-catching cow theme. Not only is it a whimsical reminder of a hilarious stunt, it honors Ohio State's agriculture tradition and history as a land grant institution.

Almost forgotten from Ohio State's 1926 homecoming was the football game itself. In one of the finest contests ever staged between Ohio State and Michigan, the Wolverines won 17-16 to deal the Buckeyes their only loss of the season. It also was the only Ohio State-Michigan game to be decided by a single point until the Buckeyes won 42-41 at Ann Arbor in 2013.

Double Delight!

The only thing better than one team from Ohio defeating Michigan is TWO teams from Ohio defeating the Wolverines, both in the same season.

Ohio Wesleyan University won 17-7 at Michigan on Oct. 6, 1928. Two weeks later on Oct. 20, Ohio State won at home over Michigan, 19-7. Ohio Wesleyan finished the season at 8-1, Ohio State at 5-2-1 and Michigan at 3-4-1.

GREAT GAMES REMEMBERED
Ohio State 6 – Princeton 6
Nov. 3, 1928 – Columbus, Ohio

A homecoming crowd of 72,496 witnessed one of the most prominent non-conference games ever played in Ohio Stadium, as Ohio State and Princeton battled to a 6-6 deadlock. At 4-0, the Buckeyes had given up only one touchdown, while the 3-0-1 Tigers entered the match-up unscored upon.

> SUPREMACY OF EAS
>
> *PRINCETON AND OHIO STATE BATTLE EVEN*
>
> Each Eleven Misses Opportunities to Put the Game on Ice—Stars Numerous.

Courtesy The Columbus Dispatch, Nov. 4, 1928

The Nov. 5 *Columbus Citizen's* description of the game included the following:

> *Ohio and Princeton supporters will never reach an agreement on who should have won the game. But they'll always agree on one point. It was one of the greatest games played anywhere by any two teams.*

Princeton's excellent halfback Al Wittmer scored in the third period, while Buckeye star Byron Eby retaliated with less than three minutes remaining. Ohio State finished the year at 5-2-1; Princeton at 5-1-2.

CHAPTER FOUR

1929-1933

Football and
The Great Depression

Sam Willaman, John Wilce's top assistant from 1926 through 1928, was generally assumed to be Wilce's replacement as head coach in 1929. Columbus newspapers referred to his appointment as "merely a formality." However, Athletic Director L.W. St. John told the Athletic Board at a meeting on Dec. 22, 1928, that he needed more time to evaluate other candidates and provided few details.

St. John was confidentially aware that Notre Dame coach Knute Rockne had an interest in the Ohio State position. In December of 1928, while visiting the Big Ten offices in Chicago, Rockne had quietly informed Big Ten Commissioner John Griffith that he would like to talk with Ohio State. Griffith immediately called St. John, told St. John he had a young coach sitting in his office that wanted to meet with the Ohio State Athletic Director, then handed the telephone to Rockne. Rockne explained to St. John that he would like to be considered for the Ohio State job.

Notre Dame was still playing home games at Cartier Field that seated fewer than 30,000 spectators, while other programs like Ohio State and Michigan recently had built new stadiums that each seated more than 60,000. Rockne was not happy when he was unable to obtain any commitment from his school that a larger stadium would soon be constructed.

St. John and Rockne met at the American Football Coaches Association annual meeting in New Orleans in early January of 1929. The two apparently reached an agreement for Rockne to become Ohio State's new coach, under the condition that Rockne could be released from his current contract.

When Rockne returned to South Bend, however, he was convinced to remain at Notre Dame and not take the Ohio State position. The Notre Dame administration promised a new stadium and construction began immediately, close to the site of Cartier field which was torn down to make room for the new stadium. The Fighting Irish played their home games in 1929 at Soldier Field in Chicago, affectionately called Notre Dame's "back yard home field." Notre Dame Stadium was completed in time for the 1930 season with a capacity of nearly 60,000.

EXTRA

Columbus Evening Dispatch.

OHIO'S GREATEST HOME DAILY

VOL. 58, NO. 200   * * *   COMPLETE EDITION   WEDNESDAY, JANUARY 16, 1929.   THIRTY-FOUR PAGES   PRICE TWO CENTS.

NAME WILLAMAN OHIO COACH

Courtesy The Columbus Dispatch, Jan. 16, 1929

Whether Rockne was merely trying to gain leverage for a larger stadium or whether he seriously contemplated coaching the Buckeyes will never be known, for history states that he was "unusually silent on the matter."

With Rockne out of the picture, Sam Willaman was appointed head coach by the Ohio State Athletic Board on Jan. 16, 1929. The 39-year-old had been a star end and halfback at Ohio State from 1911 through 1913. Still very agile and slim, Willaman looked like he could still carry the football as he did when he scored four touchdowns during a 58-0 blasting of Northwestern in his last collegiate game.

College football attendance across the country dropped dramatically during 1929. On Oct. 24, known as "Black Thursday," the national stock market suffered a significant decline. The following Tuesday, Oct. 29, a record 16,410,030 shares were sold as stockholders panicked and lost huge sums of money. More than 5,000 banks in the United States closed from 1929 through 1933, and the value of domestic goods and services produced annually fell 46 percent to $56 billion from $104 billion. The unemployment rate surged to 25 percent.

Coach Sam Willaman is flanked by assistant coaches George Houser (left) and Don Miller. Hauser had been an All-American tackle and captain at Minnesota in 1917. Miller was the right halfback in Notre Dame's famed "Four Horseman" backfield of 1924. *Courtesy Ohio State University Photo Archives*

All-American end Sid Gillman, coach Sam Willaman, and two-time All-American guard Joe Gailus. Gillman and Gailus were co-captains in 1933. *Courtesy Ohio State University Photo Archives*

Ohio State averaged only 35,657 fans per game in 1929, compared with 46,451 the previous season. Season openers the next three years each drew fewer than 20,000 spectators. The Ohio Stadium attendance in 1933 dropped to an average of 27,813 per game.

Willaman coached the Buckeyes through 1933, compiling a very respectable five-year record of 26-10-5 (69.5%). But there were no Big Ten titles and a less-than-stellar record of 2-3 against Michigan.

End Wes Fesler – Three-Time All-American. *Courtesy Ohio State University Photo Archives*

Willaman was a strong fundamentalist who stressed physical conditioning and attention to details, but to many he appeared to be distant and reserved.

There was a growing discontent among alumni and fans, and even within his own athletic department. Ohio State's student newspaper, the *Lantern*, openly called for a coaching change. Willaman resigned his position as head coach on Jan. 30, 1934, then immediately announced that he had accepted an offer as head coach at Western Reserve University.

Many close to him recognized how much happier he became after his resignation. Others realized that he was eagerly looking forward to a "fresh start" with his new position.

In 1934, Willaman directed Western Reserve to its first Cleveland Big Four Conference title with a record of 7-1-1. He suffered from failing health the following spring, and passed away at age 44 on Aug. 18, 1935.

Double Duty

Ohio State opened its 1929 season on Oct. 5 with a 19-0 triumph over Wittenberg before an Ohio Stadium crowd of 27,918. Michigan's opener one week earlier was an unusual "doubleheader." It was primarily an effort to generate higher revenues. The Wolverines outscored Albion 39-0 in their first game, then defeated Mount Union 16-6 in the second contest. A Michigan Stadium gathering of 16,412 attended the two games. Michigan also opened with doubleheaders the following two seasons. The Wolverines defeated Denison (33-0) and Eastern Michigan (7-0) in 1930, and won over Central Michigan (27-0) and Eastern Michigan (34-0) in 1931.

Getting Navy's Goat

Navy was Ohio State's Homecoming opponent in 1931, with the Nov. 7 contest played in a solid downpour of sleet and rain. It would appear to be a perfect marriage — Navy and a lot of water. But from the very beginning, nothing went well for the sailors.

The Midshipmen were accompanied to Columbus by their mascot goat, whose color had become a somewhat dirty gray from all its travels throughout the season. Navy had taken a live goat to all its games since the mascot first appeared at the Army-Navy game of 1893. Navy won 6-4 that year and elected to adopt the goat for good luck.

Courtesy Tom Hayes

A group of mischievous Ohio State students found the goat bedded down in one of the campus agriculture buildings the Friday night prior to the game. They dyed a portion of the animal with mercurochrome, a bright red topical antiseptic. Saturday morning the Navy plebes were stunned when first sighting their "Scarlet and Gray" mascot. Despite a rigorous scrubbing, the plebes were unable to remove the reddish color. Fortunately the goat was not harmed through all of this.

Navy's visit to Columbus got only worse in the afternoon — Ohio State won, 20-0.

Big Ten Charity Initiative

In the 1930s, most Americans were suffering from the economic impact of the Great Depression. In an effort to help Midwestern families, the Big Ten Conference extended the 1931 season by adding three charity games between the league's top six teams, and donated the proceeds to unemployment relief funds in the seven conference states. On Sat., Nov. 28, Ohio State played at Minnesota, Michigan hosted Wisconsin, and Purdue faced Northwestern at Soldier Field in Chicago.

The Golden Gophers won easily over the Buckeyes, 20-7. On a very cold and windy afternoon in Minneapolis, approximately 25,000 fans attended and contributed $46,000 to the conference's unemployment relief effort. Michigan defeated Wisconsin 16-0, and Purdue won over Northwestern 7-0.

The three games counted in the league standings, allowing both Purdue and Michigan to share the Big Ten title with Northwestern, all at 5-1. Northwestern would otherwise have been the outright champion with a conference mark of 5-0. Ohio State finished the year at 6-3 overall and 4-2 in league action.

GREAT GAMES REMEMBERED
Ohio State 16 — Pittsburgh 7
Nov. 15, 1930 — Columbus, Ohio

The Buckeyes were 3-2-1 when they faced Pitt. The favored Panthers were 5-1-1. Three-time All-American Wes Fesler played superbly in his final game at Ohio Stadium. Normally an end, Fesler played almost the entire game at fullback. He called the offensive signals and completed eight of 11 passes. Fesler would later become head coach at both Pitt (1946) and Ohio State (1947-1950).

The Buckeye defense intercepted four Panther passes to help limit the visitors to a single touchdown. It was the Buckeyes' very first victory over the powerful Panthers.

The News Unbiased and Unbossed

SUNDAY Ohio State **JOURNAL**   *MAIN Section*

WEATHER: Occasional rain Sunday; colder Monday.   COLUMBUS, OHIO, SUNDAY, NOVEMBER 16, 1930.   EST. 1811.   VOL. CXX   NO. 320.   PRICE TEN CENTS.

BUCKS TAME PITT PANTHERS, 16 TO 7

Courtesy Ohio State Journal, Nov. 16, 1930

Michigan band performs "Script Ohio" in 1932. *Courtesy George N. Hall*

Creating "Script Ohio"

The Ohio State Marching Band celebrated the 80th anniversary of its renowned "Script Ohio" in 2016. The distinguished moving formation was first performed during halftime of a home game against Pittsburgh on Oct. 10, 1936.

Mr. George N. Hall, a 1935 graduate of Michigan, remembered that his school's marching band presented the initial Script Ohio four years earlier when Michigan played at Ohio State on Oct. 15, 1932. Mr. Hall was a member of the 1932 Michigan band and made available the accompanying picture.

Reverend Joe Hotchkiss, a Michigan graduate, related that in 1932 Ohio State asked each visiting band to recognize the 10th anniversary of Ohio Stadium during its halftime show. According to Hotchkiss, the Michigan band developed the script configuration and then gave the charts to Ohio State, since Michigan would obviously have no further use for the formation.

There are many differences of opinions whether the Michigan Marching Band actually executed a moving script formation. Hall loved to debate the controversy. "I concede that Ohio State can both write and spell and that their brass band is reasonably good," he related, "but they weren't the first to do the script. We were!"

Disappointing Trip Across The Board

Could Indiana's trip to Columbus on Nov. 4, 1933, have been any worse? The Hoosier Marching Band left Bloomington by bus very early the morning of the game. Unfortunately, the truck carrying the band instruments developed mechanical problems and did not reach Ohio Stadium until late in the third quarter.

The band had to perform its halftime show after the game.

Meanwhile, Ohio State Coach Sam Willaman's new wingback formation worked to perfection. Sophomores Stan Pincura, Dick Heekin, and John Kabealo each scored touchdowns to spark the Buckeyes to a 21-0 triumph.

It was just a "bad day all the way around" for Indiana.

Together Again

Lew Hinchman was a three-time All-American halfback and quarterback from 1930-1932. He was the team captain and MVP his senior season. Two of his 1932 backfield teammates were halfback Bill "Blond Express" Carroll and fullback Buzz Wetzel. The three had been teammates at Columbus North High School, just north of the Ohio State campus on Arcadia Avenue.

Lew Hinchman. *Courtesy Ohio State University Photo Archives*

Unexpected Assistance

In football's earlier seasons, the head linesman would fire a blank pistol into the air to signal the end of the half and the end of the game. The practice was discontinued in the early 1980s.

Ohio State faced Illinois at home on Nov. 25, 1933, the final game of the season. With the Buckeyes leading 7-6 very late in the game, the Fighting Illini had driven from their own 35 to the Ohio State 15.

A spectator sitting on the stadium's west side had brought a concealed pistol into the game. With under a minute remaining, the viewer fired a blank cartridge into the air that sounded exactly like a head linesman's shot signaling the end of the game. Players from both teams started for their dressing rooms, thinking that the game was over, and many fans headed for the exits.

After the officials were able to gain control and clear the field, the Fighting Illini's David Cook attempted a relatively short field goal of approximately 32 yards. Cook's concentration was likely affected by all the confusion. His kick was low and to the left of the goal post, and the Buckeyes survived with the single-point victory.

GREAT GAMES REMEMBERED
Ohio State 20 - Pennsylvania 7
Nov. 11, 1933 - Philadelphia, Pennsylvania

Ohio State played one of its finest games of the season before an Armistice Day crowd of more than 40,000 at Penn's Franklin Field. Senior tackle Ted Rosequist was singled out for his excellent defensive play against the Quakers.

Watching the game from the press box was noted college coach Glenn "Pop" Warner. Among the more than 1,000 Ohio State alumni attending was Bill Daugherty, composer of "Across the Field," who lived in New York City.

Changing Rituals

From 1919-1933, Ohio State's last game of the regular season was against Illinois. The Buckeyes closed out their 1934 campaign at home against Iowa. In 1935, Ohio State and Michigan began the grand tradition of squaring-off in the final game of the regular season — odd years at Ann Arbor and even years in Columbus. Some Ohio State fans say it is easy to remember that games during the odd years are played in Michigan, because they consider some Michigan people to be very odd.

Groundskeeping legend Tony Aquila and his stadium sweeping crew. For 40 seasons, from 1907 through his retirement in 1947, he took great pride in the quality of the playing fields at old Ohio Field and Ohio Stadium. Aquila was very popular with athletic officials, players and fans alike. *Courtesy Ohio State University Photo Archives*

CHAPTER FIVE

1934-1940

Mr. Razzle-Dazzle

The Great Depression reached its lowest point in 1933. Approximately 15 million Americans were jobless and nearly half of the country's banks had failed. Ohio State's average home attendance of 22,743 in 1932 is the lowest in Ohio Stadium history. By 1935 there were clear signs of economic recovery, and this upturn favorably impacted college football. Ohio State's average home crowd increased to 56,515 in 1936.

With a better economy, many schools began to court radio stations to broadcast their entire season, rather than cover only selected games as had been the practice. This new mutually beneficial relationship greatly helped popularize college football. In the warmer climates, new postseason bowl games emerged. The

Coach Francis Schmidt. *Courtesy Ohio State University Photo Archives*

Coach Francis Schmidt often added new plays to his "Razzle Dazzle" offense at halftime. *Courtesy Ohio State University Photo Archives*

first Sugar, Orange and Sun Bowls were played on Jan. 1, 1935, and the first Cotton Bowl was played on Jan. 1, 1937.

The amiable Francis Schmidt was introduced as Ohio State's new head coach on March 2, 1934. Schmidt came from Texas Christian, where his teams had achieved a splendid five-year record of 47-5-5 (86.8%) that included two Southwest Conference titles. He signed a three-year agreement at an estimated annual salary of $7,500, becoming the first Ohio State coach to receive a multi-year contract.

Recognized as an offensive genius, Schmidt endorsed a wide-open style of football that was a sharp contrast with the more conservative approach of his predecessor, Sam Willaman. His "razzle-dazzle" offense contained more than 300 plays that were run from seven different formations. Two or three laterals behind the line of scrimmage were not uncommon. An extreme eccentric with boundless energy, he continually devised new plays 12 months a year.

Schmidt immediately endeared Ohio State fans when his first team of 1934 went 7-1, outscoring its eight opponents 267-34. The single setback came at Illinois, 14-13, when OSU's extra point attempt following its first touchdown sailed right of the goal post. Fans became fond of Schmidt's style of football, and home attendance in 1934 averaged 41,019 — at the time the second-highest in Ohio Stadium history.

Beginning in 1935, the annual Ohio State–Michigan game was moved to the last game of the regular season. At Michigan Stadium that year, the Buckeyes shut out the Wolverines, 38-0. It is Ohio State's all-time largest margin of victory over Michigan. OSU led in first downs, 20-5, and total offensive yards, 447-85.

Schmidt's teams won two Big Ten championships. The first was a co-title with Minnesota in 1935 — the Buckeyes and Golden Gophers did not meet that season. The second was an outright crown in 1939, even though the Buckeyes

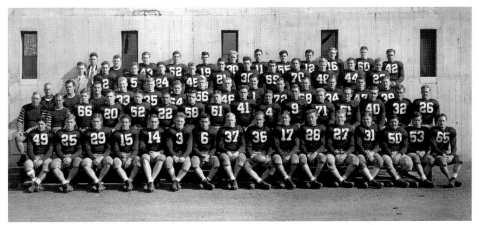

Ohio State – 1939 Outright Big Ten Champion. *Courtesy Ohio State University Photo Archives*

lost at Michigan, 21-14. It is the only time Ohio State has captured the league championship outright while losing to the Wolverines that same season.

While Schmidt was a true offensive football pioneer, he was far less talented in team organization and administration. By 1940 player morale was noticeably lower, and there was a growing dissatisfaction about the football program from within the Ohio State Athletic Department. The 1940 team's record of 4-4 included a 40-0 home loss to Michigan.

On Dec. 16, 23 days after the lopsided setback to the Wolverines, Athletic Director L.W. St. John met with Schmidt to review the condition of the football program. Schmidt resigned later that day in lieu of being removed from his position.

Schmidt's seven-year Ohio State record was a very fine 39-16-1 (70.5%). Although best known for their offensive accomplishments, his teams also registered 25 shutouts during his 56 games with the Buckeyes.

Schmidt took over as head coach at the University of Idaho in 1941. The school was one of more than 350 to suspend football beginning in 1943, because of a shortage of male students during World War II. Schmidt passed away at age 58 on Sept. 19, 1944. He was posthumously inducted into the College Football Hall of Fame in 1971.

Captains Breakfast Tradition

Each season former Ohio State captains gather for breakfast prior to a home game, normally homecoming. The concept was initiated by Columbus businessman Walter Jeffrey, who thought that past Buckeye captains should be so honored. Jeffrey was a graduate of Williams College, and held a special affection for Ohio State football. His family was deeply rooted in the Columbus business world, and Jeffrey was influential in the colossal campaign to raise funds for the construction of the Ohio Stadium.

The first Captains Breakfast was held in 1934 at the Scioto Country Club, with approximately 20 former captains and coaches attending. Today, this annual tradition is normally held the morning of the homecoming game, with new captains being welcomed by past captains. Each new captain receives a mug bearing his name and season.

Ronald Reagan Vividly Remembered Ohio State & Notre Dame

The late Jimmy Crum, longtime popular sports anchor at WCMH-TV4 in Columbus, received the Sertoma International Service to Mankind Award in 1984. Crum was recognized for his lifetime charity work and service to others. In appreciation of this honor, Crum and his wife Miriam were privileged to visit President and Mrs. Reagan at the White House. Reagan once said that as a young man he loved acting, politics and sports — and was not sure in which order.

During his early years, Reagan was Sports Director at radio station WHO in Des Moines, Iowa. When his conversation with the Crums turned to Ohio State football, Reagan recalled being in Iowa City to broadcast the Iowa-Indiana game on the same Saturday Notre Dame was playing at Ohio State in 1935. At that time, scores of other games were provided by Western Union ticker tape.

Reagan knew that the entire nation was interested in the Ohio State-Notre Dame game, so he frequently announced the score. Aware that the Buckeyes had been leading 13-0 in the fourth quarter, he was shocked to receive a ticker tape showing the final score: Notre Dame 18. Ohio State 13. "I thought it was an error. I couldn't believe Notre Dame would have been able to score three touchdowns in so little time," Reagan told the Crums, "so I never announced the final score."

That 1935 game between Ohio State and Notre Dame, noted as a "Game of the Century," is regarded as one college football's most significant games. And the Indiana at Iowa game Reagan was broadcasting? It finished as a 6-6 tie.

Fascinating Connection

The student manager of Notre Dame's 1935 team was Woody Stillwagon, father of Ohio State's two-time All-American middle guard Jim Stillwagon who captured both the Outland Trophy and Lombardi Award in 1970.

I'm the One Who Threw the Pass!

Bo Gallo of O.P. Gallo Tailoring and Formal Wear in Columbus loved to recall an incident that occurred approximately 25 years after the famous Ohio State–Notre Dame game of 1935. One Saturday morning just before Gallo opened his downtown store, a gentleman knocked at the front door and asked if he could have a button sewed on his sport coat.

Gallo took the gentleman inside and personally sewed on the button. It was a football Saturday, and Gallo asked the man if he was in town to see the Ohio State game. "Yes," he replied, "I'm one of the officials who will be working today's game at Ohio Stadium."

The two introduced themselves, with the man identifying himself as Mike Layden. Gallo asked him if he was related to the famous former Notre Dame coach, Elmer Layden. "Yes, Elmer is my older brother," Mike replied.

Gallo then recalled the 1935 Ohio State–Notre Dame game, mentioning that his brother-in-law, Frank Antenucci, had been a Buckeye fullback who made an interception that afternoon. "After the interception, Frank lateraled to halfback Frank Boucher who sped 65 yards for Ohio State's first touchdown," he remembered.

Gallo then asked Layden if he might have seen this game. Layden laughed a little, then said he had not only seen the contest, but that he played at Notre Dame when his brother was head coach, and had been one of the starting halfbacks that

GREAT GAMES REMEMBERED
Ohio State 10 — Colgate 7
Oct. 20, 1934 — Columbus, Ohio

Colgate had aspirations of capturing the 1934 national title and playing in the Rose Bowl. The visitors were guided by noted head coach Andy Kerr. Ohio State's 10 points were the highest scored against Colgate since New York University defeated the Red Raiders 13-0 at Yankee Stadium in 1931.

Halfback Jack Smith, playing with an injured knee, plunged 1 yard for Ohio State's touchdown late in the final quarter. Guard Regis Monahan's second-quarter field goal from the 22-yard line proved to be the eventual margin of victory. This was a major triumph for Ohio State's first-year coach Francis Schmidt, played before a depression-era Ohio Stadium crowd of 29,130.

Ohio State and Colgate both finished the season with records of 7-1. Illinois dealt the Buckeyes their lone setback at Champaign on Oct. 13, 14-13.

afternoon against Ohio State. With that, Gallo said, "Do you remember Frank's interception?" Layden replied, "Mr. Gallo, I remember it all too well. I'm the one who threw the pass!"

Impromptu Practice Site

Ohio State won 20-13 at Chicago on Saturday, Nov. 9, 1935. The team traveled to Chicago by train the previous Thursday, and stayed at the Windemere Hotel near the University of Chicago campus. The Michigan Wolverines were playing at Illinois that Saturday, and also stayed Thursday evening at the same hotel.

Coach Francis Schmidt had scheduled a Friday afternoon practice for his Ohio State squad at Chicago's Stagg Field. Michigan had also planned a Friday afternoon practice at Stagg Field before traveling to the Illinois campus in Champaign. The Chicago Athletic Department assumed both teams could share the stadium for their practices, but did not inform either school of the arrangement.

Schmidt was furious when he and his team arrived for practice and learned that Michigan would simultaneously be using the facility. He immediately took his players to a public park near the Chicago campus for their afternoon practice, rather than share Stagg Field with the Wolverines! Had it been any other team, Schmidt may have been willing to divide the practice field, but he definitely wanted no association with the Maize and Blue!

Delay Denied!

College teams normally traveled by train to their away games until the 1950s. In 1935, the Ohio State team stayed in Detroit the Friday evening prior to its game at Michigan the following afternoon. Saturday morning, it was planned for the train carrying the team from Detroit to Ann Arbor to arrive on a siding adjacent to Michigan Stadium. Unfortunately, the train engineer became confused and turned onto an incorrect siding six blocks from the stadium. When the engineer finally realized his mistake, it was too late to make any correction.

The Ohio State players and coaches were regrettably forced to get off the train, then carry their uniforms and equipment the six block distance to the stadium. They arrived approximately 15 minutes prior to the scheduled kickoff. Coach Francis Schmidt requested that the start of the game be delayed to allow his team sufficient time to warm up. Michigan refused! Schmidt was extremely outraged! Apparently the shortened warm up did not affect the Buckeyes. Ohio State won, 38-0.

Card Tricks

Coach Francis Schmidt was constantly designing new plays for his offense. Quarterback Tippy Dye recalled that it was almost impossible to remember all of his team's plays. With such a complex offense, the quarterbacks wrote the title and brief description of each play on a 3x5 card and carried the cards inside their helmets. During timeouts they could quickly look through the cards to remind themselves of the many plays.

Midway through Ohio State's encounter at Michigan in 1935, Dye was soundly tackled, his helmet flew off, and his play cards quickly scattered across the playing field. Michigan's curious players quickly examined some of Dye's cards — but with little benefit during Ohio State's 38-0 victory.

Shelbyville Always a Big Winner

Ohio State played at Notre Dame on Oct. 31, 1936. Dr. Chalmer Hixson, a 1937 Ohio State graduate, remembered a group of Ohio State students leaving Columbus very early that morning to attend the game. Regrettably, their car broke down near Shelbyville, Ind., and they missed the game while their car was being repaired.

While returning to the Ohio State campus late that evening, the students decided it would be amusing to tell their friends they had attended a very exciting football game that afternoon between "Shelbyville University" and "Snake Valley Normal." Many of their friends actually believed their concocted story.

The following season the group explained their tale to Mr. Leo Staley, longtime Ohio Stadium public address announcer, and asked Staley to occasionally include Shelbyville when announcing scores of other games from around the country.

Courtesy Tom Hayes

Staley always enjoyed a good practical joke, and liked the idea. For the next several seasons he occasionally included the score of the Shelbyville-Snake Valley Normal game. Shelbyville was usually a big winner, often by as much as 50-0!

The First Heisman Trophy

The Heisman Memorial Trophy is awarded annually to the most outstanding college football player whose performance best exhibits the pursuit of excellence with integrity. It was originated in 1935 by the Downtown Athletic Club in New York City, and was first titled The Downtown Athletic Club Award. Following the death of the DAC Athletic Director John Heisman on Oct. 3, 1936, the award was renamed in his honor.

Halfback Jay Berwanger of the University of Chicago was the first recipient in 1935, and his exceptional play during his team's 20-13 loss to Ohio State played a key factor with his selection. Early in the third quarter Berwanger rounded Ohio State's left end, reversed his field, then raced 85 yards for his team's second touchdown. Author Tom Perrin described it as " … the run which won the Heisman for Berwanger. He sliced through tackle at the 20-yard line, headed for the outside, then turned back toward center. At midfield, he was sandwiched between two defensive backs. He juked each one and ran between them. Once in the clear, he outran his pursuers for the touchdown."

Associated Press Poll Created

The weekly *Associated Press* college football rankings began in 1936. That season, Minnesota (7-1) was selected the mythical national champion, followed by Louisiana State (9-0-1), Pittsburgh (8-1-1), Alabama (8-0-1), and Washington (7-2-1). Northwestern (7-1) was the only other Big Ten team to finish in the *AP's* final rankings, placing seventh. Ohio State was listed only once in any of the 1936 weekly standings, ranking 18th in the Nov. 16 poll.

The initial polls from 1936 through 1960 ranked only the top 20 teams. In 1961, the number of ranked teams was reduced to 10, and then increased back to 20 from 1968 through 1988. Beginning in 1989, the poll expanded to rank the top 25 teams.

There have been a total of 1,120 weekly *Associated Press* college football polls during the 81 seasons from 1936 through 2016. Ohio State leads the nation in total

Associated Press Weekly Football Polls - 1936-2016

Total Appearances			Times Ranked #1				National Titles			
Team	#	%	Team	#	First	Last	Team	#	First	Last
1 Ohio State	870	77.7	1 Ohio State	105	1942	2015	1 Alabama	10	1961	2015
2 Michigan	823	73.5	2 Oklahoma	101	1950	2011	2 Notre Dame	8	1943	1988
3 Oklahoma	798	71.3	3 Notre Dame	98	1938	2012	3 Oklahoma	7	1950	2000
4 Notre Dame	770	68.8	4 USC	91	1939	2012	4 Miami	5	1983	2001
5 Alabama	759	67.8	5 Alabama	89	1961	2016	4 Ohio State	5	1942	2014
							4 USC	5	1962	2004

weekly appearances and times being top-ranked, and is tied with Miami and USC for fourth in national titles:

The Buckeyes were awarded *Associated Press* national titles in 1942, 1954, 1968, 2002, and 2014. Ohio State has been ranked at least once during 80 of the poll's first 81 seasons. The lone exception is 1947, when the Buckeyes finished with a record of 2-6-1.

Greatness in the Making

Two of Ohio State's fine assistant coaches during the late 1930s were Gomer Jones and Sid Gillman. Both were former Buckeye players who had been team captains and All-Americans. Jones was also twice named the team's MVP.

After Ohio State, Jones was a superb 17-year assistant to coach Bud Wilkinson at Oklahoma, where he became the architect of the Sooners' great offensive and defensive lines. Oklahoma established a college record 47-game winning streak between 1953 and 1957. After turning down many head coaching opportunities at other schools, Jones became the Sooners' head coach when Wilkinson retired after the 1963 season.

Gillman had much success as head coach at both Miami University and the University of Cincinnati, before beginning a notable 19-year professional career as head coach of the Los Angeles Rams, San Diego Chargers, and Houston Oilers. He became one of football's most innovative coaches, particularly with his creativity involving the deep passing game.

Jones and Gillman were both inducted into the College Football Hall of Fame, and Gillman was also inducted into the Professional Football Hall of Fame. Gillman is the only coach to have achieved both honors.

Assistant Coaches Gomer Jones and Sid Gillman. *Courtesy Ohio State University Photo Archives*

GREAT GAMES REMEMBERED
Notre Dame 18 — Ohio State 13
Nov. 2, 1935 — Columbus, Ohio

Ohio State and Notre Dame both entered the game undefeated and in pursuit of the national championship. The game attracted record media coverage including noted writers Grantland Rice, Francis Wallace, Damon Runyon, and Paul Gallico. It was broadcast nationally by CBS, NBC, and Mutual Radio, and Chicago's WGN-AM. The Ohio Stadium crowd totaled 81,018, but it was estimated that 200,000 tickets could have been sold for this game.

Coach Francis Schmidt's Buckeyes dominated the first half and led 13-0 at intermission. Coach Elmer Layden unexpectedly played his second team "shock troops" during the scoreless third quarter in a successful effort to wear down the larger Ohio State players. The Irish then rallied for three touchdowns in the final period for the amazing victory. The winning touchdown was a 19-yard pass from tailback Bill Shakespeare to end Wayne Milner with just 32 seconds remaining.

Ohio State finished the season at 7-1, tying Minnesota for the Big Ten title with identical league records of 5-0. Notre Dame's final record of 7-1-1 included a 14-7 loss to Northwestern and a 6-6 tie with Army at Yankee Stadium.

The 1969 season was college football's 100th anniversary. In a national poll of football writers and broadcasters, the 1935 Ohio State–Notre Dame encounter was selected the No. 1 game during the first 100 seasons of college football.

Courtesy The South Bend Tribune, Nov. 3, 1935

Totally Preoccupied with Football

Francis Schmidt concentrated solely on football 365 days a year. The eccentric coach always carried a supply of 3x5 cards and stubby pencils, and religiously made notes to himself as new plays came to mind. When in deep thought, Schmidt was completely oblivious to other actions close to him.

One winter morning in the late 1930s, Schmidt and Athletic Director L.W. St. John decided to go hunting east of Columbus. Schmidt was driving and stopped for gasoline along the way. While the station attendant was filling the car, St. John went inside to purchase some food while Schmidt stayed in the car to ponder some new

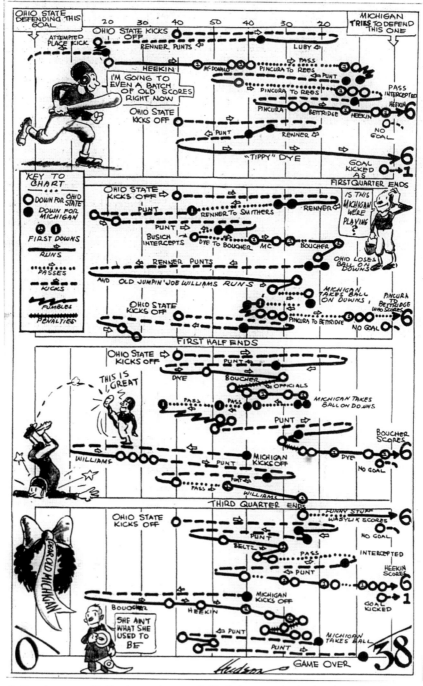

Grid grafs appeared in Sunday sports pages to illustrate a game's play-by-play action. Above grid graf describes 38-0 victory at Michigan in 1935. *Courtesy The Columbus Citizen, Nov. 25, 1935*

plays. When the attendant was finished, Schmidt paid for the gasoline and drove away. From inside the station, St. John was astonished to see Schmidt leave without him. Schmidt was several miles down the road before realizing he had left St. John, his boss, back at the service station.

GREAT GAMES REMEMBERED
No. 10 Ohio State 23 - Minnesota 20
Oct. 21, 1939 - Minneapolis, Minnesota

Ohio State and Minnesota had not met since the Buckeyes were defeated 19-7 at Minneapolis eight years earlier in 1931. Coach Bernie Bierman's Golden Gophers were national champions three of the previous five seasons, and had lost only twice in their last 32 Big Ten Conference games.

Coach Francis Schmidt's courageous squad twice came from behind for the emotional three-point victory. The Buckeyes led 16-14 at halftime, thanks to Charlie Maag's field goal at a difficult angle from the 21 near the end of the second quarter. After an exchange of second-half touchdowns, Buckeye defender Jack Graf intercepted Harold VanEvery's pass at the Ohio State 5 as the game came to a close.

Veteran *Columbus Citizen* sportswriter Lew Byrer called it "one of the greatest football games ever played anywhere by any two teams. I've never seen an Ohio State team show better blocking than the Buckeyes exhibited against the Gophers." An enthusiastic crowd of 5,000 greeted the Ohio State team train when it returned to Columbus Sunday evening.

Two-Time All-American Quarterback Don Scott Passed for Three Touchdowns at Minnesota in 1939. *Courtesy Ohio State University Photo Archives*

SiU — Ohio State's Sidewalk Fraternity

The great tradition of Ohio State is exemplified by its non-fraternity fraternity, SiU, an organization of male students that developed during the depression days of the 1930s. "It all began as a gag to impress coeds," related the late Nate Fraher, Ohio State class of 1937. "The name SiU was adopted from a wealthy fraternity at Kenyon College named Psi U, and we hoped co-eds would assume we were members of the same organization. Actually, very few of the guys could afford to belong to a real fraternity. We all shared two situations — great friendship and an acute lack of money."

Smitty's Drug Store at 16th and High Streets was a hangout for the group that included many members of the football team. The store basement became a popular spot to gather and socialize. Fraher was the store's soda jerk at the pretentious salary of 15 cents an hour. He jokingly referred to Smitty's as the international headquarters of Ohio State's sidewalk fraternity.

Two decades later Fraher and some others from the group decided it would be great fun if many of them could again get together. They scheduled a banquet for Friday, Nov. 15, 1957, the evening before a home game with Iowa. The response far exceeded even their most optimistic expectations, as over 200 returned for the first reunion. The group continued with a similar biennial get-together through the early 1990s.

Jim Smith, owner of Smitty's Drug Store, and Bob Hill of adjacent Hill Tailoring were honored at the first reunion as "SiU Men of the Year." Other subsequent honorees included track star Jesse Owens, Governor James Rhodes, cartoonist Milton Caniff, quarterback Tippy Dye, coach Woody Hayes, and Mrs. Anne Hayes. Heisman Trophy winners Les Horvath, Vic Janowicz, Hopalong Cassady and Archie Griffin were honored at the 1985 banquet.

The SiU Motto tells it all: Never had a Charter, House, Pin, or Dues. Never had a Formal Dance, Ritual, or any Extra Money. ALL WE HAD WAS FRIENDSHIP.

Schmidt's 300x7 Offense

Coach Francis Schmidt and his wife, Evelyn, lived in Columbus at 120 E. 15th Ave., just east of the Ohio State campus. The location is currently the home of Sigma Pi Fraternity.

Schmidt's wide-open offense contained more than 300 plays that were run from seven different formations. He used a small third floor bedroom at the front of the home as his office. It was there, 365 days a year, he designed much of his multiple-offense. The plays were often diagrammed on 3x5 cards that he would then spread all across the bed before filing them. Lights in the room were frequently burning all hours of the day and night.

Sid Gillman was a three-year assistant to Schmidt from 1938-1940. He later helped develop what is known as the "West Coast offense" while

Francis Schmidt home - 120 E. 15th Ave. *Courtesy Jack Park*

head coach of the San Diego Chargers in the early 1960s. He became known as the "father of the passing game" because of his innovative vertical passing attack. Gillman always believed that the foundation for his creative offense was shaped from what he learned from Schmidt during those three seasons at Ohio State.

Illegal Substitute?

Ohio State defeated Purdue 17-14 at Ohio Stadium on Oct. 5, 1940. With the score tied 14-14, placekicker Charlie Magg booted a 29-yard field goal with 19 seconds remaining to provide the thrilling three-point victory.

The following week it was revealed that Maag may have been an illegal substitution when he made the winning kick. Early in the second quarter, Magg was replaced at tackle by Jack Stephenson. Later that quarter, Magg returned to play and replaced Stephenson. College rules at that time prohibited a player from returning to action once he had played during that quarter.

When told of the possible infringement, coach Francis Schmidt reviewed the situation and acknowledged the violation. He took full responsibility for the infraction. Schmidt indicated that the Big Ten coaches had a "gentlemen's agreement" to self-govern themselves on this regulation, and that he had simply forgotten that Magg had been on the field in the early part of the second period.

It was reported that Ohio State may have contacted Purdue and offered to either forfeit the game or remove the field goal and permit the final score to remain at 14-14. If this offer was made, Purdue apparently declined the proposal. Each school reports the game as a 17-14 Ohio State victory.

Prime Pigskin Prognosticator

Friday evening, Nov. 1, 1940, noted *Columbus Citizen* sports columnist Lew Byrer covered Massillon High School's 28-0 home victory over Toledo Waite. Byrer reported that a rain-soaked capacity crowd of 21,500 saw the Tigers extend their victory string to 31 games, while at least another 20,000 Massillon fans were turned away at the gate. The following two sentences appeared in Byrer's next day column:

> *One of these fine days you'll read where Paul Brown of Massillon has been named head coach of some big college football team. When you do, make a notation in your future book to watch that college go places in football.*

Mr. Byrer had great intuition. Paul Brown replaced Francis Schmidt at Ohio State the following season, and the next year led the Buckeyes to their first national title in 1942.

In the early years the Ohio State football team traveled to away games by train. The players and coaching staff were often accompanied by football writers and others very close to the program. These autographs were obtained by youngster Nate Dawson when he and his parents accompanied the team to Michigan on Nov. 25, 1939. *Courtesy Nate Dawson*

CHAPTER SIX

1941–1950

The Graveyard of Coaches

Paul Brown, a bold architect of team effectiveness, took control of the Ohio State football program in 1941. At age 32, Brown became the Big Ten's youngest active coach. He had directed Massillon High School to an astounding nine-year record of 80-8-2 from 1932 through 1940. Brown was strongly recommended by the Ohio High School Football Coaches Association, with more than 500 of its members sending written endorsements to the Ohio State Athletic Department.

There was a noticeable contrast in coaching philosophy between Brown and his predecessor Francis Schmidt. Known as "Precision Paul, the Miracle Man from Massillon," the innovative Brown was exceptionally well organized and left nothing to chance. Practices were planned right down to the minute, and Brown relied closely on his assistant coaches who had clear-cut responsibilities for each practice.

Ohio State's 1941 team posted a fine record of 6-1-1. The season included an imposing 33-0 triumph at favored Southern California for Ohio State's very first victory over a west coast opponent. But just 15 days after a season-ending 20-20 tie at Michigan, the United States quickly plunged into World War II following Japan's Dec. 7 sneak attack on Pearl Harbor. During the next four years the country would be decidedly involved in an undertaking far more noteworthy than college football.

Coach Paul Brown. *Courtesy Ohio State University Photo Archives*

Ohio State captured its first National Title in 1942. *Courtesy Ohio State University Photo Archives*

Many major universities immediately began the training of military officers, and most military bases fielded football teams to help promote morale within the troops. Beginning in 1942, the Big Ten allowed its members to play 10 games rather than the prior limit of eight, and the league encouraged the scheduling of service teams. Ohio State added Fort Knox and Iowa Pre-Flight to its 1942 schedule.

In just Brown's second season at the helm, the 1942 Buckeyes captured the school's first national title with a record of 9-1. The squad of 43 included only three seniors. After the season, with the nation firmly immersed in World War II, most of the players soon entered the military where their talents were significantly needed and appreciated. A "football dynasty in the making" quickly was depleted.

In 1943 and 1944, most smaller colleges in Ohio and throughout the country discontinued football because of a shortage of players, as did many major programs including Alabama, Auburn, Boston College and Tennessee. The Big Ten Conference, in an effort to keep football active, temporarily made freshmen eligible for varsity competition. Ohio State's 1943 squad of 44 included only five players from the previous season, and all five had been deferred from military service.

At age 35, Paul Brown was still eligible for the military draft following the 1943 season. He was granted a Navy commission as a lieutenant junior grade, and reported to the Great Lakes Naval Training Center on April 12, 1944. Brown remained Ohio State's head coach "in absentia" with the intention of returning to the position after the war. He chose assistant coach Carroll Widdoes as "acting head coach" to direct the program until he returned.

Widdoes led the Buckeyes to a perfect 9-0 record in 1944, and became the first Ohio State coach to be selected "coach of the year," even though he was not officially the head coach. The Buckeyes were named mythical "national civilian champion," and placed second to Army in the final *Associated Press* poll. That season, quarterback Les Horvath became Ohio State's first Heisman Trophy winner.

On Feb. 8, 1945, Brown shocked the football world by accepting an offer to become head coach of Cleveland's franchise in professional football's new All-American Conference at the conclusion of World War II. His decision was not well-received by a portion of the Ohio State administration. Buckeyes fans were somewhat split on Brown's decision. Some wished him well with his new venture in Cleveland, while many others strongly believed he should have retained his loyalty to Ohio State.

Coach Paul Brown with 1942 backfield: left to right, wingback Les Horvath, fullback Gene Fekete, quarterback George Lynn, and tailback Paul Sarringhaus. Lynn was the team captain. Horvath, Fekete, and Sarringhaus all became All-Americans during their Ohio State careers. *Courtesy Ohio State University Photo Archives*

The word "acting" was immediately removed from Carroll Widdoes' title. Widdoes led the Buckeyes to a fine 7-2 mark in 1945, but did not relish the attention and pressure of being head coach. He was much happier as an assistant, and at season end asked to return to his previous position.

Athletic Director L.W. St. John promoted assistant coach Paul Bixler to head coach and granted Widdoes' request to return to his assistant coaching post. Widdoes

Ohio State was named "National Civilian Champion" in 1944. *Courtesy Ohio State University Photo Archives*

and Bixler simply switched positions. It remains one of the most unexpected and unusual coaching changes in college history.

After directing the Buckeyes to a record of 4-3-2 in 1946, Bixler abruptly resigned after just one season because of the demands and pressure of big-time college coaching. Ohio State was now developing the well-earned and unbecoming distinction as the "graveyard of coaches."

Coach Carroll Widdoes surrounded by 1944 All-Americans: end Jack Dugger, guard Bill Hackett, quarterback Les Horvath, and tackle Bill Willis. *Courtesy Ohio State University Photo Archives*

In an attempt to regain stability in its coaching ranks, Ohio State chose Wes Fesler who had been an outstanding three-time All-American end for the Buckeyes from 1928-30. Fesler guided the program four years before resigning after the 1950 season, citing how the pressure of coaching was affecting both his health and his family. There was much speculation that he accepted the opportunity to resign before being removed from his position.

Fesler compiled a very respectable four-year record of 21-13-3 (60.8%) that included Ohio State's first Rose Bowl victory, a 17-14 triumph over third-ranked

Ohio State won its first Rose Bowl in 1949. *Courtesy Ohio State University Photo Archives*

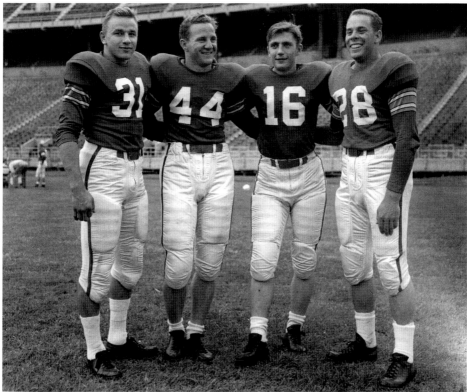

Left to right, 1949 halfbacks Vic Janowicz, Jerry Krall, Walt Klevay, Dick Widdoes. *Courtesy Ohio State University Photo Archives*

and previously undefeated California at the end of the 1949 season. Vic Janowicz became OSU's second Heisman Trophy recipient in 1950.

At age 42, Fesler proclaimed the end of his college coaching career and immediately entered the real estate business in Columbus. However, he surprisingly accepted the head coaching position at Minnesota just 47 days after leaving Ohio State. Fesler stayed with the Golden Gophers just three seasons with a record of 10-13-4. He spent the remainder of his working career in the financial services business in California. Fesler was inducted into the College Football Hall of Fame as a player in 1954.

Fesler was replaced at Ohio State by 38-year old Woody Hayes, the school's sixth different head coach over the last 12 seasons. Ohio State's reputation as the "graveyard of coaches" would soon be only a memory.

If You're Paul Brown,
I'm President Roosevelt!

Paul Brown's first game as Ohio State's new coach was a 12-7 home victory over Missouri on Sept. 27, 1941. When the team bus arrived at the south end of Ohio Stadium, Brown briefly stepped off the bus to greet some supporters from Massillon, including good friend Tink Ulrich. Meanwhile, the bus pulled inside the stadium and the gate was quickly closed, leaving Brown outside.

Brown tried to enter the stadium, but the gate attendant didn't recognize him and asked to see his ticket. "I don't have a ticket. I'm the new coach," Brown responded. "Is that right?" the attendant responded. "Well, I'm President Roosevelt, but you must have a ticket if you want to see today's game."

Brown hurried over below the stadium's southeast tower and began throwing stones against the tower windows. When one of the trainers finally looked down, Brown yelled, "Send someone out here who can get me through that gate!" The

Courtesy Tom Hayes

trainer ran down to the gate and explained that this man really was Ohio State's new coach. Brown was finally permitted to enter Ohio Stadium.

Discovering Otto Graham

Ohio State lost only one game during Paul Brown's first season as head coach in 1941. On Oct. 25, Northwestern defeated the Buckeyes 14-7 at Ohio Stadium. Brown marveled at the talented play of NU's sophomore tailback, Otto Graham, who passed for both Wildcat touchdowns.

Years later Brown remarked, "I never forgot Otto's tremendous peripheral vision, and his ability to run to his left before throwing far across the field with such strength and accuracy. His fine running ability made his passing all the more effective, and he could quickly survey the field and pick out the correct receiver."

Initially, Graham enrolled at Northwestern on a basketball scholarship, and nearly gave up football following knee surgery his freshman season. He became an All-American in each sport.

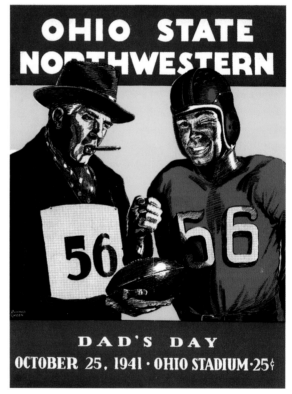

OHIO STATE NORTHWESTERN

DAD'S DAY
OCTOBER 25, 1941 · OHIO STADIUM · 25¢

After coaching a World War II service team two seasons at Great Lakes Naval Training Center in 1944-45, Brown accepted an offer from owner Art McBride to coach McBride's Cleveland Browns franchise in professional football's newly formed All-American Conference. The league began play in 1946.

Brown immediately contacted Ohio State nemesis Otto Graham, who was serving at Glenview Air Station near Chicago. They reached an agreement, and Graham became the Cleveland Browns' very first player.

Graham quarterbacked the Browns their first 10 seasons from 1946 through 1955, guiding them to the title game each year. Cleveland won seven league championships, and Graham was selected an All-Pro each season. On the 50th anniversary of their 1941 game, Ohio State and Northwestern played their 1991 contest in Cleveland's Municipal Stadium where Paul Brown and Otto Graham made professional football history.

1-2-3-4-5

During Ohio State's 46-34 victory over Wisconsin in 1941, the Badgers' second touchdown resulted from a "fifth down" 6-yard pass from left halfback Bud Seelinger to quarterback Tom Farris. After Farris had failed to score from scrimmage on fourth down, Wisconsin surprisingly called timeout. Referee Jim Masker became confused and awarded the Badgers an extra play. Coach Paul Brown intensely protested the official's miscount, but to no avail. Fortunately Masker's error did not impact the game's outcome.

Brown and Wisconsin coach Harry Stuhldreher were both from Massillon, Ohio, where they were highly regarded hometown football heroes. The 1941 game was Massillon Appreciation Day at Ohio Stadium. The Massillon High School Band appeared at halftime and spelled out "Paul" and "Harry" in honor of the two coaches.

OHIO STATE ★ WISCONSIN

NOVEMBER 8, 1941 ★ OHIO STADIUM ★ 25c

High Achievers

Halfback Les Horvath, end Dante Lavelli and tackle Don McCafferty all roomed together during the 1941-1942 school year. What a successful future each would have!

Horvath became Ohio State's first Heisman Trophy winner in 1944. Lavelli became one of the NFL's all-time greatest receivers with the Cleveland Browns, and in 1975 was inducted into the Professional Football Hall of Fame. McCafferty became the first NFL coach to lead his team to a Super Bowl title during his rookie season as head coach. McCafferty's first head coaching position was with the Baltimore Colts in 1970, the season his team defeated coach Tom Landry's Dallas Cowboys 16-13 in Super Bowl V, played at the old Orange Bowl in Miami.

A Most Unique Career

J.T. White has the distinction of playing on national championship football teams at both Ohio State and Michigan. Raised in Detroit, White played end on the Buckeyes' national title squad of 1942. After returning from military service following World War II, White elected to finish his education at Michigan where his older brother Paul had been captain in 1943. He was the starting center for the Wolverines' national champions of 1947, and was selected a second-team All-American.

White earned both bachelor's and master's degrees at Michigan. He served six seasons as a Wolverine assistant under coach Bennie Oosterbaan, followed by 26 seasons as a Penn State assistant under coaches Rip Engle and Joe Paterno. White was well loved and respected, and was very loyal to each school with which he was associated.

A Taste of Bad Water

Ohio State captured its first national title in 1942 with a record of 9-1. The lone setback came Oct. 31 at Wisconsin, 17-7, in what was soon labeled the "bad water game." The railroads committed all current railroad cars and equipment to the military during World War II, forcing the Buckeyes to travel to Madison in outdated railroad coaches that were pulled from storage for the trip. Old water had not been drained from the coaches, and many players became ill with a serious attack of dysentery. By Saturday, nearly half the squad could not play at full strength.

The Ohio State team stayed on the sixth floor of the Park Hotel in downtown Madison. The hotel's ancient elevators were closed for repair, forcing the players to navigate six flights of steps to their rooms. It was Halloween weekend and many loud parties continued outside the hotel, well into "the wee hours" of Friday night.

Ohio State at 5-0 was ranked No. 1, and Wisconsin was ranked No. 6 with a record of 5-0-1. The game was broadcast to what was believed to be, at the time, the largest radio audience ever to hear a football game. NBC's Bill Stern voiced the action for more than 200 stations that aired the game throughout the United States and to servicemen around the world.

A record Camp Randall Stadium homecoming crowd of nearly 45,000 watched the Badgers control the action most of the afternoon. Wisconsin led 10-0 at the half, and OSU's two lost fumbles in the third quarter seriously hampered any possible comeback.

The Badgers jumped to second in the following week's poll, while the Buckeyes dropped to sixth. However, Ohio State won its last four games in impressive style, and was able to regain the top spot in the Associated Press final poll at the end of the season.

Fighting Illini Move "Home Games" to Cleveland

College football attendance suffered during World War II, partly because of nationwide gas rationing that hampered fans from driving to the games. Most car owners were limited to purchasing four gallons of gasoline per week. The smaller crowds significantly impacted many athletic department budgets.

Ohio State Defeats Illinois 26 to 12; 83,627 See Eighth Straight Victory

Courtesy The Columbus Citizen, Nov. 19, 1944

Ohio State was scheduled to play at Illinois in both 1942 and 1944. Because of low home attendance, Illinois moved each of these home games to Cleveland, where Ohio State fans were having difficulty commuting to games in Columbus. The 1942 game at Municipal Stadium drew 68,586 (OSU won 44-20) and the 1944 game attracted 83,627 (OSU won 26-12). Ohio State was officially the "visiting team" each time. Illinois averaged only 19,260 fans for five games played in Champaign in 1942, and 21,039 for five games in 1944.

The Fifth Quarter Game

Ohio State's 1943 homecoming game against Illinois on Nov. 13 was thrilling from start to finish, with the lead changing hands four times. The Fighting Illini led 19-13 at halftime. The Buckeyes re-gained the lead 26-19, after scoring in each of the third and fourth quarters. Illinois retaliated with its only points of the second half to tie the game at 26-all midway through the final period.

With just 10 seconds remaining on the clock, the Buckeyes received a huge break when Illinois halfback Eddie McGovern fumbled and Buckeye quarterback Bobby McQuade recovered at the Illinois 23. With time for just one play, McQuade aimed a pass into the end zone for halfback Ernie Parks that fell incomplete. After field judge Irish Krieger fired his gun signaling that time had expired, both teams headed for their dressing rooms. Most of the Ohio Stadium crowd of 36,331 headed home, believing the game had ended in a 26-all tie.

Illinois' left tackle, however, had been offside on the game's final play. Few people, including the other game officials, had seen head linesman Paul Goebel signal the infraction. After quickly discussing the infringement, the officials agreed that the contest could not end on a defensive penalty. Referee Jim Masker went to the Ohio State dressing room and informed coach Paul Brown that his team was entitled to "one additional down." Krieger's task was much tougher. He delivered the same message to coach Ray Eliot in the Illinois dressing room. Masker was the same official who mistakenly gave Wisconsin a fifth down during the Badgers' game against Ohio State in 1941.

Nearly 15 minutes after McQuade's pass had fallen dead in the end zone, both squads returned to the field for one final down.

Johnny Stungis, a 17-year-old freshman from Powhatan Point, Ohio, calmly booted a 33-yard field goal to earn Ohio State a 29-26 "fifth quarter" victory. The historic three-pointer, which barely oozed over the middle of the crossbar, was the first and only field goal attempt of his career. Stungis had played tenor saxophone in the Powhatan Point High School Band until his senior year, when the school's coach convinced him to instead play football.

It was an extremely tough loss for Ray Eliot. His two fine halfbacks, Eddie Bray and Eddie McGovern, had combined for 249 yards rushing. Years later, Cincinnati sportswriter Pat Harmon asked Eliot about this game. Eliot stated, "If I had known there was an official knocking at the dressing room door and what he wanted, I would NEVER have allowed him to enter and talk with us!"

Not ALL In The Family

Ohio State freshman quarterback Howard Yerges, Jr. could not finish the 1943 season after getting his orders to report to the Navy on Nov. 1. Fortunately, Yerges had played enough during the season's first six games to earn a letter.

After World War II, Yerges enrolled at the University of Michigan and earned three letters from 1945-47. He was the starting quarterback for the Wolverines' undefeated national title team of 1947. His father, Howard Yerges, Sr., had been Ohio State's starting quarterback during the Buckeyes' very first two Big Ten championship seasons of 1916-17.

Exceptional Achievement Under Difficult Circumstances

"Acting Head Coach" Carroll Widdoes led the 1944 Buckeyes to a perfect 9-0 record, an outright Big Ten title and second place in the final *Associated Press* poll. Widdoes was born in the Philippines in 1903. His parents, Rev. and Mrs. Howard Widdoes, were missionaries to the Philippines for the United Brethren Church.

While Ohio State fans were enjoying the exceptional 1944 season, few knew about the personal strain Widdoes was experiencing. He was aware that his missionary parents had been captured by the Japanese and were being held as prisoners of war. Fortunately, both parents were found unharmed when rescued by United States Paratroopers in 1945.

Family Affair

Ohio State defeated Great Lakes Naval Station 26-6 at home on Oct. 21, 1944. During the third quarter, Ohio State quarterback Tom Keane attempted a short pass that was intercepted by Keane's older brother, Jim, a Bluejacket defender.

The Keane brothers were from Bellaire, Ohio. Both later enjoyed successful NFL careers, Tom with the Los Angeles Rams, Baltimore Colts and Chicago Cardinals; Jim with the Chicago Bears and Green Bay Packers. The Bluejackets were coached by Paul Brown, who had been Ohio State's head coach the previous three seasons.

GREAT GAME REMEMBERED
No. 3 Ohio State 18 – No. 6 Michigan 14
Nov. 25, 1944 – Columbus, Ohio

Ohio State thrilled its homecoming crowd of 71,958 with a masterful 18-14 triumph over Michigan. It was the first time the winner of this season-ending classic would be the outright Big Ten Conference champion. The lead changed hands after each of the game's five touchdowns.

With his team down 12-14 midway through the final period, quarterback Les Horvath led the Buckeyes 52 yards for the game-winning score with 3:16 remaining. Horvath was the game's leading rusher with 106 yards. At season end, he became Ohio State's first Heisman Trophy winner.

During its halftime show, the Ohio State Marching Band honored the 13,149 students and staff members who had left campus to serve their country during World War II.

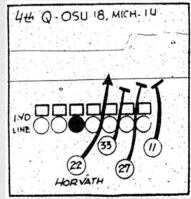

Tailback Les Horvath scores winning touchdown. *Courtesy The Columbus Citizen, Nov. 26, 1944*

Fred Taylor's Dad Honored

Ohio State began its Dad's Day tradition in 1921, when dads of all students were honored during a home game. The players' dads normally sat together behind the Ohio State bench for this game. Each year one dad with a son and/or daughter enrolled at Ohio State was recognized as the "Dad of Dads." The honored dad in

Courtesy Jack Park

1947 at the Oct. 18 game against Iowa was Mr. John F. Taylor of Zanesville, Ohio. Taylor's son, Fred, was a sophomore in the College of Education.

Fred would excel in both basketball and baseball for the Buckeyes. He was a starting forward for Ohio State's 1950 Big Ten title basketball team, and that spring became the Buckeyes' very first All-American baseball player as a first baseman. His jersey #27 was the school's first baseball number to be retired.

Taylor became Ohio State's head basketball coach in 1958-1959, and led the program to the NCAA championship in 1960. He was enshrined in the Basketball Hall of Fame in 1986. The drive on the west side of the Ohio State Schottenstein Center is named in his honor.

Losing Coach Two Years Running

Wes Fesler of Youngstown, Ohio, was one of Ohio State's finest all-around athletes, earning a total of nine letters in football, basketball, and baseball. He was a three-time football All-American from 1928-30, and a basketball All-American in 1931.

Fesler left the head football coaching position at Pittsburgh after the 1946 season to become Ohio State's head coach. Ironically, he became the losing coach in two consecutive Ohio State-Pittsburgh games. The Buckeyes defeated Fesler's Pitt Panthers 20-13 at Ohio Stadium on Nov. 9, 1946, and Pitt upset Fesler's Ohio State squad 12-0 at Pitt Stadium on Oct. 25, 1947.

Its Not Over Until Its Over!

Ohio State's 1947 clash against Northwestern, played Nov. 8 at Ohio Stadium, had one of the most bizarre and hectic finishes ever imagined. After three quarters of scoreless action, NU halfback Frank Aschenbrenner scored from the 1 on the second play of the fourth period to put the Wildcats on top 6-0. Jim Farrar's conversion attempt was wide. It was just his second miss of the season.

Later in the quarter Ohio State drove from midfield to the Northwestern 1, where the Wildcats held on downs with just one minute and 47 seconds remaining. Many of the 70,203 fans headed for the exits, apparently conceding the game to the visitors.

Then came the drama! After failing to gain a first down, Northwestern was forced to punt. Ohio State's Bob Demmel returned Tom Worthington's kick to the NU 36 with 31 seconds remaining.

On first down quarterback Pandel

Halfback Jimmy Clark and Coach Wes Fesler. *Courtesy Ohio State University Photo Archives*

Savic passed 24 yards to Demmel at the Wildcat 12. There were 13 seconds left. Savic's next pass was intercepted by L.A. Day as time expired, and Northwestern had apparently won, 6-0. The remaining fans were now pouring out of the stands, and the Ohio State Marching Band entered the field for its postgame show. However, Northwestern had 12 men on the field during the last play, and the Buckeyes were awarded one more down. Halfback Rodney Swinehart carried on a deep reverse and was tackled at the 2. But wait, Northwestern had two players lined up offside, and OSU would have yet another play. Savic fired a lobbing TD pass to Jimmy Clark in the back corner of the end zone to tie the score at 6-6.

Emil Moldea's critical extra point attempt was blocked, but AGAIN two Northwestern players were offside. Moldea's second attempt was good and Ohio State gained the victory, 7-6. Three Northwestern penalties had enabled the Buckeyes to score seven points on the second and fourth plays after time had expired.

Headlinesman E.C. Curtis, a 25-year veteran Big Ten official, called the three penalties against Northwestern after time had expired. Wildcat coach Bob Voigts might have been more disturbed if field judge Irish Krieger had flagged any of NU's infractions. Irish's son, George, was a reserve Ohio State lineman.

During a junior varsity game earlier that morning, Ohio State defeated Northwestern by the same 7-6 score.

Women At Last

Ohio State and Michigan played to a 7-7 tie at Michigan Stadium on Nov. 19, 1949. Among the 306 people packed inside the Michigan Stadium press box were eight women who operated the Western Union printing machines. This was the first season women had been allowed in this part of the stadium. Michigan's

GREAT GAME REMEMBERED
No. 6 Ohio State 17 - No. 3 California 14
Jan. 2, 1950 - Rose Bowl - Pasadena, Cal.

This was Ohio State's first Rose Bowl appearance since the Big Ten and Pacific Eight conferences agreed in 1946 to have their respective league champions meet in this New Year's Day classic. The Buckeyes entered with a record of 6-1-2.

The Golden Bears at 9-0 were coached by Lynn "Pappy" Waldorf, who had been very successful as coach at Northwestern from 1935-1946.

California controlled the first half and threatened to increase its 7-0 lead early in the third period. Buckeye defender Vic Janowicz significantly changed the game's momentum with a leaping interception at the Ohio State 25, followed by a 44-yard return to the California 31 to set up his team's first touchdown.

With the score tied 14-14 late in the final quarter, Jimmy Hague kicked a 35-yard field with 1:55 remaining to earn the Buckeyes a stirring 17-14 victory. It was the first Rose Bowl to be decided by a kick. Ohio State fullback Curly Morrison gained 119 yards on 25 attempts and was chosen the game's MVP.

Courtesy The Ohio State Journal, Jan. 3, 1950

working press box, like most other schools, had previously been a "men only" area.

First TV

Ohio State's thrilling 35-34 season-opening victory over Missouri on Sept. 24, 1949 was the first game televised from Ohio Stadium. Columbus station WLWC (now WCMH/NBC4) did the telecast that was sponsored by four Columbus Chevrolet dealerships. The Mutual Radio Network also broadcast the game nationally with admired sportscaster Russ Hodges describing the action.

MISSOURI OHIO STATE

25¢

SEPTEMBER 24, 1949

Name Game

Earle Bruce was a star halfback at Allegany High School in Cumberland, Md. Bruce was strongly recruited in 1949 by his namesake, Penn State assistant coach Earl Bruce. Bruce eventually elected to play at Ohio State under coach Wes Fesler.

First Come, First Serve

The Ohio State-Michigan game at Ohio Stadium on Nov. 20, 1948 attracted national attention. The undefeated Wolverines were ranked No. 1, while Ohio State at 6-2 was ranked No. 18.

In those years the CBS, NBC and Mutual radio networks each selected a "game of the week" for its national broadcast. Retired Ohio State Sports Information Director Marv Homan recalled that each network normally followed an unwritten policy of notifying the home school by Monday if that team's game the following Saturday had been chosen.

CBS, with well-known broadcaster Ted Husing, had selected the Ohio State-Michigan game several weeks in advance. By Monday evening prior to the game, then-SID Wilbur Snypp had had no contact from NBC, so Snypp assumed NBC was going elsewhere. However, NBC's prominent sportscaster Bill Stern called Snypp on Wednesday to request a booth. Stern was furious when he learned that the Ohio Stadium press box was full and all radio booths had been assigned, leaving no space for him to broadcast the game. There was quite a rivalry between Stern and Husing, so this likely added fuel to the fire.

To smooth things over and accommodate NBC, Snypp became creative. He had a temporary open-air platform erected adjacent to C deck and extending from Ohio Stadium's southwest corner. Two student spotters joined Stern on the stand, Ohio State's Dick Mantanaro and Michigan's Ray Collins. It was from this small makeshift dais overlooking the south end zone, that the famous "but not too happy" Bill Stern broadcasted the Ohio State-Michigan game of 1948. The Wolverines won, 13-3.

Family Matter

Ohio State traveled to Michigan in 1949, needing a win or tie to represent Ohio State in the Rose Bowl. With the Wolverines leading 7-0 midway through the final quarter, the Buckeyes marched 80 yards for a touchdown to narrow the score at 7-6. The drive's key play was a 47-yard completion from quarterback Pandel Savic to halfback Ray Hamilton. Fullback Curly Morrison bolted four yards into the end zone for the all-important touchdown.

Ohio State's condition initially looked bleak when Jimmy Hague's critical extra point attempt hooked wide to the right — but wait, Michigan was flagged for being offside. The Buckeyes may never have profited from a timelier penalty! Hague's second try was good, the game ended in a 7-7 tie, and Ohio State was headed to Pasadena.

Center Tony Momsen was the Michigan player who lined up offside on Hague's first conversion attempt. Tony's younger brother Bob played tackle for Ohio State. Because Tony had been offside, brother Bob was able to play in the Rose Bowl!

Left to right, author Jack Park, Warren Pierce-WJR Radio, Tony Momsen-Michigan, Bob Momsen-Ohio State. Pregame Detroit's WJR Radio Ohio State-Michigan game 1988. *Courtesy Jack Park*

Robert Hooey Remembered

Ohio State defeated California 17-14 in the Rose Bowl of Monday, Jan. 2, 1950. Buckeye Captain Jack Wilson and his teammates presented the Rose Bowl game ball to Mrs. Gladys Hooey, widow of former Ohio State Journal Sports Editor Robert Hooey, who died five weeks earlier from a Nov. 28 automobile accident. Hooey was a devoted sports journalist who meticulously covered the Ohio State football program for many years. He passed away before he could realize his favorite wish, covering an Ohio State victory in the Rose Bowl.

Hooey was buried in a multi-plot lot, purchased by his very close friend Billy Southworth, at Green Lawn Cemetery in Columbus. Southworth died of emphysema in 1969 and was buried next to Hooey. Southworth was a noteworthy Major League Baseball player, manager and Hall of Famer. He managed the St. Louis Cardinals to World Series titles in 1942 and 1944. Hooey's wife, Gladys, was laid to rest next to her husband following her death in 2001.

"Jim Zabel, Where Are You When I Need You?" — Jack Buck

The late Jim Zabel, longtime Sports Director at WHO Radio in Des Moines, Iowa, was a legend in his own time. Zabel followed Ronald Reagan as the sports voice at WHO, and began broadcasting University of Iowa football in 1950.

Zabel's first trip to Ohio Stadium to air the Ohio State-Iowa game of Oct. 28, 1950, developed into a "long afternoon" in more ways than one. Zabel began his pregame show without taking into consideration the one-hour time difference between Columbus and Des Moines. As the pregame show progressed, Zabel soon realized he had an additional hour of air time to fill.

Jack Buck, an Ohio State graduate who was doing the Buckeyes' play-by-play on WCOL Radio in Columbus, was in the adjoining radio booth. Zabel quickly brought Buck into his booth for an interview. During commercial breaks, Buck arranged for other media people in the press box to be Zabel's guests. "It was a really long pregame show," Zabel recalled, "but with Jack's help, we made it."

The game was also a long one for Zabel and his Iowa listeners. The Buckeyes completely outclassed the Hawkeyes, 83-21. It is Ohio State's all-time highest score in a Big Ten Conference game.

Jack Buck became a Baseball Hall of Fame announcer as the popular voice of the St. Louis Cardinals over KMOX Radio. He never forgot the 1950 Ohio State-Iowa game. Years later, when Buck was trying to fill air time during a baseball rain delay, he was known to say, "Jim Zabel, where are you when I need you? You still owe me one!"

The Unforgettable "Snow Bowl"

Words cannot explain the playing conditions at Ohio Stadium, when No. 8 Ohio State hosted Michigan on Nov. 25, 1950. With winds swirling at 40 miles per hour and the temperature hovering near 10 degrees, Columbus became paralyzed by one of the fiercest snowstorms ever in central Ohio.

Most other games in central Ohio were cancelled, but athletic directors Dick Larkins of Ohio State and Fritz Crisler of Michigan elected to play the game. It was rumored that Larkins wanted the game postponed, but Crisler insisted that Michigan would not return at a later date. It was homecoming, and more than 80,000 tickets had been purchased. Amazingly, 50,535 fans braved the weather to watch what would be a bizarre encounter.

With the playing conditions strongly neutralizing the running attacks, each team frequently punted on first down and waited for the other to commit a turnover. An NCAA record of 45 punts was established that afternoon, 24 by Michigan's Chuck Ortmann for 723 yards and 21 by Ohio State's Vic Janowicz for 685 yards.

Near halftime, Michigan center Tony Momsen blocked a Janowicz punt and recovered the ball in the end zone for the game's only touchdown. Ohio

Three of many unused tickets. Courtesy Estate of Emmett and Amelia Park

Playing in blizzard conditions, Ohio State and Michigan combined for only 43 yards rushing. *Courtesy Ohio State University Photo Archives*

State coach Wes Fesler was strongly criticized for punting on third down with just 47 seconds remaining in the second quarter, rather than running out the clock.

The Buckeyes rushed for 16 yards and completed just three of 18 passes for 25 yards. The Wolverines rushed for 27 yards and were unable to complete any of nine passes. Michigan won 9-3 without registering a single first down — Ohio State had just three.

Lost Boy Scout

The Ohio Stadium grounds crew had a very difficult assignment in removing the canvas from the frozen field prior to the 1950 "Snow Bowl." Many fans and Boy Scouts came down from the stands to assist the crew with clearing the field.

Early in the game a rumor spread that a Boy Scout named Roy Case fell on the slick surface, and was wrapped in the canvas as it was being rolled off the field. Fortunately, the rumor was not entirely true. He did fall, but managed to roll aside and avoid being trapped in the rolling tarp. Case remained active with the Boy Scouts for many years. He frequently supervised scouts who served as ushers for the home games.

Courtesy Tom Hayes

"Snow Bowl" Connection

Miss Marilyn Soliday braved the blizzard-type weather to attend the 1950 "Snow Bowl." Marilyn's ticket was in section 18C, but she sat under cover in 18B because of the icy aisles on C deck.

After halftime she noticed one of the portal men was very cold, and offered to share one of her blankets with him. His name was Barney Atkinson. When Marilyn told Barney she needed to leave to catch a bus home to Bexley, he offered to drive her since he drove through Bexley on his way home to Pataskala.

The drive to Bexley took nearly three hours through the heavy snow, and the couple became better acquainted. The following Tuesday Barney asked Marilyn for a date. They began to see each other regularly, and were married the following May 11.

GREAT GAME REMEMBERED
No. 6 Ohio State 83 - Iowa 21
Oct. 28, 1950 - Columbus, Ohio

Ohio State tailback Vic Janowicz put together one of the most outstanding performances in all of college football. The talented junior scored two touchdowns, passed for four touchdowns, kicked 10 extra points, punted twice for a 42-yard average, recovered an Iowa fumble, and played a stellar game at defensive safety. At season end, he became Ohio State's second Heisman Trophy winner.

Halfback Bob Demmel's 87-yard punt return for a second-quarter touchdown was an Ohio State record until Brian Hartline scored with a 90-yard punt return against Kent State on Oct. 13, 2007. The 83 points is the third highest ever for Ohio State, exceeded only by a 128-0 win over Oberlin in 1916 and an 85-7 win over Drake in 1935.

Courtesy Ohio State University Photo Archives

Keepsake Mistake

For many seasons Mr. John Hummel was responsible for distributing the footall programs at Ohio State's home games. A total of 28,000 programs were printed for the 1950 homecoming game against Michigan, the famous Snow Bowl. Not surprisingly, because of the heavy snow, only 4,000 of the 28,000 were sold.

The following week, Hummel had the remaining 24,000 programs destroyed. "This was a huge mistake," Hummel commented years later. "Many fans wanted one of the programs as a souvenir. Just think of the money that could have been raised for charity if we had kept at least a few thousand."

A Buckeye Replaces Bernie Bierman

In 1950, it was strongly rumored that Minnesota head coach Bernie Bierman would retire at the end of the season. The future College Football Hall of Fame coach had been extremely successful, posting a record of 93-35-6 (72.7%) while leading the Golden Gophers to three national titles during his 16 seasons as head coach.

The Nov. 19, 1950, *Columbus Citizen* stated the possibility of coach Paul Brown leaving the Cleveland Browns to replace Bierman. Citing a reliable source, columnist Lew Byrer reported that Minnesota Chancellor J. Louis Morrill was possibly in favor of Brown, and that Brown had indicated he wouldn't turn down returning to the college game if sufficient financial incentives were included.

Ironically, Bierman's replacement would be a former Buckeye head coach, but it wouldn't be Paul Brown. After resigning as Ohio State's head coach on Dec. 9, 1950, Wes Fesler accepted the same position at Minnesota on Jan. 25, 1951.

Southwest tower of Ohio Stadium

CHAPTER SEVEN

1951-1960

Three Yards and a Cloud of Dust

More than 60 candidates applied for Ohio State's head coaching position following Wes Fesler's resignation. A high priority was selecting a coach who would bring a severely needed stability to the program. The selection committee's first choice was Don Faurot, highly successful head coach at the University of Missouri since 1935. He nearly had been selected 10 years earlier in 1941, when Paul Brown was chosen instead. Faurot accepted Ohio State's offer during an interview in Columbus on Saturday, Feb. 10, 1951.

Head Coach Woody Hayes and his 1951 coaching staff. Front from left, Gene Fekete, Bo Schembechler, Bill Arnsparger and Bill Hess. Back from left, Doyt Perry, Harry Strobel, Hayes, Esco Sarkkinen, and Ernie Godfrey. *Courtesy Ohio State University Photo Archives*

Ohio State was National Champion in 1954 with a record of 10-0. *Courtesy Ohio State University Photo Archives*

The following Monday while Ohio State was planning a press conference to introduce its new coach, Faurot unexpectedly informed Athletic Director Dick Larkins he had "changed his mind" and decided to remain at Missouri. Faurot gave no reason for his surprise decision.

The saddened selection committee hastily reconvened and recommended Miami (Ohio) head coach Woody Hayes. Hayes immediately accepted Ohio State's offer on Sunday, Feb. 18, 1951, at a starting annual salary of $12,500. No one possibly could have foreseen the positive impact this decision would provide The Ohio State University.

At best, Hayes' first season of 1951 was very ordinary. Players had difficulty adjusting to his T-formation offense from the single-wing attack used during the

Ohio State was National Champion in 1957 with a record of 9-1. *Courtesy Ohio State University Photo Archives*

Fesler years. Many had difficulty tolerating Hayes' forceful personality and team morale was often quite low. His first squad struggled to a record of 4-3-2.

The Buckeyes improved to 6-3 in both 1952 and 1953. In his second campaign Hayes installed the split-T formation offense that, ironically, had been developed at Missouri by coach Don Faurot. That season 18-year-old freshman halfback Howard "Hopalong" Cassady began a magnificent four-year career. One of the school's all-time greats, Cassady became Ohio State's third Heisman Trophy winner in 1955.

Hayes' predictable run-oriented offense often was labeled "three yards and a cloud of dust." The jury was still out on the relentless coach after a somewhat disappointing three-year record of 16-9-2, but his status strongly accelerated after the 1954 Buckeyes became national champions. Although expected to place fifth in the league standings, Ohio State went 10-0 through an extremely rugged schedule to become the first school to win seven Big Ten Conference games since Chicago in 1913, the year Hayes was born.

Hayes' reputation grew even stronger when OSU repeated as the undisputed league champion in 1955 (7-2). The campaign concluded with an imposing 17-0 triumph at Michigan, Ohio State's first victory in Ann Arbor since 1937.

After an unsuccessful bid for a third-consecutive outright conference title in 1956 (6-3), the Buckeyes claimed the 1957 national championship with a record of 9-1. Following an 18-14 upset opening loss to Texas Christian, Hayes' squad reeled off nine straight victories to become the only Ohio State team to win all of its remaining games after losing the season opener.

Jim Herbstreit, 1960 Co-Captain. *Courtesy Ohio State University Photo Archives*

Jim Houston, 1959 Captain. Two-time All-American and two-time team MVP. Member of College Football Hall of Fame. *Courtesy Ohio State University Photo Archives*

OSU went 6-2-1, 3-5-1, and 7-2, respectively, in 1958-59-60, placing no higher than third in the Big Ten rankings. Hayes finished his first decade at Ohio State with a 10-year record of 64-23-5

(72.3 percent), two national titles and three undisputed Big Ten championships. His record against Michigan was 6-4. But the fiery 48-year-old, who had been the selection committee's "second choice," was just getting started!

Live From Ann Arbor?

The late Jimmy Crum covered Ohio State football for 41 years as the popular sports anchor at WCMH-TV4 in Columbus before retiring in 1993. Crum was well known for his charity work and his wild plaid sport coats.

In the early 1950's, Crum did the play-by-play broadcast of Ohio State football on WRFD Radio. A quandary developed when WRFD sponsors were obtained to broadcast the 1951 Ohio State-Michigan game, but WRFD was unable to secure a broadcasting booth at Michigan Stadium.

With no space available, Crum and color commentator Dave Collins viewed the game in the WRFD studios on a small black-and-white televison, and simultaneously broadcast the action as if they were inside Michigan Stadium. When reminiscing years later, Crum stated that if these details had been revealed at that time, WRFD likely would have lost its broadcasting license.

Victory Bell

The Ohio State victory bell, located in the southeast tower of Ohio Stadium, is rung after every home win and also following Ohio State's spring commencement. The bell was a gift from the graduating classes of 1943, 1944 and 1945.

The bell originally was to be located on the oval and sounded after every athletic victory, not just football. After several delays the bell finally was cast and placed in its present location nearly 10 years later. It cost $2,500 to cast and install — and it weighs 2,420 pounds.

The first ringing followed a 21-13 victory over California on Oct. 2, 1954. The ringing lasts 15 minutes after all victories except a win over Michigan, when the bell is rung for 30 minutes.

At the request of Coach Woody Hayes, members of Alpha Phi Omega, a national co-ed service fraternity, have the honor of ringing the bell. On a still day the sound can be heard as far as 5 miles from campus.

Courtesy Jack Park

Success On and Off the Gridiron

One of the most noteworthy plays during Woody Hayes' 28 seasons at Ohio State was executed by a somewhat unknown reserve linebacker during the Buckeyes' decisive clash with Michigan in 1954. Near halftime, Hubert Bobo injured his foot. Jack Gibbs, a senior with little game experience, replaced Bobo at linebacker.

On his second play, Gibbs intercepted a pass at the Michigan 43 thrown by Wolverine quarterback Jim Maddock, and returned the ball to the 10-yard line. Gibbs' timely interception set-up Ohio State's first touchdown to tie the game 7-7 at halftime. This play completely changed the game's momentum and Ohio State won, 21-7.

Jack Gibbs' story is one of amazing success that extended well beyond the gridiron. Gibbs had not played football at Columbus West High School after being told he was too small. After graduation he worked two years to help support his family before attending Ohio State. Coach Woody Hayes encouraged Gibbs to play college football, even without high school experience.

Gibbs made steady progress until a broken ankle idled him most of his junior season of 1953. By Michigan week of his senior year he had advanced to the second team. Gibbs attended classes during the day, practiced football in the late afternoon, and worked a 40-hour-week night shift at North American Aviation on the east side of Columbus. He graduated summa cum laude in the fall of 1954.

Gibbs joined the Columbus Public Schools faculty and rapidly developed into a high achiever. He became Principal at East High School and later served as the first Director of the Fort Hayes Career Center. Lee Williams, a 1954 Ohio State teammate who also taught at East High School, described Gibbs as "one of the best educators I've ever known."

Gibbs was a member of the Ohio State University Board of Trustees in the late-1960s. He passed away in 1982 at age 51. The boulevard in front of the Fort Hayes Career Center in Columbus is named in honor of Gibbs.

Courtesy Jack Park

Greatest Rose Bowl NEVER Played!

The "Dream Rose Bowl" of Jan. 1, 1955, would have matched undefeated Ohio State (9-0) and undefeated UCLA (9-0). Ohio State was awarded the 1954 *Associated Press* national title, and UCLA was chosen national champion by the *United Press International*. The Bruins of coach Red Sanders featured All-American linemen Jim Salsbury and Jack Ellena, and excellent running backs Bob Davenport and Primo Villanueva.

This was one of UCLA's all-time finest teams, but the "no repeat" rule at that time prevented teams from appearing in consecutive Rose Bowls. UCLA had lost to Michigan State 28-20 in the previous season's classic. With UCLA unable to play, Ohio State faced second-place Southern California and defeated the Trojans 20-7.

This game was unique for another reason. It was the first Rose Bowl to be covered by a female sportswriter. Miss Faye Lloyd analyzed the game for the *United Press International*.

GREAT GAME REMEMBERED
Ohio State 23 - No. 1 Wisconsin 14
Oct. 11, 1952 - Columbus, Ohio

Unranked Ohio State scored on well-executed drives of 88, 64 and 55 yards to surprise the heavily favored Badgers. It was the Buckeyes' first-ever victory over a No. 1-ranked opponent, and coach Woody Hayes' first "big win" at Ohio State. Led by the dominant play of linebacker Tony Curcillo, the Buckeye defense held coach Ivy Williamson's powerful offense on downs five times inside the Ohio State 20.

Freshman halfback Howard "Hopalong" Cassady made his first Ohio State start and rushed for 113 yards. The Badgers finished the season ranked No. 11 with a record of 6-2-1, and the Buckeyes finished at No. 17 with a record of 6-3.

Sportsmanship Unmatched

Late during the Jan. 1, 1955, Rose Bowl, Woody Hayes began substituting liberally, providing each player the opportunity to play at least one down. One player who had not yet played was senior co-captain John Borton, who had lost his starting quarterback position that season to senior Dave Leggett. As Hayes beckoned Borton to relieve Leggett, Borton very unselfishly suggested that third-team quarterback Bill Booth enter the game instead. Borton knew that Booth's father, Dick Booth, had played fullback for the Pitt Panthers against Stanford in the 1928 Rose Bowl.

Hayes proudly shook Borton's hand then inserted Booth, who quarterbacked the last three plays of the game. John Borton was Ohio State's only able-bodied player not to see action that afternoon, but his thoughtfulness was always remembered by Booth as "the greatest act of sportsmanship I have ever seen."

Booth's proud father was in attendance that afternoon. They became the first father-son combination to play in the Rose Bowl.

Together One Last Time

A game between the prior year's NFL Champions and a College All-Star team comprised of prominent seniors from the previous season was played in August at Soldier Field in Chicago from 1934 through 1976. The proceeds from this pre-season event benefitted various Chicago area charities. The game was the brainchild of sports editor Arch Ward of the Chicago Tribune, who also was instrumental in developing Major League Baseball's All-Star game.

Placekicker Tad Weed, an Ohio State senior in 1954, paced the College All-Stars to a 30-27 upset victory over the Cleveland Browns on Aug. 12, 1955. Weed scored 11 of the All-Star's 30 points with three field goals and two extra points. The game's MVP was College All-Star quarterback Ralph Guglielmi, a Notre Dame All-American. Weed and Guglielmi had been teammates at Grandview Heights High School, a Columbus suburb, from 1947 through 1950. The 1955 All-Stars were coached by Curly Lambeau, founder and longtime coach of the Green Bay Packers.

Nation's Elite

Ohio State's 1955 home finale against Iowa featured the opposing play of the nation's two most talented guards, the Buckeyes' Jim Parker and the Hawkeyes' Calvin Jones. Both would capture the Outland Trophy (Jones-1955, Parker-1956), both were consensus All-Americans, both hailed from Ohio (Parker-Toledo, Jones-Steubenville), and both wore jersey No. 62. Ohio State won the Nov. 12 contest, 20-10.

Stressful Visit

Buckeye Tackle Dick Guy was an extremely gregarious player who loved "having a good time!" Woody Hayes wanted Guy to be more serious about football, so he had Guy move into the Hayes home on the Monday prior to the 1955 Ohio State-Michigan game.

Guy was not pleased to spend the next three nights with the Hayes family. Woody drilled him on his assignments until late at night, asking "what do you do on this play" and "how would you react in this situation." Early the following morning the coach assertively would commence the routine all over again.

On Thursday, Hayes finally permitted the senior lineman to return to his campus room after being convinced Guy knew his assignments. "Man, was I glad to get out of there," Guy recalled years later. Guy played arguably his finest game at Ann Arbor that Saturday. Ohio State won, 17-0.

GREAT GAME REMEMBERED
No. 4 Ohio State 31 - No. 2 Wisconsin 14
Oct. 23, 1954 - Columbus, Ohio

This was a major victory during Ohio State's successful run for the 1954 national title. The Buckeyes played well in the early going but trailed 7-3 at halftime. Late in the third quarter, the Badgers had a second-and-4 at the Ohio State 20, and were in good position to increase their four-point lead. Quarterback Jim Miller's pass was intercepted by Howard "Hopalong"

Cassady at the 12. With the aid of three key blocks, the talented junior thrilled the homecoming crowd with a magnificent 88-yard touchdown return that completely changed the game's momentum.

In the final quarter the Buckeye offense scored three more TDs while the defense grew stronger, but the game was really much closer than suggested by Ohio State's 17-point margin of victory. Badger fullback Alan Ameche, that season's Heisman Trophy winner, was held to 42 yards in 16 attempts. Cassady finished third to Ameche in the Heisman balloting, then captured the award the following season.

Howard "Hopalong" Cassady.
Courtesy Ohio State University Photo Archives

Safety First

Ohio State's defense executed one of football's all-time most bizarre plays during the Buckeyes' 17-0 triumph at Michigan in 1955. Trailing 9-0 in the final period, the Wolverines had possession deep in their own territory. Quarterback Jim Maddock faded back into his own end zone, then flipped a short pass into the flat to halfback Terry Barr. Barr immediately was brought down behind the Michigan goal line for a safety by OSU's Bill Michael and Aurealius Thomas.

It is one of the most abnormal moments in this storied series — catching a pass and being tackled for a safety, both on the same play.

Spartan Support!

The winner of the 1955 Ohio State-Michigan game would capture the outright Big Ten title. The Buckeyes entered the Nov. 19 contest 5-0 in league play while the Wolverines were 5-1 after losing 25-6 at Illinois two weeks earlier. Since Michigan played seven conference games compared with six for Ohio State, a victory over the Buckeyes would earn the Wolverines the Big Ten title and Rose Bowl appearance.

Ohio State had defeated Southern California, 20-7, in the previous season's Rose Bowl and could not return to Pasadena because of the then "no-repeat" policy. Michigan State had already completed its 1955 conference schedule at 5-1, and hosted Marquette in a nonconference game the same afternoon as the Ohio State-Michigan clash in Ann Arbor. The Spartans would be Rose Bowl-bound if the Buckeyes defeated the Wolverines.

To encourage an Ohio State victory, one of Michigan State's cheerleaders joined the Ohio State cheerleaders on the Michigan Stadium sidelines. Maybe this

Courtesy Tom Hayes

obvious show of support helped! The Buckeyes won, 17-0, dropping Michigan to 5-2 and third place in the final league standings. The Spartans with their 5-1 conference mark rose to second place and headed for Pasadena.

In one of the Rose Bowl's most exciting games, Michigan State came from behind for a remarkable 17-14 victory over talented UCLA to finish the year with an overall record of 9-1. Ironically, Michigan had dealt the Spartans their only setback of the season with a 14-7 victory in Ann Arbor on Oct. 1.

Last Laugh

Penn State's 7-6 triumph at Ohio State in 1956 was especially sweet for Nittany Lion senior guard Sam Valentine, a 5'11", 200-pounder from DuBois, Pa. Valentine had wanted to play for Ohio State but was told by the Buckeye coaches he was too small. What a mistake! Valentine was elected Penn State's 1956 team captain, and at season end became an All-American.

Abundant Ability

Jim Parker was truly one of Ohio State's all-time finest. The 6'3", 248-pounder from Toledo was equally talented at offensive guard and defensive linebacker during his three seasons of 1954-56. A two-time All-American, Parker became the Buckeyes' first Outland Trophy winner in 1956. After Ohio State, Parker became a 10-time All-NFL offensive lineman with the Baltimore Colts. Many consider him the NFL's all-time finest pass blocker. Parker was inducted into the Professional Football Hall of Fame in 1973 and the College Football Hall of Fame in 1974.

Attendance Mark

For the first time in Ohio Stadium history, Ohio State in 1955 drew more than 80,000 fans for each home game. A total of 490,477 fans attended the six home contests.

Jim Parker. *Courtesy Ohio State University Photo Archives*

"Fill-In" Shockers

Penn State's 7-6 upset victory in 1956 broke an Ohio State eight-game winning streak. It was the Buckeyes' first loss since underdog Duke startled OSU 20-14 in the fourth game of 1955. Both games were played at Ohio Stadium. Ironically, the Blue Devils and Nittany Lions had been late "fill-ins" on the Ohio State schedule, replacing Navy, which had canceled a two-game series.

Prized Achievement

Ohio State offensive guard Bill Jobko of Bridgeport, Ohio, is the only player in Big Ten history to play on three undisputed league champions. During Jobko's sophomore and junior seasons of 1954 and 1955, the Buckeyes won outright conference titles with league records of 7-0 and 6-0, respectively.

After being out of school in 1956, Jobko returned to lead Ohio State to the outright 1957 league championship with a 7-0 league mark. The Buckeyes were 20-0 in Big Ten contests his three seasons, and also were national champions in 1954 and 1957.

Jobko was Ohio State's 1957 MVP. From 1958 through 1966 he played professional football with the Los Angeles Rams, Minnesota Vikings and Atlanta Falcons.

Lineman's Dream

At home against Purdue on Nov. 8, 1958, Ohio State defensive tackle Jim Marshall snatched up a blocked punt and scurried 22 yards for a first quarter touchdown. Late in the second period, Marshall returned an interception 25 yards for his second touchdown. The OSU offense struggled, but the Buckeyes held a 14-0 halftime lead, thanks to Marshall's two defensive scores. End Jim Houston aided with both of Marshall's touchdowns by blocking the punt and deflecting the pass.

In the second half, OSU's troubled offense

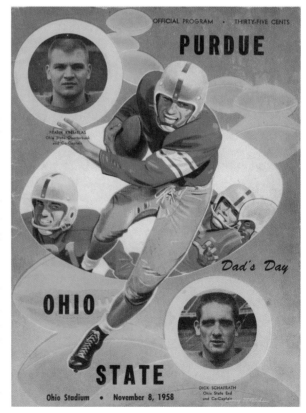

OFFICIAL PROGRAM · THIRTY-FIVE CENTS

PURDUE

FRANK KREMBLAS
Ohio State Quarterback
and Co-Captain

Dad's Day

OHIO STATE

Ohio Stadium · November 8, 1958

DICK SCHAFRATH
Ohio State End
and Co-Captain

continued to have difficulty, generating just one first down and a mere 37 yards of offense. The Boilermakers scored twice, and the contest finished in a 14-14 tie.

Scoring Enhancement

The two-point conversion option became a part of college football in 1958. Ohio State's very first two-pointer came on a pass from quarterback Frank Kremblas to halfback Dick LeBeau following the Buckeyes' first touchdown in the 1958 season-opening 23-20 home victory over Southern Methodist.

GREAT GAME REMEMBERED
No. 1 Ohio State 21 - No. 12 Michigan 7
Nov. 20, 1954 - Columbus, Ohio

More than 500 media credentials were issued, at the time the largest contingent to ever cover a Big Ten football game. Michigan took charge early and led 7-0 near halftime. A vital interception late in the second quarter by linebacker Jack Gibbs enabled the Buckeyes to tie the game 7-7 with a 15-yard scoring pass to end Fred Kriss from quarterback Dave Leggett.

After a scoreless third period and the score still 7-7, Michigan opened play in the final quarter with a first down at the Ohio State 4. With great strength and confidence, the Buckeyes held the Wolverines on downs just inches short of the end zone. Ohio State promptly marched nearly 100 yards for the go-ahead touchdown, and ultimately a trip to the Rose Bowl. This was one of the most significant victories during Woody Hayes' 28 seasons at Ohio State.

The Columbus Citizen

SUNDAY EDITION 15¢

VOL. 55—No. 366   Phone CA. 4-1111   COLUMBUS 15, OHIO, SUNDAY, NOVEMBER 21, 1954   ★ ★ ★

Rose Bowl Bound On Big Ten Title · · ·

Bucks Clobber Michigan, 21-7

Courtesy The Columbus Citizen, Nov. 21, 1954

Buckeyes and Hawkeyes

Ohio State and Iowa dominated the Big Ten Conference during the mid-1950s. Their annual clash usually had more impact on the Big Ten title than the Ohio State-Michigan game. Head coaches Woody Hayes and Forest Evashevski were extremely competitive, and there was definitely no love lost between the two.

There was an outright Big Ten champion during each of the five seasons from 1954 through 1958. The Buckeyes won titles in 1954, 1955 and 1957, and the Hawkeyes in 1956 and 1958.

After the 1958 season, the struggling Green Bay Packers of the NFL offered Evashevski their head coaching position. After meeting twice with the Packers, Evashevski decided to remain at Iowa. Green Bay then selected a candidate who, at the time, was not nearly as well known as Evashevski — his name was Vince Lombardi!

Mr. Hospitality!

Midwest sportswriters and broadcasters who covered Big Ten football during the 1950s and 1960s were commonly known as the Big Ten skywriters. As a group, they visited practices at conference schools to preview the teams prior to the season openers.

When the skywriters arrived at Ohio State in early September of 1958, they were stunned when Coach Woody Hayes refused to meet with them or allow

Courtesy Tom Hayes

them access to his team's practice. Visibly insulted, the offended sportswriters and broadcasters abruptly departed for their next city.

Ohio State's athletic administration was totally embarrassed by Hayes' action and immediately issued a letter of apology to the Big Ten Conference. The following season, Hayes could not have been more charming, and extended his hospitality to the skywriters by serving lemonade and cookies.

Impromptu Halftime Adjustment

Ohio State opened its 1959 season Sept. 26 against Duke. Starting quarterback Jerry Fields injured his right arm late in the second quarter and was out for the rest of the game. Backup Jack Wallace was a sophomore and lacked game experience.

As the teams headed to their dressing rooms at halftime, coach Woody Hayes unexpectedly took four of his players to the practice field outside the south end of Ohio Stadium for a very spontaneous workout. Hayes was considering an instant conversion of starting right halfback Tom Matte to quarterback. Matte practiced taking snaps from center Jene Watkins, and handing off to halfbacks Dave Tingley and Ronny Houk.

Matte returned to his halfback position for most of the second half. The Buckeyes' 7-0 halftime advantage eventually vanished after the Blue Devils scored

Courtesy Tom Hayes

twice to lead 13-7 late in the fourth quarter. Hayes immediately made his move. As Ohio State took possession at its own 37-yard line, he shifted Matte to quarterback.

Matte responded like a veteran, leading his team 63 yards in nine plays for the winning touchdown, that came on a fourth down 22-yard rollout pass from Matte to end Chuck Bryant. Placekicker Dave Kilgore converted and Ohio State won, 14-13.

Matte, a junior, played both positions the remainder of the 1959 season. He became the starting quarterback in 1960, and was chosen All-Big Ten and named Ohio State's MVP.

Only Once

The 1959 season is the only time Ohio State and Michigan *both* finished with losing records, during the 113 years they have clashed through 2016. The Wolverines finished 1959 with a record of 4-5, while the Buckeyes were 3-5-1. Michigan won at home over Ohio State that season, 23-14.

GREAT GAME REMEMBERED
No. 6 Ohio State 17 - No. 5 Iowa 13
Nov. 16, 1957 - Columbus, Ohio

In a gigantic clash that would determine the Big Ten champion, the talented Hawkeyes were favored by six points. Using a wide open offense with multiple reverses and laterals, Iowa was on top 13-10 when Ohio State took possession at its own 32 with 7:51 left to play.

With near perfect execution, the Buckeyes drove 68 yards for the winning touchdown and the outright conference title. It was one of the classic drives in school history. The Ohio State offensive line was flawless, allowing fullback Bob White to plunge between the tackles for 66 of the 68 yards.

Ohio State captured the 1957 national title with an overall record of 9-1. The Buckeyes completed the season with a 10-7 victory over Oregon in the Rose Bowl. Iowa finished No. 7 at 7-1-1.

Brotherly Love

Ohio State's 7-2 record in 1960 included a 34-7 victory at Illinois and a season-ending 7-0 home triumph over Michigan. Illinois was led by first-year head coach Pete Elliott. Pete's older brother, Bump, had taken charge of the Michigan program one year earlier.

On Nov. 5, 1960, Michigan edged Illinois 8-7 at Ann Arbor. It marked the first "brother against brother" coaching encounter in Big Ten history.

Bump had been an All-American halfback who led Michigan to the national title in 1947 with a record of 10-0. Pete was an All-American quarterback who directed Michigan to the 1948 national championship with a 9-0 record. After extensive coaching careers, Bump served as Director of Athletics at the University of Iowa from 1970 through 1990, and Pete was Executive Director of the Professional Football Hall of Fame in Canton, Ohio, from 1979 through 1995.

History Repeats Itself

Ohio State's 20-0 win over Southern California in 1960 marked the Trojans first game at Ohio Stadium since 1948, when they lost by the same exact score.

Short on Words!

Unranked Purdue shocked third-ranked Ohio State, 24-21, at West Lafayette on Oct. 15, 1960. Senior fullback Willie Jones, who had never before scored a collegiate touchdown, tallied three times for the Boilermakers with runs of 2, 3 and 26 yards. Purdue quarterback Bernie Allen, a senior from East Liverpool, Ohio, passed effectively in clutch situations and kicked a 32-yard, third period field goal that became Purdue's eventual margin of victory.

Coach Woody Hayes was visibly disturbed with his team's play, particularly the defense, and barred all reporters from the Ohio State dressing room after the game. He finally met with the press outside the dressing room for all of 45 seconds and simply stated, "Both teams moved the ball well, but Purdue moved it better." Hayes took no questions and promptly left. The writers were noticeably insulted and had a few "choice words" to say about Hayes in their Sunday columns.

The Purdue Athletic Department apologized to the press and quickly issued the following brief statement: "Woody Hayes, noted as possibly the most outspoken coach in the United States, was all but speechless. He made a brief, almost fruitless appearance in the corridor outside the dressing room."

As might be expected, Ohio State's practices the following week were especially demanding!

Planning Ahead

Before freshmen players became eligible for varsity competition in 1972, they normally sat together at home games in section 17 behind the Ohio State bench. Two very talented freshmen in 1960 were halfbacks Paul Warfield and Matt Snell.

As the two reached their seats for the season's final game against Michigan, they were instructed to see coach Woody Hayes in the Ohio State dressing room after the game.

Approximately an hour after the Buckeyes had defeated the Wolverines, 7-0, Hayes brought his two prize freshmen onto the stadium playing field dressed in sweat suits. Senior quarterback Tom Matte's college career was now complete, and Hayes already was considering a shift of either Warfield or Snell to quarterback. The two worked out for approximately an hour, throwing passes and practicing handoffs.

After careful analysis, Hayes decided to keep both Warfield and Snell at halfback and named them starters for 1961. John Mummey, Bill Mrukowski and Joe Sparma shared the duties at quarterback. The 1961 Buckeyes captured the outright Big Ten title with an overall record of 8-0-1 and were chosen national champions by the Football Writers Association of America.

GREAT GAME REMEMBERED
No. 16 Ohio State 38 - No. 2 Iowa 28
Nov. 15, 1958 - Iowa City, Iowa

Coach Forest Evashevski's Hawkeyes were a 14-point favorite, and had already secured the outright Big Ten title. The game was fast and furious from the very start. The two rivals alternated touchdowns until the fourth quarter, when OSU was able to put the game out of reach with 10 unanswered points. The Buckeyes took the lead after each of their five touchdowns, but the Hawkeyes responded after the first four to knot the score at 7-7, 14-14, 21-21, and 28-28.

Fullback Bob White and halfback Don Clark scored all five OSU touchdowns and rushed for 209 and 157 yards, respectively. Coach Woody Hayes strongly recognized quarterback Jerry Fields, who flawlessly directed the offense while substituting for an injured Frank Kremblas. This was Iowa's only loss of the 1958 season.

CHAPTER EIGHT

1961-1970

Woody and the Turbulent Sixties

The 1960s was a decade of vast transformation that included widespread industrial expansion, far-reaching development of computer technology, growth of the civil rights movement, involvement in the Vietnam War and extensive campus unrest. Ohio State football also experienced significant change during this period, as well as a severe disappointment by its own administration. The Buckeyes also would rebound and capture a national title with a team dominated by sophomores.

The disappointment came at the end of the excellent 1961 season. Ohio State earned the outright Big Ten title and a partial national championship with a record of 8-0-1, but the school's faculty council rejected an invitation to the Rose Bowl. The vote was reported to be 28 to 25. Many faculty members believed the university was gaining too strong a reputation as a "football factory," and that the college game was becoming too commercialized. This momentous decision immediately weakened Ohio State's ability to attract many of Ohio's top high school players. From 1962 through 1966, the Buckeyes compiled a five-year record of 29-15-1 and finished no higher than second in the Big Ten rankings.

After the Buckeyes started the 1967 season at 2-3 with three consecutive home losses, coach Woody Hayes told his staff their coaching future at Ohio State would seriously be in question unless they could win their remaining four games.

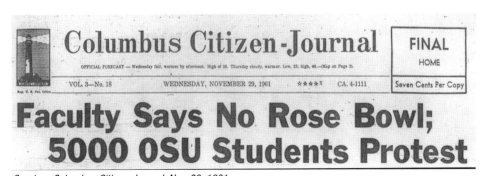

Courtesy Columbus Citizen-Journal, Nov. 29, 1961

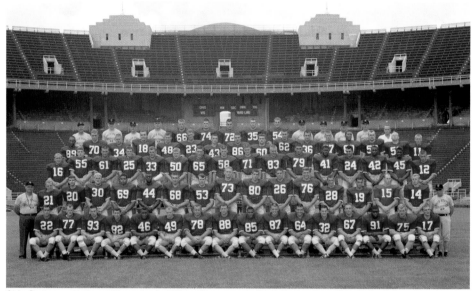

Ohio State was National Champion in 1961 with a record of 8-0-1. *Courtesy Ohio State University Photo Archives*

The following weekend his much improved squad defeated Michigan State 21-7 in what would become a major "turning-point" for the program and for Hayes' career. Ohio State closed out the season with three additional victories to finish on the upswing at 6-3.

In 1967, Hayes and his staff began targeting out-of-state high school talent in addition to the top prospects within Ohio. As a result, Ohio State's freshman class of 1967 would become one of the finest ever assembled. This group became eligible for varsity competition in 1968, and led Ohio State to the national title with a record of 10-0.

The team really came together during a 13-0 triumph over No. 1 ranked Purdue in the season's third game. Nicknamed the "super sophomores," as many as 16 of them started one or more games on offense and defense. Key sophomores included cornerback Jack Tatum; middle guard Jim Stillwagon; quarterback Rex Kern; halfbacks John Brockington, Larry

Head Coach Woody Hayes and his 1968 coaching staff. *Courtesy Ohio State University Photo Archives*

Jack Tatum *Courtesy Ohio State University Photo Archives*

Jim Stillwagon *Courtesy Ohio State University Photo Archives*

Zelina and Leo Hayden; defensive backs Tim Anderson and Mike Sensibaugh; linebacker Doug Adams; guard Phil Strickland; and ends Jan White and Bruce Jankowski.

With most of the 1968 team returning, Ohio State was even more imposing in 1969, winning its first eight outings by outscoring its opponents, 371-69. While the Buckeyes were aiming for their second consecutive national championship, a major makeover was taking shape at Michigan. Bo Schembechler, who had been both a player and an assistant coach under Hayes, became Michigan's head coach in 1969.

Ohio State was National Champion in 1968 with a record of 10-0. *Courtesy Ohio State University Photo Archives*

Players and coaches crossed this rug prior to each practice in 1970. It was a constant reminder of Michigan's 24-12 victory in 1969. *Courtesy Ohio State University Photo Archives*

During Hayes' first 18 seasons at Ohio State from 1951 through 1968, the Wolverines' single conference title came in 1964.

Coach Schembechler immediately changed the culture of Michigan football. Everything was elevated to a higher level of achievement, both on and off the football field. Top-ranked Ohio State at 8-0 traveled to Michigan in 1969 as a 17-point favorite, while No. 12 Michigan entered the game at 7-2. In one of the college game's all-time most significant upsets, the Wolverines shocked the Buckeyes, 24-12. The scoring all took place in the first half. Ohio State's winning streak had been snapped at 22 games, at the time the longest in school history.

Ohio State's entire 1970 season centered on retribution. The "super sophomores" of '68 were now seniors. The 1970 showdown marked the first time the Buckeyes and Wolverines both entered "the game" undefeated and untied since the annual clash was moved to the last game of the regular season in 1935. Before one of the most spirited Ohio Stadium crowds ever, the Buckeyes won 20-9 for one of the school's most cherished victories!

Ohio State's Rose Bowl clash against underdog Stanford was not nearly as pleasing. Heisman Trophy winner Jim Plunkett directed his team to a very unexpected 27-17 triumph, handing the Buckeyes their only loss of the 1970 season. Ohio State nevertheless enjoyed a three-year record of 27-2 from 1968 through 1970, with a winning rate of 93.1 percent — highest of any three consecutive seasons in school history.

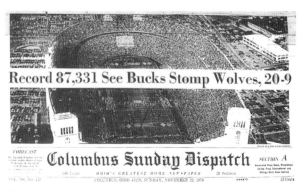

Record 87,331 See Bucks Stomp Wolves, 20-9

Columbus Sunday Dispatch

Courtesy The Columbus Dispatch, Nov. 22, 1970

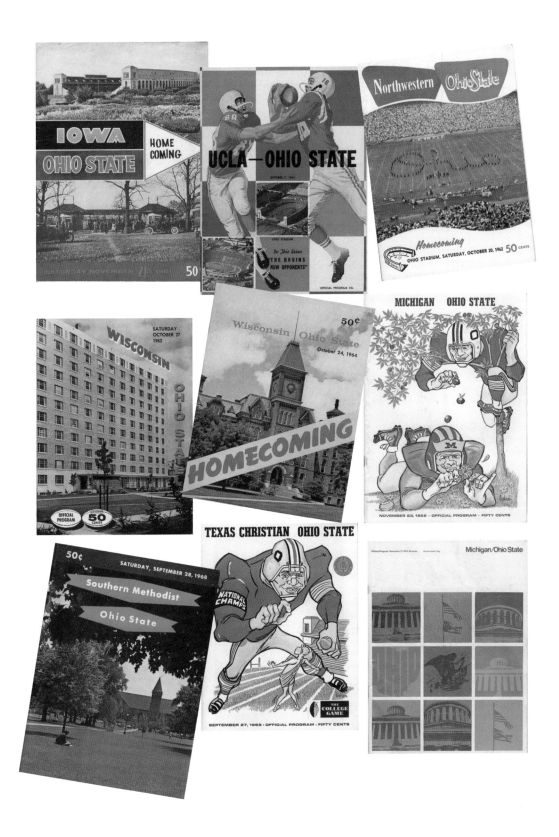

Hayes' Profound Influence

Coach Woody Hayes had such an impact on end Tom Perdue, Ohio State co-captain in 1961, that Perdue later named his son Hayes Perdue in honor of his college coach. Tom Purdue was an Academic All-American selection his senior year. He also was an All-American outfielder in baseball. Perdue's 1960 batting average of .469 remains an Ohio State single-season record.

After college, Perdue played four seasons in the minor league systems of the Cincinnati Reds and Chicago White Sox. He was inducted into the Ohio State Athletics Hall of Fame for both football and baseball in 1988.

Appropriate 100th

Coach Woody Hayes passionately treasured his sound ground attack. During his 100th game at Ohio State, three backs fittingly each rushed for more than 100 yards to pace a 22-12 home victory over Oregon on Nov. 18, 1961. Quarterback John Mummey ran for 116 yards, halfback Bob Klein raced for 103 and fullback Bob Ferguson added 101. Hayes' record through his first 100 games was 71-23-6 (74.0 percent).

Extraordinary Change of Sidelines

Ohio State assistant coach Bo Schembechler was in the Michigan Stadium Press Box, calling the offensive plays that led to the Buckeyes' substantial 50-20 triumph over the Wolverines in 1961. Few attending that Nov. 25 encounter (including Woody Hayes) could have predicted that in eight years, Schembechler would begin a 21-year stint as one of Michigan's all-time most successful head coaches.

Triple Fullback Supremacy

Woody Hayes' patented fullback-dominated ground offense propelled Ohio State to a 28-0 trouncing of Michigan at Ohio Stadium on Nov. 24, 1962. The Buckeyes' talented senior fullback trio of Dave Francis, Dave Ketterhenrich and Bob Butts scored all four touchdowns — Francis two, Ketterhenrich and Butts one each. Chuck Mamula kicked the four extra points. Hayes could not have been more proud!

Ohio State led in first downs, 19-9, and in rushing yards, 330-74. Michigan was not able to advance beyond the OSU 21-yard line. Hayes' record against "That Team Up North" then stood at 8-4. Through the 2016 season, this is the last time the Buckeyes have shut out the Wolverines.

Adaptability-Plus

Versatile Matt Snell, 1963 co-captain, was a starter at Ohio State three consecutive seasons at three different positions. Snell started at fullback in 1963, defensive end in 1962, and right halfback in 1961.

A Nation in Mourning

The United States was grief-stricken after the assassination of President John F. Kennedy in Dallas on Friday, Nov. 22, 1963. The 46-year old Kennedy, who was inaugurated as the nation's 35th president on Jan. 20, 1961, had been in office just 34 months.

The Ohio State team was in Michigan, and learned of the tragedy while preparing for the following day's encounter against the Wolverines. Many college games scheduled for Sat., Nov. 23, were either immediately postponed or cancelled

Courtesy The Columbus Dispatch, Nov. 22, 1963

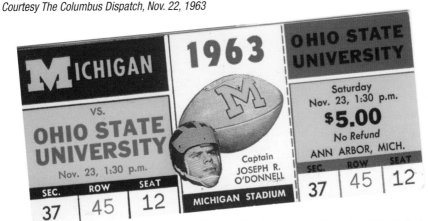

One of many unused tickets. *Courtesy Estate of Emmett and Amelia Park*

altogether. The decision to postpone the Ohio State–Michigan game until the following weekend was not made until 10:00 a.m. Sat. morning, just a little more than three hours prior to the scheduled start of the game. The Ohio State team learned of the postponement while on its way to Michigan Stadium from its hotel in nearby Ypsilanti.

The Ohio State Marching Band left for Ann Arbor by bus very early Saturday morning. When news of the postponement was received later that morning, Ohio State officials sought help from the Michigan Highway Patrol to inform the band. The patrol soon sighted the buses just north of the Ohio-Michigan line, and informed the band of the rescheduling. The buses immediately turned around and headed back to Columbus.

On Sat., Nov. 30, Ohio State defeated Michigan 14-10 before a crowd of just 36,424, smallest to ever attend an Ohio State-Michigan game at Michigan Stadium.

GREAT GAME REMEMBERED
Ohio State 14 - No. 5 Wisconsin 7
Oct. 27, 1962 - Columbus, Ohio

Underdog Ohio State handed talented Wisconsin its only setback of the regular season. With the game tied 7-7 midway through the final quarter, Ohio State took possession at its own 42. Coach Woody Hayes alternated carries by his three senior fullbacks — Dave Francis, Bob Butts, Dave Katterhenrich — eight times for a total of 57 yards to the Wisconsin 1. Quarterback John Mummey sneaked through for the winning touchdown.

The stingy Ohio State defense held Wisconsin All-American end Pat Richter to only two receptions, and broke his streak of at least one touchdown reception at eight games. The outright league champion Badgers were directed by senior quarterback Ron VanderKelen, who became the conference's MVP.

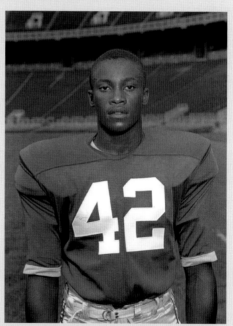

Halfback Paul Warfield was very effective against the Badgers, playing offense, defense and returning punts. *Courtesy Ohio State University Photo Archives*

For most players and fans it was an "empty victory." The great thrill of defeating Michigan was overshadowed by the terrible occurrence of just eight days earlier.

To the surprise of many, professional football did not entirely follow suit with postponing or cancelling games that weekend. The American Football League postponed all games scheduled for Sun., Nov. 24, just two days after the assassination, but the National Football League played its games as scheduled. NFL Commissioner Pete Rozelle made the decision, partly to honor Kennedy who had been a very avid football fan. Rozelle later expressed some regret that he chose not to postpone the games. The AFL added a week at the end of its regular season, and on Dec. 22 played the games that were originally scheduled for Nov. 24.

The Cleveland Browns hosted the Dallas Cowboys on Nov. 24. The mood was especially somber for the visiting team, traveling from the city that now had the attention of the entire world. Just prior to the start of the game, Lee Harvey Oswald, who was in police custody for the assassination, was fatally shot by Dallas nightclub owner Jack Ruby during a transfer from one Dallas jail to another.

The game was not broadcast, since television coverage focused exclusively on the news of the assassination. The Browns won, 27-17, in front of a low-energy Cleveland Municipal Stadium crown of 55,096.

Resourceful Solution

The late Roger Stanton, Publisher of the *Football News,* stated that the coldest game of his 40-plus years of covering football was the Nov. 21, 1964, encounter between Ohio State and Michigan. The temperature hovered near 18 degrees as strong winds whipped throughout the horseshoe. "The Ohio Stadium press box was so cold that the copying machine wouldn't work," Stanton recalled, "and the staff had no way of providing game statistics for the sportswriters. Finally, a resourceful individual poured some vodka into the machine's gears. The lubricant got it going, and the machine hummed along reasonably well the remainder of the afternoon."

The Wolverines won, 10-0, handing the Buckeyes their only conference loss of the season. Michigan won the Big Ten title with a league record of 6-1, compared with Ohio State's 5-1. Ohio State was denied a share of the conference championship because of playing one less league encounter.

Ohio's 'Team Up North' Goes West

Michigan claimed the 1964 Big Ten championship and trip to the Rose Bowl. That season Ohio State's four starting offensive backs were all from Ohio — quarterback Don Unverferth of Dayton, fullback Will Sander of Cincinnati, and halfbacks Bo Rein and Tom Barrington of Niles and Lima, respectively. Ironically, Michigan's entire starting offensive backfield was also from Ohio — All-American quarterback Bob Timberlake hailed from Franklin, halfback Jim Detwiler was from Toledo, and fullback Mel Anthony and halfback Carl Ward were both from Cincinnati.

Ohio's "Team Up North" played well in Pasadena, defeating Oregon State, 34-7.

GREAT GAME REMEMBERED
No. 4 Ohio State 26 - No. 2 Illinois 0
Oct. 10, 1964 - Champaign, Illinois

Ohio State shocked an Illinois homecoming contingent of 71,227 with near-perfect execution on both sides of the ball. Quarterback Don Unverferth surprised everyone with a 24-yard scoring bootleg around left end on Ohio State's very first play from scrimmage. Coach Woody Hayes called two "tackle-eligible" pass plays, and both were completed to tackle Jim Davidson for a total of 37 yards.

An overwhelming pass rush, keyed by linebacker Ike Kelley, tackle Ed Orazen, middle guard Bill Ridder and end Bill Spahr, silenced the Illinois offense the entire afternoon. The favored Fighting Illini were unable to advance beyond the Ohio State 31-yard line. Hayes was now 7-0 in games played at Memorial Stadium in Champaign.

Celebrity Admirer

Supporting Ohio State during a 20-10 victory at Wisconsin on Oct. 23, 1965, was comedian Bob Hope. The Cleveland, Ohio, native was performing at the Badgers' homecoming in Madison.

Thirteen years later, Hope had the honor of dotting the "i" in Script Ohio during a 31-7 homecoming victory over Iowa at Ohio Stadium on Oct. 21, 1978.

Sharp Eye

Ohio State faced Minnesota at homecoming on Sat., Oct. 30, 1965. Apparently a prankster had gained access to the field the previous night, and strung a fine nylon fishing line between the goal post uprights at the stadium's north end. Saturday morning Stadium Superintendent Ralph Guarasci noticed the mesh shining in the sunlight and had it removed. Late that afternoon, with 1:17 remaining in the fourth quarter,

placekicker Bob Funk booted an 18-yard field goal through this goal post to lift the Buckeyes to an 11-10 come-from-behind victory.

Victory Bell Silent

Ohio State's Victory Bell was noticeably silent after the Buckeyes' 38-0 home victory over Iowa on Nov. 13, 1965. The bell's clapper was mysteriously missing. The clapper was sighted the following week, dangling from a rope around the William Oxley Thompson statue in front of Ohio State's Main Library.

Talented Toe

Thanks to accomplished placekicker Bob Funk, Ohio State's 1965 record was 7-2 rather than 4-5. Three of Funk's eight field goals that year spelled the difference between victory and defeat:

- A 27-yarder with 59 seconds remaining provided a 23-21 victory at Washington on Oct. 2.
- An 18-yarder with 1:17 left afforded an 11-10 homecoming triumph over Minnesota on Oct. 30.
- A 28-yarder with 1:15 remaining granted a 9-7 win at Michigan on Nov. 20.

Academic Delight

Woody Hayes was extraordinarily proud when three former players finished first in The Ohio State College of Medicine's freshman class three consecutive years: All-American defensive halfback Arnie Chonko in 1966, quarterback Don Unverferth in 1967 and halfback John Derbyshire in 1968.

Chonko, from Parma, Ohio, was a two-time Academic All-American. A standout athlete, he was eyed by both professional baseball and football teams after graduation, but chose instead to attend medical school at Ohio State. Chonko became a very successful physician and a faculty member of the Kidney Institute at the University of Kansas Medical Center.

Unverferth, from Dayton, Ohio, established what was then a career Ohio State passing record with 2,518 yards from 1963 through 1965. He became a world-renowned cardiologist at the Ohio State Medical Center, overseeing Ohio State's first heart transplants in 1986. Unverferth died from a brain tumor in 1988, at the young age of 43. The Unverferth House, a residence facility near campus for families of out-of-town patients undergoing prolonged treatment at the Ohio State Medical Center, is named in his honor.

Derbyshire, from Edon, Ohio, graduated from the Ohio State Medical School and completed his residency at the Duke University Medical Center. He remained in North Carolina and became a highly respected internal medicine physician. Derbyshire was awarded the Distinguished Citizen of the Year Award from the Rocky Mount Area Chamber of Commerce in 2013. The award was presented by Dr. Gaylord Lehman, who commented while presenting the award, "Every year on the last weekend of the football season, John still wears a big button that says Beat Michigan! The button leaves most of his patients puzzled and doesn't mean a lot to us in Atlantic Coast Conference country."

Determination Galore

End Billy Anders started at offensive left end all 27 games from 1965 through 1967. At the time, Anders was Ohio State's all-time leading receiver with a three-year career record of 108 catches for 1,318 yards and six touchdowns. His 55 receptions for 671 yards in 1966 was a single-season record.

Anders was from Sabina, Ohio, a village of 2,200 south of Columbus in Clinton County. Since Sabina High School was too small to field a football team, Anders walked on at Ohio State without any high school football experience. He had earned 11 high school letters in sports other than football. Anders and defensive halfback Sam Elliott were the Buckeyes' co-captains in 1967.

Peak Embarrassment

Purdue solidly defeated Ohio State 41-6 at Ohio Stadium on Oct. 14, 1967, after leading 41-0 very late in the fourth period. The 35-point setback was the Buckeyes' largest margin of defeat during Woody Hayes' 276 games at Ohio State from 1951 through 1978.

Sensational Season Opener

Ohio State opened its 1968 season at home with a thrilling 35-14 triumph over Southern Methodist. The two teams combined for a total of 178 plays and 859

In his first varsity game for the Buckeyes, quarterback Rex Kern led his team like a veteran against SMU. *Courtesy Ohio State University Photo Archives*

yards of total offense. The Buckeye defense held the Mustangs on downs five times inside the OSU 21.

Mustang quarterback Chuck Hixon and backup Gary Carter combined for a total of 76 passes, the most even thrown by one team in an NCAA game until Houston launched 78 against Arizona State in 1989. Turnovers were the key to OSU's victory. SMU threw five interceptions and lost three fumbles, while Ohio State had no interceptions and one lost fumble. The Mustangs were coached by Hayden Fry, who later enjoyed great success as head coach at Iowa from 1978 through 1998.

Lou Holtz. *Courtesy Ohio State University Photo Archives*

Holtz Heroes

Lou Holtz was defensive backfield coach during Ohio State's undefeated national championship season of 1968. All four of the Buckeyes' starting defensive backs that season would become All-Americans: halfback Ted Provost (1969), cornerback Jack Tatum (1969-1970), safety Mike Sensibaugh (1970) and halfback Tim Anderson (1970).

Buckeyes' No. 1 Fan!

Ed Linser was raised in New York City and joined the Navy in 1948 at age 19. Linser became good friends with Bill Wade while stationed at Great Lakes Naval Training Station north of Chicago. Wade was a fellow enlistee from Chauncey, Ohio, and an avid Ohio State football fan.

After the two were discharged from the Navy, they roomed together in Columbus for a short time. Linser quickly became a Buckeye fan but never attended a game at Ohio Stadium. He met his wife, Shirley, while living in Columbus, and the Linsers soon moved to New York City in 1951.

After 17 years of supporting the Buckeyes from afar, the Linsers visited Columbus to see their very first game — OSU's unforgettable 13-0 triumph over No. 1 Purdue on Oct. 12, 1968. For Linser, it was the most exciting event he had ever experienced.

The following spring, against the advice of many close friends, Linser quit his job, sold his home and moved his family to Columbus. He had a wife and four school-age children to support, with no job waiting in Columbus. The family lived with Shirley's parents until Linser found a job and purchased a home. Beginning in 1969, Linser missed only five games at Ohio Stadium over the next 30 seasons. Wow, what some fans will do to follow the Buckeyes!

GREAT GAME REMEMBERED
Ohio State 24 – Michigan 14
Nov. 25, 1967 – Ann Arbor, Michigan

Ohio State continued to get stronger during the second half of the 1967 season, finishing with a fine 24-14 win at Michigan before a crowd of 64,411. The Buckeyes scored on their first two possessions, then tallied their third touchdown just seven minutes into the second period. Halfback Rudy Hubbard, playing his final game for the Scarlet and Gray, scored on runs of 22 and 12 yards. Quarterback Bill Long accounted for the second-quarter touchdown with a one-yard sneak. Placekicker Gary Cairns added a 35-yard field goal late in the final period.

Coach Woody Hayes was extremely pleased with the turnover margin; Michigan had four, Ohio State none. After 17 seasons, his coaching record against Michigan of 11-6 included victories in six of the last eight meetings.

The Legendary Fullback Chinstrap

Bob Ferguson was a two-time All-American fullback in 1960-61. He finished a close second to Syracuse's Ernie Davis in the Heisman Trophy balloting his senior year. Jim Otis was an All-American fullback in 1969. His career rushing total of 2,542 yards is the highest of any fullback in Ohio State history.

In his last collegiate game, Ferguson scored four touchdowns as Ohio State blasted Michigan 50-20 at Ann Arbor in 1961. It was the Buckeyes' 400th all-time victory. Fifty is the most points ever scored by Ohio State in this storied rivalry. While leaving the playing field following this major victory, Ferguson gave his chinstrap to a very young Buckeye fan named Scooter, who requested it as a keepsake.

Seven years later, Ohio State was preparing for its 1968 home encounter against Michigan. With both teams possessing league records of 6-0, the winner would emerge as the outright Big Ten champion. At a spirited pep rally on campus the evening prior to the game, Scooter approached Otis, told the Buckeye fullback the history of the chinstrap and gave it to him.

Saturday morning for "good luck," Otis taped his new keepsake inside his shoulder pads. That afternoon Otis incredibly scored four touchdowns against the Wolverines, just like Ferguson in 1961. The Buckeyes again scored 50 points, defeating the visitors 50-14. Otis now lives in St. Louis, and still cherishes that famous chinstrap — the one that crossed the Michigan goal line eight times.

Scooter is the nickname of Jon Hall, who has continued to be an avid Ohio State fan throughout his entire adult life.

Courtesy Tom Hayes

OSU BLASTS WOLVES, 50-20; BADGERS TRIP MINNESOTA, 23-21

Buckeyes Win Big Ten Title

Ohio State   7 14 0 29---50
Michigan   0   6 6   8---20

*Courtesy The Columbus Dispatch,
Nov. 26, 1961*

BUCKEYES WIN IT ALL - - - BIG

Bury Michigan, 50 - 14 for Title, Rose Bowl

Courtesy The Columbus Dispatch, Nov. 24, 1968

Domination Defined

Ohio State opened the 1969 season at home on Sept. 27, trouncing Texas Christian 62-0. This was the largest margin of victory during Woody Hayes' 276 games as head coach from 1951 through 1978.

#41 and #41 — a Coincidence?

The New York Jets stunned the 18-point favored Baltimore Colts, 16-7, in Super Bowl III at the old Orange Bowl in Miami on Jan. 12, 1969. Three days before the game, Jets quarterback Joe Namath boldly predicted a victory when speaking to the Miami Touchdown Club.

Two notable former Buckeyes were the game's leading rushers. Tom Matte (OSU 1958-60) led the Colts with 116 yards and Matt Snell (OSU 1961-63) was the Jets' leading rusher with 121 yards. Matte and Snell each wore jersey #41 in the NFL, the same number they had each proudly worn at Ohio State.

Tom Matte. *Courtesy Ohio State University Photo Archives*

Matt Snell. *Courtesy Ohio State University Photo Archives*

A "First Lady" First

Mrs. Anne Hayes became the first woman to address the Chicago Quarterback Club when she dazzled them with her wit and charm at their luncheon on Mon., Nov. 3, 1969. Mrs. Hayes impressed the accomplished group with her insight and knowledge of college football, and she provided many "humorous insights" about her husband.

The next day, the *Chicago Tribune* wrote: "Another male bastion tumbled yesterday under a crescendo of anecdotes and humorous mutterings from Mrs. Woody (Anne) Hayes. Mrs. Hayes was the first woman speaker in the history of the Quarterback Club, and she had the audience in the Sherman House in the palm of her hand, just as Hayes has college football in his palm with his No. 1 ranked squad in the nation."

She was quoted as saying how she keeps her mouth shut when people criticized her husband, but speaks out against people who attacked the players. She said, "They're young men out there doing the best job they can. The criticism should go to the coaches."

Anne sprinkled humor liberally throughout her talk. When someone asked her what it was like to be married to a football coach, she replied "Woody has never been anything but a football coach, so I don't know anything else. When we first

GREAT GAME REMEMBERED
No. 4 Ohio State 13 – No. 1 Purdue 0
Oct. 12, 1968 – Columbus, Ohio

Many Ohio State fans refer to this game as their school's greatest victory, especially when recalling the embarrassing 41-6 home loss to Purdue the previous season. It set the stage for the season's undefeated national championship.

BUCKS UPSET NO. 1 PURDUE, 13-0

Details in Sports Section

Columbus Sunday Dispatch SECTION A

Courtesy The Columbus Dispatch, Oct . 13, 1968

On the fourth play of the second half, halfback Ted Provost intercepted Boilermaker quarterback Mike Phipps' outcut pass and raced 35 yards for Ohio State's first score. Later in the third period, quarterback Bill Long dropped back to pass, then dashed 14 yards right up the middle for the game's other touchdown. Ohio State sophomore cornerback Jack Tatum was splendid defending Purdue's Leroy Keyes, holding the talented runner to a mere 18 yards.

Ted Provost's interception return for the game's first touchdown was one of the season's key plays. *Courtesy Ohio State University Photo Archives*

This was the Buckeyes' second all-time victory over a top-ranked opponent. It was the first time Purdue had been shut out in its last 28 games, dating back to a 21-0 loss at Illinois on Oct. 30, 1965.

came to Columbus 19 years ago, it was called the 'Graveyard of Coaches.' Well, a couple of times they've had the 'H-A' on the tombstone!"

The audience loved her, and she was invited back the following year, when she again wowed and wooed the audience with her charm. The day after that event, the Chicago Tribune ran a story with the headline, "Witty Wife of Woody is a Big Hit."

GREAT GAME REMEMBERED
No. 1 Ohio State 27 – No. 2 Southern Calif. 16
Jan. 1, 1969 – Pasadena, California

This was the first Rose Bowl between unbeaten teams since the Big Ten and Pacific Eight Conference joint agreement became effective beginning with the 1946 season. The Buckeyes were 9-0; the Trojans 9-0-1. It also was Ohio State's first time to appear in a game between the nation's two top-ranked teams.

Down 10-0 in the second period, the Buckeyes struck back with 27 consecutive points to flip the lead and create a wide point spread. Fullback Jim Otis plunged 1 yard for the Buckeyes' first touchdown, Jim Roman kicked two field goals, and quarterback Rex Kern (game MVP) threw touchdown passes of 4 and 16 yards to halfbacks Leo Hayden and Ray Gillian, respectively. OSU's offense did not commit a turnover, while the Buckeye defense made two interceptions and recovered three fumbles.

CHAPTER NINE

1971-1978

Archie's Impact and "The Ten Year War"

The 1970s was a decade of cultural changes, technological innovation and economic struggle. Political tumult accompanied the Watergate scandal, the Vietnam War and the women's movement. Home video games appeared, led by Magnavox and Atari's wildly successful Pong. They forever changed our relationship with electronics from one of strictly business to also entertainment.

Archie Griffin's last game in Ohio Stadium was a 38-6 triumph over Minnesota on Nov. 15, 1975. *Courtesy Ohio State University Photo Archives*

Economically, the nation stumbled into a "stagflation" period of slow growth and increased inflation.

In 1965 all other Big Ten Conference teams began playing a 10-game regular-season schedule, while Ohio State remained at nine. The Buckeyes finally went to 10 games in 1971, when other conference members increased their schedules to 11. Ohio State began playing 11 regular-season games in 1974.

Two major policy changes in 1972 were extremely favorable for Ohio State. Freshmen players were now eligible for varsity competition, and the Big Ten Conference eliminated its "no repeat" rule when selecting its annual Rose Bowl representative. Archie Griffin, a talented freshman tailback from Columbus Eastmoor High School, quickly impacted the offense by rushing for a team-leading 867 yards in 1972.

Ohio State won outright or shared Big Ten titles in each of Griffin's four seasons through 1975, and played in the Rose Bowl each year. The Buckeyes were 24-0 at home and 3-0-1 against the Michigan Wolverines. Griffin captured the Heisman Trophy his junior and senior years to become the only two-time recipient of the coveted award. He finished his outstanding career with 5,589 yards on the ground, including 31 consecutive games of rushing for more than 100 yards. Ohio State's four-year record was 40-5-1 for a winning rate of 88.0 percent, the third-highest of any four consecutive seasons in school history (exceeded only by 2012-2015 at 92.6 percent and 2013-2016 at 89.1 percent).

Woody Hayes suffered a heart attack on June 6, 1974, exactly 100 days prior to the Sept. 14 season opener at Minnesota. The 61-year-old coach used the summer to recuperate. By September he had lost 25 pounds and was completely cleared to resume his coaching responsibilities.

Ohio State shared Big Ten championships with Michigan in 1976 and 1977 to establish a league-record six consecutive titles. Hayes would conclude his tenure as head coach in 1978. His final victory in Ohio Stadium was a 45-7 triumph over

Illinois on Nov. 11. The Fighting Illini were coached by Gary Moeller, who had been an Ohio State co-captain under Hayes in 1962.

Hayes' career quickly ended after he struck Clemson linebacker Charlie Bauman on the sideline near the end of a 17-15 loss to the Tigers in the Dec. 29 Gator Bowl. The following morning Hayes telephoned his good friend Paul Hornung, Sports Editor of *The Columbus Dispatch*, and told Hornung, "I have resigned as of now."

Woody Hayes' 28-year record at Ohio State was an excellent 205-61-10 (76.1 percent), and his 33-year career mark was 238-72-10 (75.9 percent). His Ohio State teams captured 13 Big Ten championships and five national titles. He also was an associate professor who took great pride in teaching classes on football coaching methods at Ohio State during the offseason.

During World War II, Hayes rose to the rank of Lieutenant Commander and commanded the USS Rinehart in both the Atlantic and Pacific. After football, Hayes continued to be a very visible goodwill representative for Ohio State. He delivered the university's winter commencement address on March 22, 1986, and considered that opportunity "the greatest day of my life." Hayes passed away at his home at 1711 Cardiff Road in Columbus at age 74 on March 12, 1987. His positive influence will be felt for many future generations.

OSU Cagers Top No. 1 Duke In Overtime — Page B-1

WEATHER
Rain and snow mixed tonight.
Low in low 30s. Rain with
high in mid-40s Sunday.

(Map, Data on Page A-2)

The Columbus Dispatch

**HOME
FINAL**
Associated Press, United Press,
International and
Copley News Services

32 Pages   *OHIO'S GREATEST HOME NEWSPAPER*   3 Sections

VOL. 108, NO. 183   COLUMBUS, OHIO 43216, SATURDAY, DECEMBER 30, 1978   15 Cents

WOODY HAYES RESIGNS

Courtesy The Columbus Dispatch, Dec. 30, 1978

Route 88

Ohio State defeated Wisconsin 31-6 on Oct. 23, 1971. Halfback Morris Bradshaw electrified the homecoming crowd with two 88-yard scoring runs — one from scrimmage in the second quarter and a kickoff return in the final period. Bradshaw's efforts brought to mind Hopalong Cassady's treasured 88-yard scoring interception return that keyed the Buckeyes' 31-14 homecoming win over the Badgers 17 years earlier in 1954. Interestingly, these two victories over Wisconsin each took place on Oct. 23 at Ohio Stadium.

Woody - Bo and "The Ten Year War"

Woody Hayes' last 10 seasons (1969-1978) as head coach were highlighted by his teams' fiercely fought games against the Michigan Wolverines, coached by Bo Schembechler. The conference title or co-title was on the line for both schools during each of these 10 battles, with the exception of OSU in 1971.

Bo Schembechler and Woody Hayes. *Courtesy Ohio State University Photo Archives*

Ohio State won four of the contests (1970-72-74-75), Michigan won five (1969-71-76-77-78), and the two battled to a bitter 10-10 tie in 1973. It is unlikely that 10 consecutive games between two major college football programs were ever played at the same level of desire and intensity as these 10 between the Buckeyes and Wolverines.

Just Keep Driving!

Coach Woody Hayes and assistant coach Ed Ferkany were recruiting in Detroit on a very snowy evening in February of 1972. When the two started their return trip to Columbus, Ferkany mentioned that their car was almost out of gas. Hayes told him to keep driving until they crossed back into Ohio, because he didn't want the tax portion of their gas purchase to go to the state of Michigan. After driving a few more miles with the gas needle now pointing directly at zero, Ferkany again said that they needed to get gas. Hayes forcefully told him to just keep driving until they were in Ohio. Fortunately, the two made it to a gas station about a mile south

GREAT GAME REMEMBERED
No. 9 Ohio State 14 – No. 3 Michigan 11
Nov. 25, 1972 – Columbus, Ohio

Michigan dominated the game, running 83 plays from scrimmage while Ohio State ran only 44. The Wolverines led in first downs, 21-10, and total offensive yards, 344-192. But two remarkable Buckeye goal-line stands on this chilly, wet afternoon — one near halftime and the other early in the fourth quarter — helped secure the thrilling three-point triumph. Ohio State's opportunistic defense was spearheaded by its linebackers: Arnie Jones with 24 tackles followed by Rick Middleton with 17 and Randy Gradishar with 15.

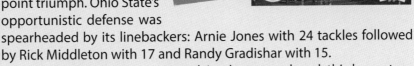

All of the scoring occurred in the second and third quarters. Fullback Champ Henson scored OSU's first touchdown from the 1, and tailback Archie Griffin raced 30 yards over right tackle for the second score. With the victory, Ohio State shared the Big Ten title with Michigan and represented the conference in the Rose Bowl. This was the fourth game of the "Ten Year War" between Woody Hayes and Bo Schembechler, with the games now tied at 2-2.

of the state line. Years later, when recalling this venture, Ferkany stated that it was a miracle they make it out of Michigan. Their trip to Detroit was very beneficial, since the player they were recruiting was Bruce Ruhl from Southfield-Lathrup High School. Ruhl became a very fine defensive back for the Buckeyes from 1973 through 1976, finishing with seven career interceptions.

All Night History Lesson

After speaking in Philadelphia on Wednesday evening, March 29, 1972, Woody Hayes was very unhappy to learn that his late evening return flight to Columbus had been canceled. As Hayes was making arrangements for a rental car, a young Air Force sergeant named David Buller overheard Hayes and asked if he could ride with him. Hayes gladly agreed, and Buller explained his need to get to the Dayton Airport for a flight to his home in Ogden, Utah.

The two drove throughout the night, reaching Columbus at approximately 3 a.m. Hayes then called junior varsity coach John Mummey, and asked Mummey to drive Buller from Columbus to the Dayton airport. During their drive, Buller told Mummey how much Mr. Hayes impressed him with his knowledge and understanding of history, and how much Buller enjoyed their conversation.

Mummey soon asked Buller, "Do you know who you were riding with?" Buller replied, "He said his name was Hayes and he sure sounded like a history professor." Mummey responded, "Are you aware that the Mr. Hayes you rode with is Coach Woody Hayes of Ohio State?" The surprised sergeant answered, "You're kidding, THE Woody Hayes? He never once even mentioned football. I can't believe it. Just wait until I tell my parents!"

After taking Buller to the Dayton airport, Mummey headed back to Columbus for an 8 a.m. coaches' meeting — and there was Hayes, eager to prepare for spring football practice after a very short night's sleep.

Sensational Debut

Ohio State opened the 1972 season at home with a 21-0 victory over Iowa on Sept. 16. With freshman now eligible for varsity play, a record 114 players were in uniform. Freshman tailback Archie Griffin was in for one play late in the fourth quarter, a play that resulted in a fumble when Griffin and quarterback Dave

NORTH CAROLINA
OHIO STATE
September 30, 1972

Purdy did not connect on a pitchout. Aware that Woody Hayes detested turnovers, Griffin was worried how this fumble might affect his future.

After a bye week, highly-favored Ohio State faced North Carolina on Sept. 30. The Buckeyes started slowly, gained only 13 yards on their first two possessions, and trailed 7-0 after the visiting Tar Heels recovered a blocked punt in the end zone. Late in the first period, Hayes followed the advice of backfield coach Rudy Hubbard and line coach Ed Ferkany, and inserted Griffin at tailback. That week Griffin had been listed with the fifth team. He was so stunned that Hayes would put him in the game, he was halfway to the huddle before realizing he had forgotten his helmet.

Griffin responded impressively by rushing for what was then a school single-game record of 229 yards. Ohio State won 29-14. Long-time *Columbus Dispatch* sports editor Paul Hornung stated, "Probably never in the 50-year history of Ohio Stadium has there been so sensational a debut as that of 18-year-old Eastmoor grad Archie Griffin."

GREAT GAME REMEMBERED
No. 4 Ohio State 42 - No. 7 Southern Calif. 21
Jan. 1, 1974 - Rose Bowl - Pasadena, Cal.

After trailing 21-14 early in the third period, Ohio State scored the game's last 28 points to achieve the cherished victory, before a crowd of 105,267. It was the Big Ten's first Rose Bowl triumph in five years. Sophomore tailback Archie Griffin was the game's leading rusher with 149 yards. Freshman fullback Pete Johnson added 94 yards and scored three touchdowns on short plunges. An exhilarating 56-yard punt return by junior Neal Colzie set up OSU's fourth touchdown late in the third quarter. Sophomore quarterback Cornelius Greene was selected the game's MVP. Ohio State finished the 1973 season at 10-0-1, placing second behind Notre Dame (11-0) in the final *Associated Press* poll.

Godfrey Saluted

Coach emeritus Ernie Godfrey was honored for his induction into the National Football Foundation Hall of Fame during a ceremony prior to the Oct. 14, 1972, home game against Illinois. The Ohio State Marching Band spelled out "Ernie," while Godfrey was presented with his Hall of Fame plaque by former Buckeye All-American Bill Willis and Mr. John W. Galbreath, who represented the Hall of Fame.

Godfrey served the Buckeyes with distinction as an assistant coach for 33 seasons, from 1929 through 1961, under seven different head coaches. He is credited with developing many of Ohio State's fine placekickers. The Columbus Chapter of the National Football Foundation is named in Godfrey's honor.

Golden Anniversary

Ohio State scored in each quarter to defeat Indiana 44-7 at Ohio Stadium on Oct. 21, 1972. Quarterback Greg Hare and fullback Champ Henson each tallied twice. The victory commemorated the exact 50th anniversary of the Ohio Stadium dedication game, a 19-0 loss to Michigan on Oct. 21, 1922. Fourteen former Buckeyes who had played in the dedication game were honored on the field at halftime.

GREAT GAME REMEMBERED
No. 4 Ohio State 12 – No. 3 Michigan 10
Nov. 23, 1974 – Columbus, Ohio

It is the only time Ohio State has defeated Michigan without scoring a touchdown. The game featured one of Ohio State's all-time finest kicking exhibitions. All 22 points were scored at the north end of Ohio Stadium. Michigan opened strongly and quickly tallied on its first two possessions to lead, 10-0. With a strong wind at their backs, the Buckeyes retaliated with second quarter field goals of 47, 25, and 43 yards by placekicker

The Dispatch   SPORTS SECTION

Bucks' Toe Beats Bo, 12-10

Klaban's Four Field Goals Victory Margin,

Courtesy The Columbus Dispatch, Nov. 24, 1974

Placekicker Tom Klaban and holder Brian Baschnagel.
Courtesy Ohio State University Photo Archives

Tom Klaban, to tighten the halftime score at 10-9. Early in the third period, Klaban kicked his fourth three-pointer to give Ohio State its first lead of the afternoon at 12-10. With just 16 seconds remaining in the final quarter, a field-goal attempt of 33 yards by Michigan's Mike Lantry was wide to the left by a mere 18 inches. OSU's Tom Skladany averaged 45.2 yards on five timely punts and was a major factor in the game's outcome. Ohio State had been held without a touchdown for the first time in its last 81 games.

Rose Bowl Firsts

Ohio State All-American tackle John Hicks became the first player to appear in three Rose Bowls (1970, 1972, and 1973 seasons). Two-time Heisman Trophy winner Archie Griffin is the only player to have started four Rose Bowls (seasons 1972 through 1975).

Overwhelmed!

After playing Southern California to a 7-7 standoff at halftime, Ohio State lost 42-17 in the Rose Bowl on Jan. 1, 1973. The Trojans' 42 points are the most ever scored against the Buckeyes during the 276 games coached by Woody Hayes from 1951 through 1978.

Banner Breakers

A Michigan football tradition is the Wolverine team running under a blue M Club banner as they take the field prior to each game at Michigan Stadium. Led by tackle John Hicks, the Ohio State team surprisingly tore down the banner as they raced onto the field prior to the 1973 encounter. It is one of the most iconic moments in this storied history.

Michigan radio announcer Bob Ufer was noticeably upset as he told his listening audience, "They're tearing down Michigan's coveted M Club banner! They will meet a dastardly fate here for that. There isn't a Michigan Man who wouldn't

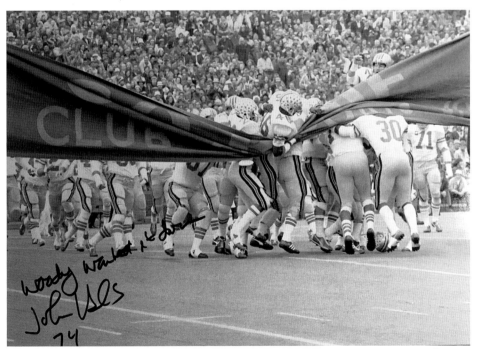

The 1973 Buckeyes tear down the M Club banner. Autographed by John Hicks who led the charge. *Courtesy Ohio State University Photo Archives*

like to go out and scalp those Buckeyes right now. They have the audacity, the unmitigated gall to tear down the coveted M banner!"

The Big Ten's Most Controversial Vote

After battling to a 10-10 tie at Ann Arbor, Ohio State and Michigan shared the 1973 Big Ten title with league records of 7-0-1. The co-championship forced the league's 10 Athletic Directors to vote for their representative to the Rose Bowl.

To the complete surprise of many, including most Buckeye fans, Ohio State was selected. Michigan coach Bo Schembechler was extremely bitter, stating that his team had outplayed Ohio State — leading in first downs, 16-9, and in total offensive yards, 333-204. He also emphasized that Ohio State had been to Pasadena the previous year. Ironically, the Big Ten's "no repeat" policy was abolished just one year earlier, and Michigan Athletic Director Don Canham had actively helped promote the change.

The Big Ten office would not release the official count, but the *Detroit Free Press* reported the vote to be six to four. The *Free Press* indicated that Ohio State received votes from Illinois, Michigan State, Northwestern, Purdue, and Wisconsin. Michigan received the support of Indiana, Iowa, and Minnesota.

Michigan was visibly disturbed that its "sister school," Michigan State, had voted for Ohio State. MSU's vote was cast by Athletic Director Burt Smith, who was a graduate of Michigan. Chicago had dropped out of the Big Ten after the 1939 season, and that void was finally filled by Michigan State in 1953. Michigan openly had supported Pittsburgh to fill the opening in an obvious attempt to keep Michigan State out of the conference. Some veteran Big Ten media representatives suggested that Michigan's action some 20 years earlier helped sway Michigan State's vote in favor of Ohio State.

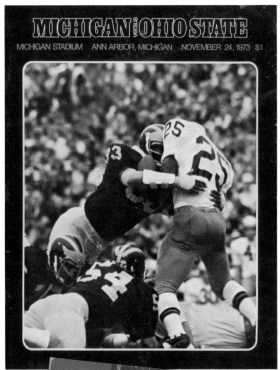

Senior Leadership

Ohio State's 1973 team was one of the very finest in school history, going 10-0-1, placing second in the final *Associated Press* poll, and outscoring its 11 opponents, 413-64. Linebacker Randy Gradishar and offensive tackle John Hicks provided excellent senior leadership. Both were two-time All-Americans, and each is one of the Buckeyes' all-time most outstanding players at his respective position.

Hicks placed second in the 1973 Heisman Trophy voting, Gradishar finished sixth, and sophomore tailback Archie Griffin was fifth. All three are now members of the College Football Hall of Fame.

That season's Heisman Trophy winner was Penn State running back John Cappelletti, who also is a member of the College Football Hall of Fame.

Randy Gradishar and John Hicks. *Courtesy Ohio State University Photo Archives*

Leader on Both Sides of the Ball

Bruce Elia distinguished himself as Ohio State's single-season leader in both scoring and total tackles.

Starting fullback Champ Henson was lost for the remainder of the 1973 regular season after sustaining a torn knee cartilage against TCU in the second game of the year. Coach Woody Hayes immediately moved junior reserve linebacker Elia to fullback, a position he played as a sophomore. Elia led the Buckeyes in scoring in 1973 with 84 points on 14 touchdowns.

In 1974 Elia returned to linebacker and led the Buckeyes in total tackles with 144 — 74 solos and 70 assists.

Bruce Elia. *Courtesy Ohio State University Photo Archives*

Abnormal Opening

Ohio State opened its 1974 season with a 34-19 victory at Minnesota on Sept. 14. Playing at old Memorial Stadium on the Minnesota campus, the Golden Gophers were quarterbacked by sophomore Tony Dungy. Ohio State junior tailback Archie Griffin was the game's leading rusher with 133 yards. This was the Buckeyes' first season opener on the road in 62 seasons. Their last opener away from home had been a 55-0 victory over Otterbein College in Westerville, Ohio, on Oct. 5, 1912.

Fascinating Dates

Woody Hayes and Bo Schembechler have very intriguing birthdays. Hayes was born in Clifton, Ohio, on Valentine's Day — Friday, Feb. 14, 1913. Schembechler was born in Barberton, Ohio, on April Fool's Day — Monday, April 1, 1929.

Neighborly Support

While addressing a gathering of *The Columbus Dispatch* Quarterback Club during the mid-1970s, coach Woody Hayes recalled an experience during the summer of 1954 that impacted his career. While he was relaxing by himself one summer evening on his home's side porch, his neighbors were enjoying a small cook-out nearby. It was dark and the neighbors apparently were unaware of Hayes' presence.

The people were talking about Ohio State football, and Hayes heard one neighbor suggest that, "This is the year we get Woody!" During Hayes' first three seasons his teams had a combined record of 16-9-2. The neighbor seemed to be predicting that the coach would be fired after the 1954 season.

Hayes told the Quarterback Club that this incident definitely provided him with additional motivation. "I even got up an hour earlier each day, so I could prepare all the more for our season," he related. That year became the turning point during Hayes' tenure at Ohio State. The Buckeyes went 10-0 through a very rugged Big Ten schedule to claim the 1954 national title.

Woody Hayes family home at 1711 Cardiff Road in Columbus. *Courtesy Jack Park*

Hey, You're Sitting in MY Seat!

One week after opening the 1974 season at Minnesota, the Buckeyes' talented offense scored in each quarter to shellac Oregon State 51-10 at Ohio Stadium. Junior tailback Archie Griffin led all rushers with 134 yards, and his younger brother, freshman tailback Ray Griffin, scored his team's final two TDs with runs of 9 and 12 yards. Speedster Lenny Willis returned the second half kickoff 97 yards for OSU's fourth score of the afternoon.

There was also a lot of action that afternoon in Ohio Stadium's section 9B. Shortly after the stadium opened, Portal Chief Kenny Tinkler was stunned to learn that tickets for many seats in this section had been double-printed and double-sold. The Ohio State Ticket Office had computerized its ticket distribution system that year, and an unknown flaw in the program allowed duplicate tickets to be printed for certain seats. Tinkler estimated 700 seats were duplicated.

Many patrons with duplicate tickets were seated on top of the press box, some sat in the aisles, and the remainder used folding chairs placed on the stadium's running track. Years later, Portal Superintendent Dick Weber remarked, "Those displaced fans probably can't recall the opponent, the final score, or even the season. But they'll always remember the confusion associated with the double-printing of game tickets for section 9B."

Who Won?

Top-ranked Ohio State (8-0) faced always-rugged Michigan State on Nov. 9, 1974, at spirited Spartan Stadium. The Buckeyes had outscored their eight opponents, 360-75, and had surrendered no more than one touchdown in each of their last seven outings. MSU's record was 4-3-1.

The game was tied 3-3 at halftime, after Ohio State's offense had been hampered with an interception and two lost fumbles. Placekicker Tom Klaban's second field goal of the day put the Buckeyes on top 6-3 early in the third quarter. During an afternoon when yards were difficult to obtain, fullback Champ Henson plunged 1 yard over right tackle for the game's first touchdown early in the final period. With 9:03 left in the tense contest, Ohio State's 13-3 lead appeared to be secure.

On the following possession, Spartan quarterback Charlie Baggett passed 44 yards to end Mike Jones for a touchdown to tighten the score at 13-9. A two-point conversion attempt failed. After the Buckeyes were unable to sustain their next possession, Tom Skladany punted 55 yards to push the Spartans deep at their own 12. On first down fullback Levi Jackson broke through right tackle, eluded three tacklers, then raced down the Spartan sideline to score standing up with 3:17 remaining. Jackson's 88-yard gallop gave the Spartans their first lead of the game at 16-13. Ohio State's stellar defense was noted for rarely giving up a long play — yet in a span of just over six minutes the Buckeyes had surrendered two lengthy scores.

Ohio State rapidly drove 66 yards to the MSU 5. Henson plunged to within inches of the end zone. There were 29 seconds remaining and the Buckeyes were out of timeouts. The Spartan defenders were very deliberate getting up after

Henson's carry, and Ohio State had difficulty executing one last play. After the ball was finally snapped, it shot between the legs of quarterback Cornelius Greene and was picked up and carried into the end zone by wingback Brian Baschnagel. Headlinesman Ed Scheck signaled touchdown, but field judge Robert Dagenhardt indicated time had expired before the ball was snapped.

There was total confusion on the field, in the press box, and among the partisan crowd of 78,533. Did Baschnagel score? Who won? After much deliberation and several viewings of the final play, Big Ten Commissioner Wayne Duke announced that Michigan State was the winner, 16-13. Approximately one-half of the crowd was still in the stadium when Duke made his announcement 46 minutes after the game's final play.

Referee Gene Calhoun told Duke that time had expired before Ohio State's final play. Calhoun also stated that if time had not expired, the Buckeyes would have been penalized when they did not come to a required one-second set before the ball was snapped. Ohio State's No. 1 ranking abruptly was gone!

The Buckeye offense was weakened with the loss of All-American tackle Kurt Schumacher, who was injured and not able to play. Ohio State finished the 1974 season with a very impressive 10-2 record and a fourth place ranking in the final *Associated Press* poll. Michigan State won its remaining two games to conclude the year at 7-3-1.

Wolverine Woes

Michigan's excellent three-year record from 1972 through 1974 was 30-2-1. The three games the Wolverines did not win were their three against Ohio State. The Buckeyes won in 1972 (14-11) and 1974 (12-10), and the two battled to a 10-10 tie in 1973.

Fullback Delight

The fullback off-tackle play was a key element of Woody Hayes' ground-oriented offense. Two of the best at this position during Hayes' tenure were Harold "Champ" Henson (1972-73-74) and Pete Johnson (1973-74-75-76). Each plunged for numerous first downs when the count was third-and-short. Henson rushed 308 times for 1,335 yards and 36 touchdowns during his three-year career, even though he missed most of the 1973 season with a knee injury. Henson was never tackled for a loss. Johnson rushed 548 times for 2,308 yards and a school-record 58 touchdowns during his four seasons.

Champ Henson. *Courtesy Ohio State University Photo Archives*

Pete Johnson. *Courtesy Ohio State University Photo Archives*

Maybe Not Such a Good Idea

The Buckeyes were 7-0 and had outscored their opponents 251-42 as they prepared for a Nov. 1 home encounter with Indiana in 1975. The Hoosiers had won only two of their first seven starts, and had been beaten 55-7 at Michigan the previous Saturday.

Since Indiana apparently appeared to be an easy win for his team, Woody Hayes cancelled the Monday practice prior to the game. He thought a day of rest would be best for his players at this stage of the season, especially when considering the opponent.

Saturday afternoon, Indiana played far more impressively than Hayes ever anticipated. OSU won 24-14 after leading just 17-14 late in the final period, and the game was even closer than suggested by the final score. Hoosier fullback Rick Enis (Hayes had tried to recruit Enis out of Union City, Ind.) punished the Buckeye defense for 148 yards and both Hoosier TDs.

Indiana head coach Lee Corso told the press, "We just gave them our full shot. I feel like my team played as well as any I have ever seen against a great team." Hayes said, "Maybe we were fortunate not to get bumped off. We'll just go on from here."

Woody Hayes was never again known to cancel a Monday practice.

Bo's "Home Cooking"

Ohio State's thrilling 21-14 come-from-behind triumph at Michigan on Nov. 22, 1975, was the Wolverines' first Big Ten loss at home under Bo Schembechler, who was in his seventh season as head coach. Michigan had played 26 league games at Michigan Stadium under Schembechler since 1969, with a record of 25-0-1. It also was the Wolverines' first loss in their last 42 games at home, dating back to a 40-17 loss to Missouri in Ann Arbor on Oct. 4, 1969.

Duplicates

UCLA upset top-ranked and previously undefeated Ohio State, 23-10, in the Rose Bowl of Jan. 1, 1976. Exactly 10 years earlier in the Rose Bowl of Jan. 1, 1966, UCLA defeated No. 1-rated and previously undefeated Michigan State, 14-12.

Ironically, the Buckeyes and Spartans both had defeated UCLA in each of those two regular seasons. Ohio State won at UCLA, 41-20, on Oct. 4, 1975, and Michigan State defeated UCLA, 13-3, at Spartan Stadium on Sept. 18, 1965.

Five Seasons Between Home Setbacks

Ohio State's all-time home winning streak is 25 games. It began with a 21-0 season-opening triumph over Iowa on Sept. 16, 1972, and finished with a 49-21 season-opening victory over Michigan State on Sept. 11, 1976. The Buckeyes lost to Missouri, 22-21, on Sept. 25, 1976, to end the streak. It was the Tigers' very first triumph over Ohio State after 10 previous unsuccessful attempts.

Eventually

Ohio State suffered a home loss to Michigan 22-0 on Nov. 20, 1976, and a 14-6 setback in Ann Arbor a year later on Nov. 19, 1977. It was the first time the Wolverines had been able to defeat the Buckeyes two years in a row, during Woody Hayes' first 27 seasons at Ohio State from 1951 through 1977. Michigan added a third consecutive win in 1978, with a 14-3 victory in Columbus on Nov. 25.

GREAT GAME REMEMBERED
No. 1 Ohio State 21 - No. 4 Michigan 14
Nov. 22, 1975 - Ann Arbor, Michigan

With both teams undefeated and untied in league play, the winner would claim the outright Big Ten title and a trip to the Rose Bowl. The first half was poorly played with each team committing three turnovers. When Michigan grabbed a 14-7 lead with 7:11 left in the game, Ohio State had not had a first down since early in the second period. Things changed quickly! Quarterback Cornelius Greene engineered an 80-yard scoring drive to tie the score at 14-14. On Michigan's ensuing possession, quarterback Rick Leach was intercepted by safety Ray Griffin, who streaked 29 yards to the Michigan 3. Fullback Pete Johnson bolted across for his third touchdown of the afternoon and a seven-point victory. Johnson's final two scores came within a span of 59 seconds. Griffin's two-handed interception was likely the team's key play of the season.

Ray Griffin. *Courtesy Ohio State University Photo Archives*

Fullback Pete Johnson scores the deciding touchdown, his third of the game. *Courtesy Ohio State University Photo Archives*

Woody in a Hurry

While opening up his Upper Arlington barber shop one summer morning in the late-1970s, Howard Warner noticed Woody Hayes driving east on Lane Avenue with his briefcase resting on top of his car. The coach was headed to his campus office and apparently did not realize he had placed it there as he was leaving home.

Warner quickly telephoned Anne Hayes and explained what he had just seen, then lightheartedly told her he was concerned that Ohio State's plans for the Michigan game might be inside the briefcase. Mrs. Hayes promptly contacted her husband at his office. Hayes went outside and, fortunately, found his briefcase still sitting on top of his car. The Buckeyes' plans for the Michigan game were secure!

Looking For Clues at 1711 Cardiff Road

Dale Keitz, a defensive lineman at the University of Michigan from 1976 through 1979, played his high school football at Upper Arlington on the edge of Columbus. During the summers, Keitz worked on one of the Upper Arlington Sanitation Department trucks, picking up garbage.

One of his "customers" was the Woody Hayes family at 1711 Cardiff Road. Keitz took a lot of good natured kidding about sorting through Woody's trash, looking for clues to Ohio State's game plan for the Michigan game.

Dale likely also talked with his father, Dick, to gain an insight into Hayes' game planning techniques. The elder Keitz had played football under Hayes at Denison University in 1947-48.

Clancy's Homecoming Rite

Ohio State's popular "Block O" card section was the brain-child of Clancy Issac, head cheerleader in 1938. Issac developed the concept after viewing a similar student activity at the University of Southern California when the Buckeyes played in Los Angeles in 1937. Issac grew up in the Columbus suburb of Bexley, and after graduation lived most of his adult life as an advertising executive in New York City.

For 40 consecutive seasons from 1939 through 1978, Issac returned for Homecoming and passionately led his annual cheer, "Yea Ohio, Yea Ohio, Let's Go, Let's Fight, Let's Win!" His final appearance was at the homecoming game against Iowa on Oct. 21, 1978. It was a very emotional moment for Issac, when the marching band spelled out CLANCY in tribute to his many years of loyalty and enthusiasm. Issac was honored by his alma mater in 1970 as "one of 100 distinguished alumni selected during The Ohio State University's first 100 years."

Highest High

Ohio State scored in each quarter to overwhelm Northwestern, 63-21, at Ohio Stadium on Oct. 28, 1978. It was the most points scored by the Buckeyes in a single game during Woody Hayes' 28 seasons as head coach from 1951 through 1978.

The Rest of the Story

Near the end of Clemson's 17-15 victory over Ohio State in the Gator Bowl of Dec. 29, 1978, a frustrated Woody Hayes struck Clemson linebacker Charlie Bauman after Bauman intercepted quarterback Art Schlichter's pass and was run out of bounds in front of the Ohio State bench. This immediately ended Hayes' notable 28-year Ohio State coaching tenure.

Announcers Keith Jackson and Ara Parseghian were doing the television broadcast of the game. A few days later, Jackson was a guest on John Gordon's nightly "Sportstalk" call-in show on WBNS Radio (1460 AM) in Columbus. Jackson recounted how Schlichter had tried to connect with tailback Ron Springs over the middle when Bauman made the interception.

While watching a replay after the game, Jackson discovered that Buckeye receiver Doug Donley had been wide open several yards behind the Clemson secondary. Jackson stated, "Schlichter apparently did not see Donley. Had he noticed him, Schlichter would likely have thrown to Donley for an easy touchdown, Bauman's interception would never have occurred, Ohio State would have won the game, and Woody Hayes would still be coaching the Buckeyes!"

GREAT GAME REMEMBERED
No. 3 Oklahoma 29 - No. 4 Ohio State 28
Sept. 24, 1977 - Columbus, Ohio

This highly anticipated match-up developed into three separate episodes. Oklahoma quickly scored the game's first 20 points, Ohio State painstakingly retaliated with the next 28, and Oklahoma completed the physically tense afternoon by tallying the final nine. It was one of the most  dramatic struggles ever staged at Ohio Stadium. All but three of the game's 57 points were scored at the north end of Ohio Stadium, primarily because of a strong 15-mile-per-hour wind blowing from the south. With his team down 28-26, Sooner placekicker Uwe von Schamann calmly booted a 41-yard field goal with just three seconds remaining. Many Buckeye fans remained glued to their seats for several minutes after the game ended, too emotionally drained to leave.

"Let's Meet at Doyt's"

The 1978 Gator Bowl was played on Friday night, Dec. 29. Michigan's coaches and players learned that Woody Hayes' coaching career had come to an end the night before, while they were in Pasadena preparing for the following Monday's Rose Bowl against Southern California.

Soon after the Wolverines returned from the Rose Bowl to Ann Arbor, Bo Schembechler called Hayes to arrange a visit with him in Columbus. Apparently Mrs. Anne Hayes had suggested to Schembechler that her rather distressed husband would really benefit from seeing him. Hayes told Schembechler that a trip from Ann Arbor to Columbus would consume too much of Schembechler's time, especially with Schembechler's need to concentrate on recruiting, and that they should instead get together at a later time.

Schembechler strongly insisted that they meet very soon, so Hayes suggested a compromise — "Let's meet at Doyt's." Doyt Perry, a very close friend of both Hayes and Schembechler, lived in Bowling Green, Ohio, approximately halfway between Columbus and Ann Arbor. Hayes realized it would take Schembechler far less time to drive to Bowling Green than Columbus. Perry had been Ohio State's backfield coach under Hayes before becoming an extremely successful head coach at Bowling Green State University in 1955. He later was Director of Athletics at the school before retiring in 1970. Schembechler had been Perry's freshman coach at BGSU in 1955.

The following weekend, Hayes and Schembechler enjoyed a delicious Sunday dinner at the home of Doyt and Loretta Perry. Yes, there really are no friends like your old friends, especially during times of difficulty and change.

CHAPTER TEN

1979-1987

Earle Arrives

Tremendous economic, social and political change characterized the late-1970s and 1980s. The conservative policies of President Ronald Regan stimulated exceptional economic growth. Cable television introduced MTV, ESPN and CNN, providing music, sports and politics 24 hours a day. Significant events included Sandra Day O'Connor becoming the first female United States Supreme Court Justice in 1981, the tragic explosion of the Shuttle Challenger in 1986, and the 1989 crash of the Exxon Valdez oil tanker that caused the largest oil spill in United States history.

During the twilight years of Woody Hayes' coaching career, many Ohio State fans ardently speculated about his successor. Their curiosity was answered on Jan. 12, 1979, with the hiring of one of Hayes' former assistants, 47-year-old Earle Bruce. "It's a dream come true," Bruce stated when informed of his selection.

Bruce had elected to play at Ohio State in 1949 under coach Wes Fesler after a star-studded career at Allegheny High School in Cumberland, MD. During fall practice in 1951, Hayes' first year at Ohio State, the speedy Bruce reinjured a knee that ended his playing career.

After graduation in 1953, Bruce coached a total of 13 seasons at Mansfield, Salem, Sandusky, and Massillon high schools before returning to campus in 1966 as a Hayes assistant. He finished his high school coaching career with a 42-game winning streak, and three times was selected Ohio High School Coach of the Year. After six seasons on the Ohio State staff, Bruce became head coach at Tampa for one year followed by six seasons at Iowa State before returning to Columbus.

Bruce hit the ground running! His 1979 spring practice was quite vigorous, and players became excited about their new coaching staff. Bruce's first team far

Bruce Succeeds Woody At OSU | Complete Details In Sports Section

WEATHER
Snow, freezing rain tonight. Saturday. Low mid-30s tonight. High Saturday in mid-30s.
(Map, Data on Page B-5)

The Columbus Dispatch

HOME FINAL
Associated Press, United Press International and Copley News Services

VOL. 108, NO. 196 | 60 Pages | *OHIO'S GREATEST HOME NEWSPAPER* | COLUMBUS, OHIO 43216, FRIDAY, JANUARY 12, 1979 | 4 Sections | 15 Cents

Courtesy The Columbus Dispatch, Jan. 12, 1979

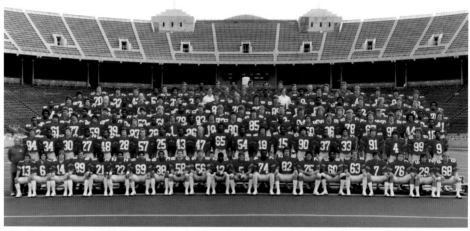

Ohio State was outright Big Ten Champion in 1979. *Courtesy Ohio State University Photo Archives*

exceeded practically everyone's expectations when they claimed the undisputed Big Ten championship with a regular-season record of 11-0. He became college football's Coach of the Year and only a single-point Rose Bowl setback to Southern California, 17-16, prevented Ohio State from claiming the 1979 national title.

The Buckeyes finished each of the next six seasons from 1980 through 1985 with identical records of 9-3. Highlights of this period included three Big Ten titles, a thrilling 45-38 triumph over Illinois in 1984, and a superbly executed 22-13 victory over top-ranked Iowa in 1985.

Bruce's tenure as head coach ended unexpectedly and without explanation. On Monday, Nov. 16, 1987, five days prior to the regular-season finale at Michigan, OSU Athletic Director Rick Bay was informed by OSU President Edward Jennings that Bruce's contract would not be renewed for 1988. Jennings told Bay to inform the media of this decision after the Michigan game. Bay strongly opposed the judgment and immediately resigned. The AD quickly called a press conference and by late that Monday afternoon the entire public now knew about Bruce's future.

Emotions soared among Bruce's loyal players as they rallied for a very moving 23-20 triumph over the favored Wolverines after trailing 13-0 very late in the second quarter. The victory was exceptionally heartwarming for the 56-year old coach

1984 All-American Guard Jim Lachey. *Courtesy Ohio State University Photo Archives*

who stated in his postgame press conference, "We teach our players that when they get knocked down, they have to get up and go again...I guess this was the ultimate test for me." Ohio State finished the 1987 season at 6-4-1.

Earle Bruce's excellent Ohio State record of 81-26-1 (75.5 percent) was the best in the Big Ten during his nine seasons with the Buckeyes. His teams won four conference titles, were 5-4 against Michigan, and posted a mark of 5-3 in postseason bowls.

After Ohio State, Bruce coached a total of five seasons at Northern Iowa and Colorado State. He was inducted into the College Football Hall of Fame in 2002.

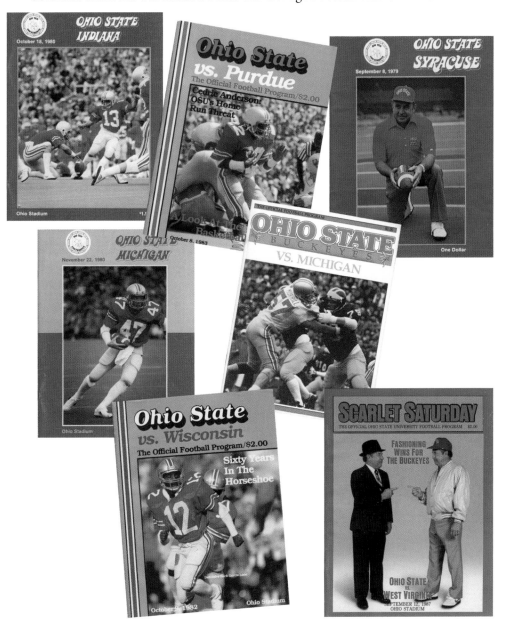

Coach Earle Bruce. *Courtesy Ohio State University Photo Archives*

Finish Your Education!

Earle Bruce was a junior offensive halfback at Ohio State in 1951, Woody Hayes' first season as head coach. His playing career ended abruptly when he reinjured his knee during fall practice. Bruce was greatly discouraged, left school, and hitchhiked back to his home in Maryland.

When Hayes learned of Bruce's departure, he directed assistant coach Harry Strobel to seek Bruce's return to finish his education. Bruce came back and graduated in June of 1953 — 26 years later he would again return to Ohio State, this time as Woody Hayes' successor!

Invading Enemy Territory

An established tradition on football Saturdays is banner towing above Ohio Stadium to communicate individual messages and for commercial advertising. Pilot Bill Watts began towing banners in 1969, and towed all kinds of messages including "Happy 50th Birthday, Harry," "Joe Loves Sue," and "Judy, Will You Marry Me?"

On Nov. 17, 1979, Ohio State needed a victory at Michigan to maintain its perfect record. Three Columbus businesses hired Watts to fly to Ann Arbor and tow a "Go Bucks Go" banner over Michigan Stadium. Watt's banner may have helped! The Buckeyes defeated the Wolverines 18-15 to capture the outright Big Ten title with a regular-season record of 11-0.

Big Two Supremacy

The Big Ten Conference from 1968 through 1980 was commonly labeled the "Big Two and Little Eight." In that span, Ohio State and Michigan were 6-6-1 against each other, with each team scoring exactly 176 points over the 13 games. Additionally, during that time the Buckeyes and Wolverines each were 83-5 against the "Little Eight." Ohio State and Michigan each lost more games to the other than against the other eight conference teams combined. The Big Ten title chase those seasons clearly was a two-team race.

Off to the Races!

Ohio State opened its 1981 campaign with a 34-13 home triumph over Duke on Sept. 12. Tailback Tim Spencer raced 82 yards for a touchdown down the east sideline and into the north end zone on Ohio State's very first play from scrimmage of the season. It is the sixth-longest run from scrimmage in Ohio State football. The talented junior finished the afternoon with 172 yards on 19 carries and three touchdowns.

Spencer rushed for 3,553 during his fine college career, sixth-highest in Ohio State history. He was the team's MVP in 1982, and later served 10 years as Ohio State's backfield coach from 1994 through 2003. His son Evan was a starting wide receiver on Ohio State's 2014 national title team. Evan is well remembered for his lone collegiate pass, a 13-yard scoring toss to Michael Thomas 12 seconds before halftime to help the Buckeyes secure a 42-35 Sugar Bowl victory over Alabama.

Hayes Family Returns

Coach and Mrs. Woody Hayes watched the 1981 season-opening victory over Duke from the Ohio Stadium press box. It was the first game they had attended since his departure as head coach following the 1978 season. Hayes consistently had declined to attend games the preceding two seasons, feeling that his attendance would detract from the efforts of new head coach Earle Bruce and the Ohio State players.

GREAT GAME REMEMBERED
No. 2 Ohio State 18 - No. 13 Michigan 15
Nov. 17, 1979 - Ann Arbor, Michigan

The undefeated Buckeyes needed a victory at Michigan to secure an outright Big Ten title and a trip to the Rose Bowl. Ohio State was inside the Michigan 40-yard line five times in the first half, but scored only two field goals and trailed 7-6 at the intermission. The Wolverines hung tough and led 15-12 when forced to punt with four minutes remaining. Ohio State's Jim Laughlin rushed hard and blocked Brian Virgil's punt, Todd Bell grabbed the bouncing ball and scampered 18 yards for the winning score. In many ways, this was the Buckeyes' "play of the year." Ohio State rushed 10 men, and Laughlin was able to go through untouched. The Michigan Stadium attendance of 106,255 was, at the time, the largest regular-season crowd in college football history.

Movable Mic

Rick Rizzs, then Sports Director at WBNS Radio in Columbus, broadcast the 1981 Ohio State-Wisconsin game from Camp Randall Stadium in Madison. His color commentator was former Buckeye All-American middle guard Jim Stillwagon.

"Jim was really great to work with," recalled Rizzs. "He was a very enthusiastic broadcaster with a tremendous knowledge of the game. That afternoon, while vigorously protesting an official's call, Stillwagon pounded so hard on the table in front of us, his microphone flew out of our radio booth's open window while we were on the air." Rizzs continued to describe the action while Stillwagon fished the microphone back into the booth by pulling it up by the cord.

Wisconsin's 24-21 victory that afternoon broke Ohio State's 21-game winning streak against the Badgers. Wisconsin's last win over the Buckeyes had been 12-3 at Madison in 1959.

GREAT GAME REMEMBERED
No. 7 Ohio State 49 - Illinois 42
Nov. 8, 1980 - Columbus, Ohio

Ohio State led 28-0 midway through the second period, then hung on for dear life to preserve the single-touchdown victory. At the time it was the most points Ohio State had ever surrendered while still winning the game. The Buckeye defense was no match for Illinois quarterback Dave Wilson, who established or tied five NCAA records. Wilson completed 43 of 69 passes for 621 yards and all six Fighting Illini touchdowns. Five of Wilson's scoring tosses and 344 of his passing yards came in the second half.

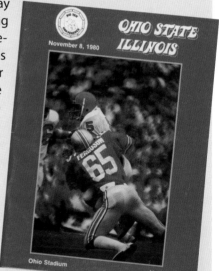

Ohio State quarterback Art Schlichter also was very effective, completing 17 of 21 attempts for 284 yards and four TDs. Illinois led in first downs, 36-17, and total offensive yards, 659-398. But the Fighting Illini had seven turnovers — four lost fumbles and three Wilson interceptions. It was the most points scored against the Buckeyes at home in 34 seasons.

Scheduling Snafu

The 1981 Big Ten football season is best remembered for the single league game that was not played. Eight of the 10 conference teams played each of the other nine members, while Ohio State and Iowa played only eight games. The Buckeyes and Hawkeyes were the only league teams not to face each other that season. There obviously had been an oversight in that season's scheduling.

Who would have guessed? Ohio State and Iowa tied for the 1981 Big Ten title with identical league marks of 6-2. The Buckeyes outscored their eight conference foes, 271-157, while the Hawkeyes outscored their eight conference opponents, 218-92. Had Ohio State and Iowa faced each other, they would have been battling for the outright conference title. What should have been the conference's most important game, was instead the only one not played.

Playing only eight conference contests also negatively affected Ohio State the following season. Michigan won the 1982 outright title with a conference record of 8-1, compared with Ohio State's 7-1 mark. Ohio State and Iowa again were the only two Big Ten teams not to meet.

Busy Times

Quarterback Brent Offenbecher came off the bench to direct Ohio State's offense the last two-and-a-half quarters against Florida State at home on Oct. 2, 1982. It was an eventful week for Offenbecher. Two days earlier, wife Jacquie gave birth to daughter Amy at nearby University Hospital. Offenbecher had been an All-Ohio quarterback at Massillon High School, and first enrolled at Wake Forest before transferring to Ohio State.

Finally!

Wisconsin's 6-0 victory on Oct. 9, 1982, was the school's very first at Ohio Stadium after 18 losses and three ties. The Buckeyes began play at the Horseshoe 60 years earlier in 1922. Wisconsin's last win in Columbus had been by the score of 14-3 at old Ohio Field on Nov. 23, 1918.

48 Straight

Buckeye wide receiver Gary Williams established what was then an NCAA record with one or more receptions in each of Ohio State's 48 games from 1979 through 1982. His four-year career statistics include 154 receptions for 2,792 yards and 16 touchdowns. Central Michigan's Bryan Anderson now owns the NCAA record with one or more receptions in 54 consecutive games from 2006 through 2009.

GREAT GAME REMEMBERED
No. 8 Ohio State 45 - Illinois 38
Oct. 13, 1984 - Columbus, Ohio

The Buckeyes really came together for this treasured homecoming triumph, after trailing 24-0 early in the second quarter. Tailback Keith Byars led the impressive comeback, scoring five touchdowns and establishing a then-Ohio State single-game rushing record with 274 yards on 39 carries. Byars' fourth score was a 67-yard excursion down the east sideline and into the north end zone. The powerful tailback never broke stride, even after losing his left shoe at the Illinois 40-yard line. The Fighting Illini led in first downs, 27-23, and the Buckeyes led in total offensive yards, 564-509. Played before a partisan crowd of 87,952, the game lasted three hours and 22 minutes.

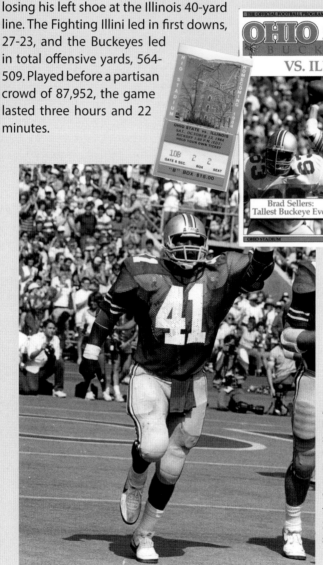

All-American tailback Keith Byars finished second to Boston College's Doug Flutie in the 1984 Heisman Trophy voting. Byars rushed for 1,764 yards and 22 touchdowns that season. *Courtesy Ohio State University Photo Archives*

Record Setter

Linebacker Marcus Marek of Masury, Ohio, is Ohio State's all-time leading tackler with a total of 572 — 256 solo tackles and 316 assists. Marek started four seasons from 1979 through 1982, when the Buckeyes' record was 38-10.

New Tradition is Born

Ohio State's first annual Cheerleading Alumni Reunion was held on Sept. 10, 1983, during the season opener against Oregon. More than 60 former cheerleaders, ranging from as far back as the 1947 squad, were active on the Ohio Stadium sidelines.

Linebacker Marcus Marek. *Courtesy Ohio State University Photo Archives*

Lane to the Rescue

Ohio State led visiting Purdue 12-7 at halftime on Oct. 8, 1983. Three Buckeye scoring drives were cut short by penalties and an interception. Garcia Lane aided the struggling offense with two third-quarter touchdowns on punt returns of 63 and 71 yards. Lane is the only Ohio State player to score twice on punt returns in one game. The Buckeyes defeated the Boilermakers, 33-22.

Unforgettable Script

Tom Hamilton, play-by-play radio voice of the Cleveland Indians and former sportscaster with Sports Radio 97.1 the Fan in Columbus, was the color analyst for the University of Wisconsin Football Radio Network in 1983. Tom's very first game at Ohio Stadium was the Buckeyes' Oct. 29 homecoming game that season against the Badgers.

"I was doing a halftime interview," recalls Hamilton, "when suddenly the crowd's applause became so deafening, I simply couldn't continue with the interview. We all looked out of the radio booth to see what was happening down on the field — Woody Hayes had just dotted the "i" in Script Ohio!"

Unexpected Interruption

In the 1980s, the Ohio State football programs were published each week by Fred and John Zimmerman's public relations firm. The Zimmermans were required to guarantee that the programs would be at the stadium by the Friday prior to each home game, otherwise they were liable for the lost income that would have been generated from the sale of the programs at $2 each.

The programs were printed in Dayton and were normally delivered to the stadium before noon on Friday. One Friday morning in 1983, Fred received an unexpected call from the driver of the truck bringing the programs to Columbus. His truck was stranded with a broken axle on Interstate 70, approximately 25 miles east of Dayton. Fred quickly drove to the scene, only to discover that the driver had unloaded the programs onto the ground, even though there was a strong threat of rain.

After a couple of troubled delays, another truck finally was acquired and loaded, and the programs reached Ohio Stadium at 7 p.m. The stadium maintenance crew that normally unloaded the programs was gone for the day and the stadium was locked. The only known opening was a ticket window near gate 28 that, fortunately, was just large enough for a person to get inside. Fred and his crew began the tedious process of passing all 500 of the 20-pound boxes through the ticket window, one by one. Tired, sore and hungry, they finally finished around 11 p.m.

Better Result 50 Years Later

Oct. 13, 1984, was the date of Ohio State's treasured 45-38 come-from-behind homecoming triumph over Illinois. Exactly 50 years earlier on October 13, 1934, Illinois defeated Ohio State at Champaign, 14-13. It was the only loss that year for the Buckeyes of first-year coach Francis Schmidt, and the single-point setback prevented Ohio State from claiming the 1934 outright Big Ten title.

Quarterback Mike Tomczak in action against Illinois in 1984.
Courtesy Ohio State University Photo Archives

GREAT GAME REMEMBERED
No. 8 Ohio State 22 – No. 1 Iowa 13
Nov. 2, 1985 – Columbus, Ohio

This was the third time Ohio State defeated a top-ranked opponent, the first being Wisconsin in 1952 (23-14) and the second Purdue in 1968 (13-0). Iowa had lost its last 11 games in Columbus, dating back to 1961. The Buckeyes possessed the nation's longest home winning streak at 19, and were underdogs at home for the first time in eight years. Tailback John Wooldridge, playing for an injured Keith Byars, sped 57 yards on his first carry of the afternoon to put Ohio State on top, 12-0, early in the second quarter. It was one of the key plays of this memorable afternoon. The Buckeyes' dominating defense forced the Hawkeyes to start their first seven possessions inside Iowa's own 27. Linebackers Pepper Johnson and Chris Spielman led the Buckeye defense with 19 tackles each. Iowa's Chuck Long, the nation's top-rated passer, was intercepted four times.

OHIO STATE vs.
IOWA
OHIO STADIUM
Sat., Nov. 2, 1985 - 1:30 P.M.
TIME SUBJECT TO CHANGE WITHOUT NOTICE

SEC.	ROW/BX	SEAT
10B	2	3
	B-BOX	

GAME 5

Timing Is Everything!

Tom Burris, former reporter and news anchor at WSYX-TV6 in Columbus, vividly recalled the happenings of Nov. 16, 1984, the Friday before the Ohio State-Michigan game at Ohio Stadium.

Brutus Buckeye Eric Mayers was doing Columbus traffic reports that week at WSNY-Sunny 95 Radio as part of Michigan week activities. As Mayers was leaving for the station early Friday morning, he discovered his Brutus head had been stolen from his car sometime during the night. There was no other Brutus head available, and the following day's big game would be his last home appearance as Brutus Buckeye.

That morning, WSNY immediately announced a $500 reward for the return of the Brutus head. Later that day Mayers joined Burris at the Ohio Union and explained his dilemma on Burris' noon news telecast. The GTE Corporation soon added $1,000 to the reward fund. WSNY and WSYX-TV received a lot of tips that afternoon, but none led to the location of the Brutus head.

At approximately 3:30 p.m., a gentleman named Eli telephoned to report he had the missing item. Eli saw the head in a trash dumpster near the Ohio State campus and took it home to his children thinking it was a doll. Fortunately, Eli's wife had heard Burris and Mayers on the noon news and recognized the item as the missing Brutus head. Eli returned the item, collected his $1,500 reward, and gave details of his discovery on the 6 p.m. news with Burris and Mayers, live from Ohio Stadium.

Mayers was so thankful! He had his Brutus head in time for the Friday evening pep rally and the following day's "big game." And Ohio State won, 21-6.

GREAT GAME REMEMBERED
Ohio State 23 - Michigan 20
Nov. 21, 1987 - Ann Arbor, Michigan

A very determined Ohio State team sent Earle Bruce out a winner in his final game for the Scarlet and Gray. Down 13-0 shortly before halftime, the Buckeyes rebounded to tie the score at 20 entering the final quarter. Placekicker Matt Frantz had missed the extra-point attempt following Ohio State's third touchdown, breaking his string of successful kicks at 52. With 5:18 left in final period, Frantz booted a 26-yard field goal to secure his team's three-point triumph. Quarterback Tom Tupa was excellent, completing 18 of 26 passes for 219 yards and two touchdowns with no interceptions. Tupa also punted six times for a 42.0-yard average.

Courtesy Ohio State University Photo Archives

History Repeats Itself

The Michigan football team stayed at the same Columbus hotel the Friday evenings prior to their games in 1982 and 1984. During the Friday night in 1982, a water main close to the hotel burst and the entire hotel was without water Saturday morning. Two years later in 1984 it happened again. On Friday night the water main outside the hotel burst, and the hotel again was without water Saturday morning.

Steve Held, the hotel's maintenance manager, recalled that the Michigan players totally believed they had been sabotaged the second time, if not on both occasions. As expected, Michigan Coach Bo Schembechler chose an entirely different hotel for his team's Friday night stay in Columbus in 1986.

First Night Encounter

Ohio State played its first home night game on Sept. 14, 1985. The Ohio Stadium crowd of 88,518 watched the Buckeyes defeat the Pitt Panthers, 10-7. Quarterback Jim Karsatos passed one yard to split end Cris Carter for the winning touchdown with 4:19 remaining in the final period. The game kicked off at 8:08 p.m. under clear skies with a temperature of 59 degrees.

Linebacker Eric Kumerow (14) tackles Pitt quarterback John Congemi (15). Other defenders are Rover Sonny Gordon (7), Linebacker Scott Leach (8) and Linebacker Byron Lee (82). Pitt tailback is Charles Gladman (32).
Courtesy Ohio State University Photo Archives

Highest High from Lowest Low

Ohio State's exceptional 22-13 victory over No.1 ranked Iowa was played at Ohio Stadium on Nov. 2, 1985. It also was the exact 50th anniversary of one of the school's most agonizing losses. On Nov. 2, 1935, the Buckeyes suffered a heartbreaking 18-13 setback during their famous home encounter against Notre Dame, hailed as the "Game of the Century."

Lanese Saluted

At halftime of Ohio State's Sept. 20 home opener against Colorado in 1986, graduated wide receiver Mike Lanese received a standing ovation when he was honored as the first Ohio State football player to earn a Rhodes Scholarship. Lanese was one of 32 American college seniors to be selected to study at Oxford University in England. The native of Mayfield, Ohio, was an honor student with a dual major in Political Science and English.

Accurate Prognosticator

In 1986, Will McClure, a 15-year-old freshman at Upper Arlington High School, was seriously injured while playing football. Ohio State linebacker Chris Spielman

Linebacker Chris Spielman. *Courtesy Ohio State University Photo Archives*

visited McClure at his hospital, and promised McClure an interception in Ohio State's next game against Illinois. The following Saturday, Oct. 4, Spielman made an interception during the Buckeyes' 14-0 victory over the Fighting Illini. As promised, Spielman returned to the hospital and presented McClure with the football.

Unusual First

Ohio State's 13-13 tie at Louisiana State on Sept. 26, 1987, was Earle Bruce's 100th game as Ohio State's head coach. It also was Bruce's first tie game as a head coach at the college level. He was 10-2 during his single season at Tampa in 1972, and 36-32 over a six-year period at Iowa State from 1973 through 1978. Bruce entered the game against the LSU Tigers with an Ohio State coaching record of 77-22.

Accomplished Celebration

Freshman tailback Carlos Snow celebrated his 19th birthday in grand style, scoring four touchdowns to pace Ohio State to a 42-9 homecoming victory over Minnesota on Oct. 24, 1987. Snow's first three scores were runs of 3, 6, and 5 yards, and his final TD came on a 45-yard pass from quarterback Tom Tupa.

Every 28 Years

Nov. 14 was the date of Iowa's dramatic come-from-behind 29-27 triumph at Ohio Stadium in 1987. It had been exactly 28 years since the Hawkeyes had won in Columbus — a 16-7 victory over the Buckeyes on Nov. 14, 1959.

"All is Well at Ohio State!"

At halftime of the 1987 Ohio State-Iowa game, Ohio State President Edward Jennings and Athletic Director Rick Bay both were halftime guests of veteran Iowa broadcaster Jim Zabel over WHO Radio in Des Moines. Both were good friends of Zabel. Jennings previously held faculty and administrative positions at the University of Iowa, and Zabel knew Bay because of Bay's many years in college athletics.

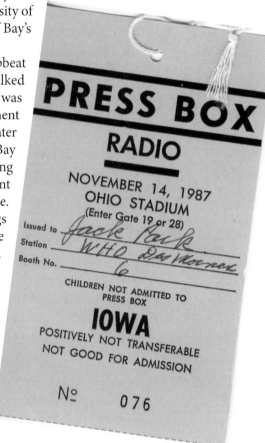

The two interviews were very upbeat and positive. Jennings and Bay each talked about "how smoothly everything was operating within Ohio State's Department of Athletics." Really? Just two days later on Monday, Nov. 16, Jennings and Bay would become the foremost opposing figures in the untimely announcement of Coach Earle Bruce's forced departure. Early that Monday afternoon, Jennings directed Bay to dismiss Bruce after the following Saturday's game at Michigan. Bay completely disagreed with this directive for Ohio State to sever ties with Bruce, and immediately resigned his own position in protest.

CHAPTER ELEVEN

1988-2000

Cooper at the Helm

Economic growth and social progressiveness continued throughout the late 1980s and into the 1990s. The Dow Jones Industrial Average grew by more than 300 percent, and median household income increased by more than 10 percent. Generation Xers, those born to Baby Boomers between 1965 and 1980, were filling the workforce. The largest mall on earth opened in Minneapolis in 1992, online blogging was introduced in 1994, and the first Harry Potter novel was released in 1997.

John Cooper took charge of the Ohio State program in 1988. The 51-year old native of Powell, Tenn., had been an assistant at five different schools before being named head coach at Tulsa in 1977 and Arizona State in 1985. Tulsa was the Missouri Valley Conference champion each of Cooper's last five years with the

John Cooper with wife Helen being introduced as Ohio State's new head coach on December 31, 1987. *Courtesy Ohio State University Photo Archives*

Golden Hurricanes. While at Arizona State, he was the college game's Coach of the Year in 1986.

After a 4-6-1 record in 1988, Ohio State improved to 8-4 in 1989. After records of 7-4-1 in 1990, 8-4 in 1991, and 8-3-1 in 1992, the Buckeyes at 10-1-1 shared the 1993 conference championship with Wisconsin. A 17-6 home triumph over Bowling Green in 1992 was Ohio State's first encounter against an opponent from within Ohio since winning 76-0 over Western Reserve at old League Park in Cleveland in 1934. Penn State joined the Big Ten in 1993, increasing the conference membership to 11 teams.

College football celebrated its 125th anniversary in 1994, and this season was also noteworthy for Ohio State. After a crushing 63-14 setback at top-ranked Penn State in late October, Ohio State's record under Cooper registered 51-25-4 (66.1 percent). Beginning with a convincing 24-3 home triumph over Wisconsin the following weekend, Cooper's teams amassed a record of

Quarterback Kirk Herbstreit was John Cooper's first Ohio State recruit. He was chosen team MVP in 1992. *Courtesy Ohio State University Photo Archives*

46-8 (85.2 percent) over the following four-and-a-half seasons through 1998. The Buckeyes twice placed second in the final *Associated Press* poll and shared two Big Ten titles.

Tailback Eddie George established an Ohio State single-game rushing record with 314 yards during a dominating 41-3 home triumph over Illinois in 1995. It is

Ohio State 1998 Coaching Staff. *Courtesy Ohio State University Photo Archives*

the only time an Ohio State player has rushed for more than 300 yards in a single game. George became the Buckeyes' first Heisman Trophy winner since Archie Griffin received his second Heisman in 1975. George finished his Ohio State career with 3,768 yards rushing, third highest in school history.

Ohio State finished 6-6 in 1999 and 8-4 in 2000. After a disappointing 24-7 loss to South Carolina in the Outback Bowl at the end of the 2000 season, Cooper was removed from his head coaching position by Athletic Director Andy Geiger. The Dean of the Big Ten coaches was saddened and surprised by the announcement, indicating he would have preferred to coach at least one additional year. He guaranteed complete support for his successor, and vigorously stated he would always be a Buckeye.

Cooper finished his 13 seasons at Ohio State with a notable record of 111-43-4. His winning record of 71.5 percent is the ninth-highest in Big Ten history for coaches with 10 or more years within the conference. His all-time 24-year coaching record is 192-84-6 (69.1 percent). John Cooper was inducted into the College Football Hall of Fame in 2008.

Eddie George. *Courtesy Ohio State University Photo Archives*

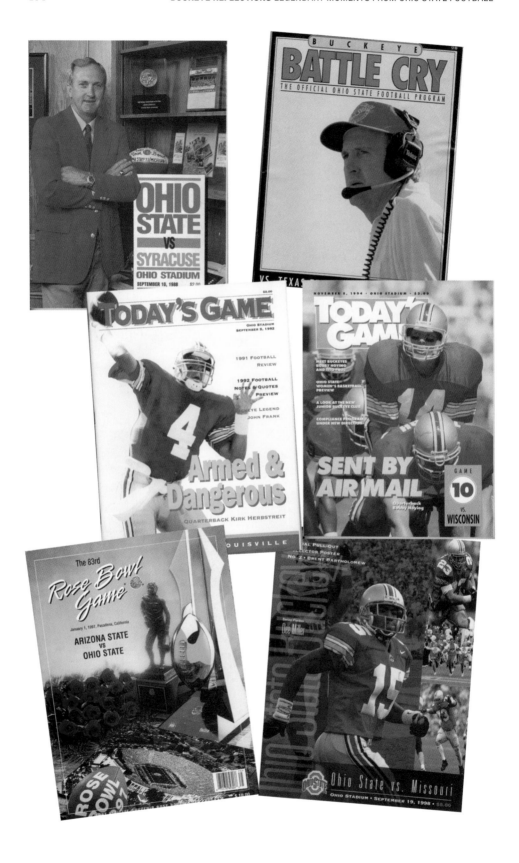

Woody Remembered During 20th Reunion

Sixty members of Ohio State's 1968 national champions were honored during halftime of the homecoming game against Purdue on Oct. 15, 1988. In a fitting tribute to their late coach Woody Hayes, the team presented their university with a $1.2 million endowment to be used for scholarships.

Tops in Last 27

The 1988 Ohio State–Michigan game's combined score of 65 points (UM 34 – OSU 31) was the highest in the series since a combined score of 70 points in 1961 (OSU 50 – UM 20).

Century Mark

Ohio State celebrated its 100th season of football in 1989. Over their first 100 years the Buckeyes played 930 games with a record of 626-254-50, good for a winning rate of exactly 70.0 percent. Ohio State had won or shared 25 Big Ten titles since joining the conference in 1913.

Comeback Delight!

Trailing 31-0, Ohio State rebounded mightily for a 41-37 triumph at Minnesota on Oct. 28, 1989. Tailback Carlos Snow scored the Buckeyes' very first points with a 1-yard touchdown burst just 10 seconds before halftime. Quarterback Greg Frey led the second half resurgence, completing 21 of 30 passes for 362 yards and three TDs.

The game tied what was then an NCAA record for the largest turnaround in a major college game. Michigan State now holds the NCAA record. The Spartans trailed at Northwestern by 35 points (38-3) with 9:54 remaining in the third period, then bounced back for a 41-38 victory on Oct. 21, 2006.

Greg Frey. *Courtesy Ohio State University Photo Archives*

Two-Sport Star

Derek Isaman grew up in Fremont, Ohio, where at age eight he fell in love with both boxing and football. He was coached in boxing by his father, and sparred regularly with his brother. He enjoyed the aggressiveness of both sports and found that excelling in one helped him excel in the other. While in high school, he faced Mike Tyson in a Golden Glove bout, and became the first boxer to lose to Tyson in a points decision. Tyson had knocked-out every other opponent in the first round. In football, Isaman won all-state honors at Fremont Ross High School.

After winning three letters as an Ohio State linebacker from 1985-1987, Isaman sat out the 1988 season to pursue his dream of qualifying for the United States Olympic Boxing Team. He won the 1988 Golden Gloves Heavyweight title,

GREAT GAME REMEMBERED
Ohio State 36 - No. 7 LSU 33
Sept. 24, 1988 - Columbus, Ohio

Ohio State went up 14-3 with 12:46 remaining in the second quarter, then was outscored 30-6 over the next 38 minutes of play. With the Buckeyes trailing 33-20 at the 4:29 mark of the final period, many of the rain-drenched crowd of 90,584 quickly headed for the exits. They left too soon! Ohio State responded with two touchdowns and a safety within one minute and 18 seconds for the remarkable come-from-behind triumph.

Tailback Carlos Snow scored from 5 yards out, narrowing LSU's lead to 33-27 with 1:56 left. LSU's ensuing possession consumed only 22 seconds, after coach John Cooper wisely used OSU's two remaining timeouts. Wide receiver Bobby Olive scored the winning TD with a diving catch of a 20-yard pass from quarterback Greg Frey with 38 seconds remaining. LSU had won its last 14 road games. It was the first visit to Ohio Stadium by a member of the Southeastern Conference since Ohio State defeated Kentucky, 19-6, on Oct. 5, 1935.

and was named the heavyweight alternate for the Olympics. He returned to Ohio State for the 1989 season and was chosen the team MVP.

Remembering Mom

Wide receiver Bobby Olive was presented with the game ball after catching the winning touchdown pass with just one second remaining, to provide a thrilling 27-26 triumph at Iowa. The contest was played on Nov. 10, 1990. Olive gave the game ball to his mother, Patsy, since it was her birthday.

Even Steven

During the 60 Ohio State-Michigan games from 1931 through 1990, the Buckeyes and Wolverines each scored a total of 883 points. Michigan had a slight winning advantage over these 60 encounters at 29-28-3.

The Modell Bowl

Rather than play its 1991 game against Ohio State on its Evanston campus as scheduled, Northwestern shifted this home game to Cleveland in anticipation of much higher gate receipts. The plan worked. An Oct. 19 Cleveland Municipal Stadium crowd of 73,830 (mostly Ohio State fans) watched the "visiting Buckeyes" defeat the Wildcats, 34-3. Northwestern wore its home purple jerseys, Ohio State wore the traditional visitor's white. It was Ohio State's first appearance in Cleveland since a 26-12 victory over Illinois on Nov. 18, 1944.

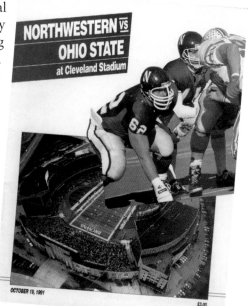

This change angered many Northwestern fans, who harshly criticized Athletic Director Bruce Corrie for "selling" the game. Corrie defended the decision, citing the financial problems facing Northwestern's athletic programs at that time. Cleveland Browns owner Art Modell had suggested to Corrie that Northwestern move the game to Cleveland. Model was looking for additional revenue opportunities, especially since the Cleveland Indians would soon be leaving Cleveland Municipal Stadium and moving to newly constructed Jacobs Field.

At home the following Saturday, Oct. 26, Northwestern defeated 17th-ranked Illinois, 17-11, before a Dyche Stadium homecoming crowd of only 25,542. Dyche Stadium's seating capacity was 49,256.

25 and Counting

The Ohio State Alumni Band held its 25th reunion during the season opener against Rice on Sept. 4, 1993. More than 600 TBDBITL alumni returned to campus to march down the field "one more time."

Band alumni over 40 years of age were not allowed to march during the first reunion in 1966 because of potential medical issues for those who were not used to this much activity. This restriction caused some of the returning members to "alter their ages." This very unpopular restriction was eliminated prior to the second reunion.

The first reunion drew 228 alumni. Since then the number has grown to over 800, with more than 600 playing on the field. This huge group of musicians emerging from the ramp at the stadium's north end has been dubbed by students as "the blob." The annual event is one of the most elaborate of all college football band performances. Halftime is highlighted by a quadruple Script Ohio — two each by the regular and alumni bands jointly (photo shown on book cover).

Big Ten Becomes Eleven

Penn State joined the Big Ten in 1993, bringing the league membership to 11 teams. It was the first conference membership change since Michigan State was added in 1953. The Spartans replaced Chicago who left the league after the 1939 season.

On a cold and snowy October 30, Ohio State solidly defeated the Nittany Lions, 24-6, in their first conference meeting. Coach Joe Paterno's squad was held without a touchdown for the first time all season. The Buckeye defense was outstanding, forcing four interceptions and a fumble recovery. Running in a sea of

Raymont Harris *Courtesy Ohio State University Photo Archives*

mud, tailback Raymont "Quiet Storm" Harris shattered the PSU defense for 151 yards — at the time a career high. Coach John Cooper told the media that this was likely his biggest win since accepting the Ohio State job in 1988.

Prior to 1993, Ohio State was 2-6 against Penn State in non-conference games. The Buckeyes are 16-8 over the 24 league tilts through the 2016 season.

College Game Turns 125

College football celebrated its 125th anniversary in 1994. Rutgers defeated Princeton, 6-4, in the first college game, played on Nov. 6, 1869 in New Brunswick, N.J. The American Football Coaches Association, NCAA and National Association of Collegiate Directors of Athletics all united to honor 1994 as a "Season of Celebration." Most teams wore a 125-year patch on their jerseys to recognize the anniversary.

GREAT GAME REMEMBERED
Ohio State 27 - No. 6 Iowa 26
Nov. 10, 1990 - Iowa City, Iowa

Iowa at 5-0 in Big Ten play was leading the league in both offense and defense. The Hawkeyes led 26-14 with just 11 minutes left in the final period and appeared to have the game under control. A 21-yard touchdown strike from quarterback Greg Frey to split end Bobby Olive made it closer at 26-21. After an exchange of possessions triggered by an interception by each team, Ohio State took possession at the Hawkeye 48 with 59 seconds on the clock and no remaining timeouts. Frey masterfully passed his team the distance for the winning TD, a 3-yard toss to Olive with just one second left.

Linebackers Steve Tovar and Jason Simmons were superb throughout the afternoon. Tovar had a career-high 14 tackles and Simmons added eight more, including three for losses totaling 26 yards. It was career win No. 100 for coach John Cooper, and his 18th victory at Ohio State.

Spielman Inspires

On Oct. 15, 1994, former Buckeye great Chris Spielman, then a star linebacker with the NFL's Detroit Lions, gave the Ohio State players a rousing pep talk at their East Lansing hotel the Friday evening prior to their game at Michigan State. Spielman especially emphasized the need to control the line of scrimmage.

The following afternoon the Buckeyes noticeably controlled the line of scrimmage, a factor that helped them defeat the Spartans, 23-7, after trailing 7-3 at halftime. Ohio State linebacker Greg Bellisari returned an interception 35 yards for Ohio State's final score late in the fourth quarter. Ironically, it was OSU's first touchdown by a linebacker's return of an interception since Spielman scored on a 24-yard interception return during Ohio State's 28-12 Cotton Bowl victory over Texas A&M on Jan. 1, 1987.

Buckeye Pride

During halftime against Purdue on Oct. 22, 1994, Ohio State's first four Heisman Trophy winners were proudly recognized by a very jubilant homecoming crowd of 92,865 — Les Horvath (1944), Vic Janowicz (1950), Howard "Hopalong" Cassady (1955), and Archie Griffin (1974-75). The Downtown Athletic Club of New York presented Horvath with a ring commemorating the 50th anniversary of his winning the coveted award. Also introduced to the delighted crowd was 1956 Outland Trophy winner Jim Parker, one of the school's all-time finest guards and linebackers.

Members of Ohio State's championship squads of 1944, 1949, and 1954 were recognized. Receiving the crowd's loudest applause was Mrs. Anne Hayes, who was introduced with Woody Hayes' first national championship team of 1954.

From left, Hesiman Trophy winners Les Horvath, Archie Griffin, Hopalong Cassady, Vic Janowicz. *Courtesy Ohio State University Photo Archives*

Century Celebration

The Big Ten Conference celebrated its 100th season of football in 1995. Ohio State's played its first conference season in 1913, when the league was in its 18th year of football.

OHIO STATE
VS
IOWA

FOOTBALL

Hall of Fame Day
OHIO STADIUM
SAT., OCT. 28, 1995
1:30 PM
Sec.   Row   Seat

10B   2   2

B-BOX

GAME 4

Abnormality

Ohio State's 56-35 home triumph over Iowa on Oct. 28, 1995, resulted from a very unusual scoring pattern. The Buckeyes scored the game's first 56 points, and the Hawkeyes tallied the last 35.

Deeply Disappointing Decision

Ohio State defeated Minnesota 49-21 at Minneapolis on November 4, 1995 — but the major sports story in Ohio that

GREAT GAME REMEMBERED
No. 5 Ohio State 28 - No. 25 Michigan State 21
Oct. 16, 1993 - Columbus, Ohio

Ohio State ran its 1993 record to 6-0, even after committing five turnovers. The Buckeyes and Spartans combined for 52 first downs and 901 yards of total offense on this festive and rainy homecoming afternoon. Wide receiver Joey Galloway seized three scoring passes, two from quarterback Bobby Hoying for 22 and 14 yards, and his third from quarterback Bret Powers that netted 64 yards. The Powers-to-Galloway TD was the Buckeyes' longest play from scrimmage of the season. Tailback Raymont Harris scored the winning touchdown from the 7 with 1:06 remaining. Linebacker Lorenzo Styles sparked the OSU defense with 18 tackles. MSU missed field-goal attempts of 34, 33, 20, and 39 yards. The afternoon was highlighted by the 25th-anniversary reunion of Ohio State's 1968 national champions.

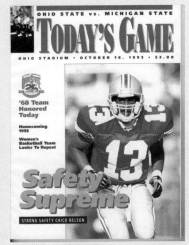

OHIO STATE
vs.
MICHIGAN STATE
(Homecoming)
OHIO STADIUM
SAT., OCT. 16, 1993 - 3:30 PM
TIME SUBJECT TO CHANGE WITHOUT NOTICE
SEC.   ROW   SEAT

10B   2   *1

B-BOX

GAME 4

weekend came from Cleveland, where owner Art Modell announced that he was moving the Cleveland Browns to Baltimore after exactly 50 seasons in the lakefront city.

Modell had just lost MLB's Cleveland Indians as tenants in aging Cleveland Municipal stadium. He subsequently reached a deal to move his franchise to Baltimore, a city that had been without NFL football since the Colts moved to Indianapolis after the 1983 season. Loyal and passionate Browns fans were furious and heartbroken. Modell was quickly regarded in Cleveland as a traitor. He passed away in 2013.

After the move was announced, the Browns name, legacy, colors, and records were allowed to remain in Cleveland to become part of an NFL expansion team in 1999.

The First 50

Beginning with the 1946 season, the Big Ten Conference and the Pacific Eight Conference (later Pacific Ten) agreed to have their respective conference champions meet in the Rose Bowl the following New Year's Day. The 50th consecutive Rose Bowl matching champions from these two conferences was played on Jan. 1, 1996. At that time the Pacific Eight/Ten had won 26, the Big Ten 24.

Following are the Big Ten member records over the first 50 Rose Bowls: Illinois 3-1, Indiana 0-1, Iowa 2-3, Michigan 6-9, Michigan State 3-1, Minnesota 1-1, Northwestern 1-1, Ohio State 5-6, Penn State 1-0, Purdue 1-0 and Wisconsin 1-3.

Two for Two

Only twice in Ohio State football have two quarterbacks each passed for more than 1,000 yards in the same season. The same two signal-callers accomplished this feat during consecutive seasons. In 1995 Stanley Jackson threw for 1,298 yards and Joe Germaine connected for 1,193, and in 1996 Germaine passed for 1,847 while Jackson threw for 1,055.

The season next closest to this record is 2015, when Cardale Jones passed for 1,460 yards and J.T. Barrett threw for 992.

Perfect Inauguration

Ohio State opened its 1996 season on Sept. 7 with a dominating 70-7 victory over Rice before a sun-baked Ohio Stadium crowd of 93,479. Freshman wide receiver Michael Wiley, playing in his first collegiate game, scored three touchdowns the only three times he touched the football. Wiley's first score came on an impressive 49-yard reverse late in the second quarter, boosting OSU's lead to 42-7 at halftime. His other two touchdowns were third-quarter post pattern receptions of 51 and 60 yards from quarterback Joe Germaine.

Seven different players scored at least once, as the Buckeyes tallied on 10 of their first 11 possessions and rolled-up 632 yards of total offense. Wiley's unveiling brought back fond memories of Howard "Hopalong" Cassady's freshman debut 44 years earlier. The 18-year-old redhead from Columbus Central High School scored three touchdowns in his first college game, leading Ohio State to a 33-13 season-opening home victory over Indiana on Sept. 27, 1952.

Finkes to the Rescue

In an emotionally played contest that was far closer than suggested by the final score, Ohio State defeated Indiana 27-17 at Bloomington on Nov. 16, 1996, to clinch its first trip to the Rose Bowl since the 1984 season. The Buckeyes had only once before earned the trip to Pasadena the week prior to their final regular season game against Michigan (1957).

With just slightly less than seven minutes to play and the score tied at 10, linebacker Andy Katzenmoyer stripped the ball from Hoosier quarterback Jay Rodgers. End Matt Finkes seized the loose pigskin, then rambled 45 yards for the go-ahead touchdown. Josh Jackson's extra point gave Ohio State a 17-10 lead with 6:18 to play.

The Hoosiers were emotionally charged for the game, partly because it was the final home game for IU head coach Bill Mallory. Mallory had been told a few weeks earlier that this would be his last season at Indiana. He had been a very fine Ohio State assistant from 1966 through 1968.

Finkes led the defense with 12 tackles, followed by Greg Bellisari with eight and Mike Vrabel with seven. In no way did the Hoosiers resemble a program that had just incurred its 15th consecutive Big Ten setback.

Matt Finkes talks with WBNS-10TV following the victory.
Courtesy Brockway Collection at The Ohio State University Photo Archives

Nifty Fifty

Nose guard Luke Fickell started a school-record 50 consecutive games from 1993 through 1996. Fickell's notable record began with a 34-7 season-opening victory over Rice at home on Sept. 4, 1993, and concluded with a thrilling 20-17 come-from-behind Rose Bowl victory over previously undefeated and second-ranked Arizona State on Jan. 1, 1997. Fickell played the entire Rose Bowl with a completely torn pectoral muscle in his left shoulder. The Buckeyes' record over those 50 games was an impressive 41-8-1 (83.0 percent).

Hometown Hero

Quarterback Joe Germaine was named the Rose Bowl's MVP after leading Ohio State's winning drive late in the final period for a 20-17 triumph over Arizona State on Jan. 1, 1997.

Germaine grew up as a Sun Devil fan in Mesa, Ariz., not far from the Arizona State campus in Tempe. ASU coach Bruce Snyder recruited him, but Germaine chose not to attend since Snyder wanted him as a defensive back. Germaine played at Scottsdale Community College in 1995, before transferring to Ohio State the following season.

Joe Germaine. *Courtesy Ohio State University Photo Archives*

John Cooper. *Courtesy Ohio State University Photo Archives*

Winner on Both Sidelines

John Cooper is the only coach to lead schools from both the Big Ten Conference and Pacific Ten Conference to victories in the Rose Bowl. Cooper led Arizona State to a 22-15 triumph over Michigan on Jan. 1, 1987. Ten years later he guided Ohio State past Arizona State, 20-17, on Jan. 1, 1997.

Arizona State quarterback Jeff VanRaaphorst passed for two touchdowns to spark the Sun Devils over Michigan. Dick VanRaaphorst, Jeff's father, had been a very proficient placekicker for Ohio State from 1961-63. The Buckeyes defeated the Wolverines each of the elder VanRaaphorst's three seasons.

GREAT GAME REMEMBERED
No. 7 Ohio State 45 – No. 15 Notre Dame 26
Sept. 30, 1995 – Columbus, Ohio

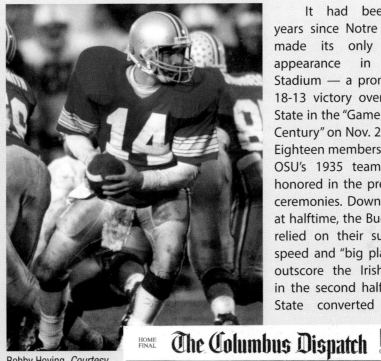

It had been 60 years since Notre Dame made its only other appearance in Ohio Stadium — a prominent 18-13 victory over Ohio State in the "Game of the Century" on Nov. 2, 1935. Eighteen members of the OSU's 1935 team were honored in the pregame ceremonies. Down 17-14 at halftime, the Buckeyes relied on their superior speed and "big plays" to outscore the Irish 31-9 in the second half. Ohio State converted three

Bobby Hoying. *Courtesy Ohio State University Photo Archives*

The Columbus Dispatch

HOME FINAL

SUNDAY   OCTOBER 1, 1995 $1.50

GORGEOUS
High 78/Low 38
Detail: 9C

OHIO STATE 45, NOTRE DAME 26

After a shaky start.

Courtesy The Columbus Dispatch, Oct. 1, 1995

ND turnovers into touchdowns within a span of fewer than six minutes to break the game wide open.

Quarterback Bobby Hoying completed 14 of 22 passes for 272 yards and four touchdowns, and tailback Eddie George ran for 207 yards and two scores on 32 carries. Terry Glenn's 82-yard third-quarter TD catch from Hoying is the fourth longest scoring reception in school history. Greg Bellisari was OSU's leading tackler with 12, followed by Luke Fickell and Ryan Miller with 10 each. Ohio State's 45 points were the most ever scored against a Notre Dame team coached by Lou Holtz from 1986 through 1996.

Buckeye-Badger Sequence Broken

Ohio State and Wisconsin did not meet in 1997, snapping the Buckeyes' third-longest continuous series. The two schools had played for 49 consecutive seasons from 1948 through 1996.

Familiar Pattern

The winner of the annual Ohio State-Michigan contest frequently has represented the Big Ten Conference in that season's Rose Bowl. The Buckeyes have played in 14 Rose Bowls (7-7), but only once after losing their regular season finale to the Wolverines. Ohio State's 20-17 victory over Arizona State in the Pasadena Classic of Jan. 1, 1997, followed a 13-9 home setback to the Wolverines on Nov. 23, 1996. It was Ohio State's only loss of the 1996 season.

Michigan has played in 20 Rose Bowls (8-12), but only three times following a regular-season loss to Ohio State. The Wolverines traveled to Pasadena after being beaten by the Buckeyes in 1982, 2004, and 2006.

Supremacy Personified

Orlando Pace anchored the Ohio State offensive line from 1994-1996, establishing himself as one of the finest linemen in college football history. At Sandusky High School in 1993 he had been chosen as an All-American offensive lineman by *Parade* magazine and an All-American defensive lineman by *USA Today*.

The term "pancake block" originated to describe Pace's dominance with knocking defenders on their backs, and Pace became known as "The Pancake Man." He was a two-time consensus All-American. Pace won the Outland Trophy as the best college interior lineman in 1996, and in 1995 and 1996 became the

Tackle Orlando Pace *Courtesy Brockway Collection at The Ohio State University Archives*

only player to twice receive the Lombardi Award as the best college lineman. He finished fourth in the 1996 Heisman Trophy voting.

Pace was the first player taken in the 1997 NFL draft, being selected by the St. Louis Cardinals. During his 13 year NFL career, he played in seven Pro Bowls and was three times chosen a first-team All-Pro. Pace was inducted into the College Football Hall of Fame in 2013 and the Professional Football Hall of Fame in 2016.

Gigantic Opener

For the first time since 1980, Ohio State entered the 1998 season as the nation's top ranked team. The Buckeyes opened September 5 with an imposing 34-17 night victory at neighboring West Virginia. Tickets for the clash against the 11th-ranked Mountaineers were so difficult to obtain that a few Ohio State faithful purchased West Virginia season tickets just to be able to attend this game.

The Buckeyes jumped to a 17-3 lead early in the second quarter, and quickly calmed the raucous Mountaineer Field crowd of 68,409. OSU cornerback Antoine Winfield led the defense with eight solo tackles. Quarterback Joe Germaine completed 18 of 32 throws for 301 yards and two touchdowns, and tailback Michael Wiley rushed for 140 yards and a TD on 17 carries. Dan Stultz booted field goals of 35 and 36 yards.

The game was just the sixth between the neighboring schools, and only the second since 1903. It was the Buckeyes' first trip to Morgantown. West Virginia won 28-0 in 1897 during a game held at Parkersburg, W. Va. The Buckeyes had triumphed four times in Columbus in 1900 (27-0), 1902 (30-0), 1903 (34-6) and 1987 (24-3).

Changing Sides

Ohio State conquered Minnesota, 45-15, in its annual homecoming game on Oct. 17, 1998. Exactly 28 years earlier on Oct. 17, 1970, the Buckeyes outscored the Golden Gophers 28-8 in that season's homecoming. Glen Mason was Minnesota's head coach in 1998. Mason had been a junior linebacker at Ohio State in 1970.

Surprise Honor

Archie Griffin's jersey No. 45 was officially retired at halftime of Ohio State's 41-11 homecoming triumph over Iowa on Oct. 30, 1999. Griffin and his 1974 teammates were being recognized on the 25th anniversary of their Big Ten title. The two-time Heisman Trophy winner was completely surprised with his number being retired. To top off the homecoming afternoon, Griffin's son, Andre, entered the game and carried three times at tailback in the final quarter.

Also recognized at halftime were Ohio State's 1949 Rose Bowl champions, 1954 national champions, and 1979 Big Ten champions.

First in 51

Minnesota spoiled Ohio State's homecoming of Oct. 14, 2000, upsetting the Buckeyes, 29-17. It was the Golden Gophers' first victory at Ohio Stadium in 51 years since winning 27-0 on Oct. 15, 1949.

GREAT GAME REMEMBERED
No. 2 Ohio State 20 - No. 4 Arizona State 17
Jan. 1, 1997 - Pasadena, California

OSU marches to Rose Bowl win

Courtesy The Columbus Dispatch, Jan. 1, 1997

With the lead changing hands five times, Ohio State dealt Arizona State its only loss of the season in one of the Rose Bowl's all-time most thrilling games. A touchdown with 1:40 left in the final quarter gave the Sun Devils a 17-14 lead.

As the ASU players began a sideline celebration as if the game were over, quarterback Joe Germaine calmly drove the Buckeyes 65 yards for the clinching score and one of Ohio State's finest triumphs. Three completions to flanker Dimitrious Stanley, two on third down, kept the drive alive. The winning TD came on a 5-yard toss to freshman wide receiver David Boston, who backpedaled across the goal line with 19 seconds remaining. Coach John Cooper described the comeback as, "The greatest moment in my 35 years of coaching." The 1996 season helped Ohio State re-establish itself as a national power.

Ohio State Rose Bowl Champion. *Courtesy Ohio State University Photo Archives*

CHAPTER TWELVE

2001-2011

Teamwork, Tenacity & Triumph

"I am so proud, so excited, and so humbled to be your football coach at The Ohio State University. I can assure you that you'll be proud of our young people — in the classroom, in the community, and most especially in 310 days in Ann Arbor, Michigan!"

This momentous declaration by Jim Tressel, when introduced as Ohio State's new head coach on Thurs., Jan. 18, 2001, passionately communicated one of his immediate objectives. Over Tressel's 10 seasons as head coach, the Buckeyes would go 9-1 against the Wolverines, marking the first time Ohio State had won 9 of 10 consecutive games in this cherished rivalry.

Tressel graduated cum laude from Baldwin-Wallace College, where he earned four letters at quarterback from 1971 through 1974. He was an all-conference selection his senior year. His college coach was his highly esteemed father, Dr. Lee

Courtesy The Columbus Dispatch, Jan. 18, 2001

Tressel, who led the Yellow Jacket program with much success from 1958 through 1980 (155-52-6, 74.2 percent). Baldwin-Wallace was the Division III national champion in 1978, and Lee was inducted into the College Football Hall of Fame in 1996.

After graduation, Tressel was an assistant coach for a total of eight seasons at the University of Akron, Miami University (Ohio) and Syracuse University, followed by three years under Earle Bruce at Ohio State from 1983 through 1985. He began an excellent 15-year head coaching stint at Youngstown State University in 1986 that included an overall record of 135-57-2 (70.1 percent) and four Division 1-AA national titles. Four times he was chosen the Division I-AA Coach of the Year. Lee and Jim Tressel

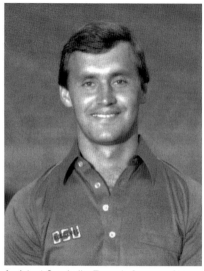

Assistant Coach Jim Tressel. *Courtesy Ohio State University Photo Archives*

are the only father-son football coaching twosome to capture NCAA national championships.

Tressel's first Ohio State game was a 28-14 home triumph over Akron on

Sat., Sept. 8, 2001. Three days later on Sept. 11, terrorists attacked New York City's World Trade Center along with the Pentagon, and football was promptly forgotten as the United States began to deal with this horrendous tragedy. All college and professional games were cancelled the following weekend. Most were rescheduled later that fall.

During Tressel's 10 seasons in Columbus, the Buckeyes won seven Big Ten titles (three outright, four shared) and were 6-4 in postseason play. His team's 31-24 double-overtime triumph over Miami (Fla.) to secure the 2002 national

Ohio State 2002 National Champion. *Courtesy Ohio State University Photo Archives*

title with a record of 14-0 will be remembered forever as one of the program's supreme achievements.

In 2006, top-ranked Ohio State used its superb speed to outscore second-ranked Michigan, 42-39, and claim the undisputed Big Ten championship. It is the only time the fierce rivals have faced off as the nation's two top teams. The contest took place on Nov. 18, just one day after Bo Schembechler, Michigan's legendary head coach for 21 seasons, passed away at age 77. OSU quarterback Troy Smith enjoyed his third consecutive spectacular performance against the Wolverines, and in December was awarded the Heisman Trophy.

Jim Tressel's tenure came to a sudden end after the 2010 season, following an NCAA investigation involving improper benefit violations by selected Ohio State players. He resigned on May 30, 2011. Defensive Coordinator Luke Fickell was promoted to lead the team for the 2011 season, just 65 days before the team reported for fall practice.

Quarterback Troy Smith - 2006 Heisman Trophy Winner. *Courtesy Brockway Collection at The Ohio State University Archives*

Fickell and his staff did a very fine job, especially under the circumstances, and the Buckeyes finished the 2011 season at 6-7. The high points were a 17-7 victory over No. 16 Illinois and a 33-29 homecoming triumph over No. 15 Wisconsin. Six of the seven losses were by seven or fewer points. Urban Meyer was announced as Ohio State's new head coach on Nov. 28, 2011. After guiding the Buckeyes against Florida in the Gator Bowl at the end of the 2011 season, Fickell returned to his position as defensive coordinator.

Tressel completed his 10-year Ohio State career with an official winning rate of 81.0 percent (94-22), the second-highest in the 121-year history of the Big Ten for those who have coached in the league for 10 or more seasons. Fielding Yost of Michigan has the highest at 88.8 percent, Bo Schembechler with 79.6 percent is third, Woody Hayes is sixth at 76.1 percent and John Cooper with 71.5 percent is ninth. Earle Bruce, with an Ohio State winning rate of 75.5 percent, is not included in the rankings since he coached the Buckeyes only nine seasons.

After Ohio State, Tressel in 2012 became Vice President of Strategic Engagement at the University of Akron, where he had obtained his first assistant coaching position and acquired his master's degree. During the Michigan game of 2012, Tressel received a standing ovation when introduced with his team on the 10-year anniversary of their 2002 national title. He was named president of Youngstown State University on May 9, 2014. He was inducted into the College Football Hall of Fame in 2015.

Golden Anniversary

Jim Tressel's first Big Ten Conference encounter was a 27-14 victory at Indiana on Sat., Sept. 29, 2001, just three weeks after the season opener against Akron. It marked the exact 50th anniversary of Woody Hayes' first Ohio State game. Hayes' first team opened its season with a 7-0 victory over SMU at Ohio Stadium on Saturday, Sept. 29, 1951.

September 11, 2001

"It was one of those days you remember exactly where you were, what time it was and who you were with." That's how Andy Groom describes his experience the day of September 11, 2001.

GREAT GAME REMEMBERED
Ohio State 26 - No. 11 Michigan 20
Nov. 24, 2001 - Ann Arbor, Michigan

Tailback Jonathan Wells carried 25 times for 129 yards and three first-half touchdowns, igniting Ohio State to its first victory at Michigan Stadium since 1987. Wells scored on runs of 1, 46, and 11 yards, leading the 11-point underdog Buckeyes to a 23-0 lead at halftime. The stunned Wolverines were able to advance no further than the Ohio State 43 in the first half. Craig Krenzel of Sterling Heights, Mich., performed very well in his first collegiate start at quarterback.

Reprinted with permission of the Akron Beacon Journal and Ohio.com., Nov. 25, 2001

Ohio State's aggressive defense forced five Michigan turnovers — four interceptions and a lost fumble. Linebacker Joe Cooper was OSU's leading tackler with eight, followed by tackle Tim Anderson and cornerback Derek Ross with seven each. This setback deprived Michigan from claiming a share of the Big Ten title and an automatic appearance in a BCS bowl.

The victory was the high mark of the season for first-year head coach Jim Tressel, who predicted that Ohio State fans would be "proud of their young people in the classroom, in the community, and most especially in 310 days in Ann Arbor, Michigan."

Groom was a junior punter and recounts what happened the day the United States was viciously attacked. "I was heading into the practice facility and I heard on the radio about the first plane. Inside the facility the whole team was in the players lounge watching everything on TV, and that's where we saw the second plane hit the second tower. We couldn't believe what was happening! It was crazy! Coach Jim Tressel told us that this day was a lot bigger than football, and he wanted us to go home and be with our family and friends."

Groom's family lived in the Canal Winchester/Groveport area just outside of Columbus. He took some of his teammates to his home for a few days so they could piece together what just happened. Two of those players were David Thompson from Patterson, N.J., and Sammy Moldonado from the Bronx in New York City. Fortunately, both of their families were fine.

The team took a few days off and a home game with San Diego State the following weekend was rescheduled to Oct. 20. Practices were suspended for several days. Coach Tressel's focus on family was paramount, and he knew that football would and should take a back seat. When the players returned to the practice field days later, they came together with the same patriotic strength and brotherly love that pulled the rest of the nation together during that crisis.

Ohio State's first game after the attack was against UCLA at the Rose Bowl on Sept. 23. Groom remembers that both teams gathered in a huddle of prayer and quiet respect prior to the game. Ohio State lost 13-6, but the game was a welcome respite from the heaviness of the nation's pain that was so personal for so many. For several weeks following the attacks, Tressel often told his players to "be in the moment, because you never know what is going to happen."

Groom was an All-American punter and a three-time Academic All-Big Ten selection. His last game was his team's 31-24 victory over Miami (Fla.) for the 2002 national championship. He played four seasons in the NFL with Tampa Bay, San Francisco, Washington, and Los Angeles. In 2007 Groom joined the Stryker Corporation in Columbus as an account manager who sells medical equipment to Ohio hospitals.

Tressel All Too Familiar With Scoring Patterns

Ohio State's 31-28 Outback Bowl loss to South Carolina on Jan. 1, 2002, was reminiscent of Youngstown State's Division I-AA title game against Marshall in Huntington, W.Va., on Dec. 19, 1992. With Marshall leading 28-0, Jim Tressel's YSU squad retaliated with 28 straight points to tie the score. Marshall finally won the game, 31-28, as left-footed senior placekicker Willy Merrick of Columbus, Ohio, connected with a 22-yard field goal in the game's last seven seconds of play. It was the first field goal attempt of Merrick's college career.

Fast forward almost two decades to the Outback Bowl on January 1, 2002. South Carolina led Ohio State 28-0 late in the third quarter before quarterback Steve Bellisari directed the Buckeyes to four consecutive TDs to tie the score at

28-28. The Gamecocks then booted a 42-yard field goal as time expired for their 31-28 victory.

Csuri Accurate Prediction

At the invitation of Jim Tressel, 1942 All-America tackle and team MVP Chuck Csuri addressed the football squad during its team meal prior to the Texas Tech season-opener in 2002. Csuri advised the players about the importance of team discipline, and told them that if they each learned to "strongly focus" on their individual responsibilities during each play, they could become national champions! Apparently the Buckeyes all heeded Csuri's excellent advice, since they won the national title that season.

Overtime Initiated

Major college football permanently adopted the overtime procedure in 1996, ending the possibility that a game could end in a tie. Over the first 21 seasons of overtime play from 1996 through 2016, there have been approximately 32 overtime games each season.

Ohio State did not play an overtime game until 2002 — a 23-16 victory at Illinois on Nov. 16. The Buckeyes' last tie had been 14-14 at Wisconsin on Nov. 6, 1993.

Gamble Did It All!

Even though football has become a game of specialization over the last 60 seasons, Chris Gamble was an excellent throwback to the early years when players played all phases of the game. During Gamble's three seasons of 2001-03, he played wide receiver, cornerback, and special teams. Over the 39 games those three years, Gamble started 12 games on offense and 18 on defense. In 2002 he started five games on both offense and defense. Following are Gamble's three-year statistics:

Chris Gamble. *Courtesy Ohio State University Photo Archives*

- Receptions – 40 for 609 yards.
- Rushing – 6 attempts for 68 yards and 1 TD.
- Tackles – 65 (51 solo, 14 assists)

GREAT GAME REMEMBERED
No. 2 Ohio State 31 - No. 1 Miami (Fla) 24
Jan. 3, 2003 - Tempe, Arizona

☆☆☆☆☆☆☆☆ **2003 FIESTA BOWL** ☆☆☆☆☆☆☆☆
31 The Columbus Dispatch **24**
SATURDAY, JANUARY 4, 2003
OHIO STATE BUCKEYES
CHAMPS!
Courtesy The Columbus Dispatch, Jan. 4, 2003

For many Ohio State fans, this is their school's "greatest victory." Ohio Sate claimed its first national championship since 1970 with a double-overtime triumph in the BCS Fiesta Bowl National Championship Game. Played at Arizona State's Sun Devil Stadium before a crowd of 77,502, the victory over the Hurricanes lasted three hours and 52 minutes.

The 13-point underdog Buckeyes led 14-7 at halftime and increased their lead to 17-7 midway through the third quarter. Miami closed the gap to 17-14 late in the final period, then tied the score 17-17 with one second remaining in regulation play.

The Hurricanes scored first in overtime to lead 24-17 — it was their first lead since early in the second quarter. Ohio State needed 10 plays to knot the score at 24. Two incredible fourth-down plays kept the drive alive — a 17-yard Craig Krenzel-to-Michael Jenkins completion on a fourth-and-14, and a pass interference penalty against Miami on a fourth-and-3 from the Miami 5.

The Buckeyes scored in the second OT to regain the lead at 31-24, then held the Hurricanes on downs at the Ohio State 1. On fourth down, linebacker Cie Grant forced quarterback Ken Dorsey into a hasty throw that fell incomplete, and Miami's 34-game winning streak had come to an end.

Quarterback Craig Krenzel. *Courtesy Ohio State University Photo Archives*

- Interceptions – 7 for 40 yards and 1 TD.
- Punt Returns – 60 for 467 yards
- Kickoff Returns – 18 for 364 yards

One of Gamble's best remembered plays was a third quarter 40-yard interception return for Ohio State's only touchdown during a key 13-7 home victory over Penn State in 2002. Gamble started both ways that afternoon, and played a total of 95 plays or nearly 70 percent of the game.

Cooper Connections

John Cooper had three distinct links with Ohio State's 31-24 double-overtime victory over Miami for the 2002 national title. First, while Cooper was the head coach at Tulsa in 1979, he gave Miami head coach Larry Coker the opportunity to move from the high school to the college level with an assistant coaching position at Tulsa. Coker had been head coach at Claremore High School in Oklahoma, and acknowledged that without Cooper's offer he might never have been able to coach at the college level.

Second, the 2002 season was Jim Tressel's second year at Ohio State, and many of the 2002 Buckeye players had been recruited to Ohio State by Cooper. Third, the BCS title game was played at Arizona State University's Sun Devil Stadium, where Cooper had been named National Coach of the Year in 1986 after leading ASU to a record of 10-1-1, that included a 22-15 Rose Bowl victory over Michigan.

January 18 — One of Tressel's Favorite Dates

Jim Tressel was introduced as Ohio State's new head football coach on Thursday, Jan. 18, 2001. The press conference was held in the recruiting room, located in Ohio Stadium's southeast tower. Back at Ohio Stadium exactly two years later on Sat., Jan. 18, 2003, Tressel, his coaching staff, and his 2002 team were honored as national champions during a ceremony attended by approximately 60,000 appreciative fans.

The Unexpected

Following their 14-0 record in 2002, the Buckeyes won their first five games of 2003 to extend their nation-leading winning streak to 19. Wisconsin broke the run Oct. 11 with a 17-10 victory on a rainy night in Madison. The Badgers' winning touchdown came from a very unexpected source.

Starting quarterback Jim Sorgi went out with an injury in the third quarter, and was replaced by back-up Matt Schabert. With the score tied at 10 late in the final period, Schabert passed 79 yards to wide receiver Lee Evans for the winning touchdown. Evans had beaten safety Chris Gamble, and Schabert hit him in stride at the OSU 48. It was Evans' only reception of the evening. Schabert played in only 12 games during his career with the Badgers, passing for three touchdowns including this epic throw to Evans.

Ohio State's first-ever victory over a No. 1 ranked opponent came against Wisconsin exactly 51 years earlier, when the Buckeyes defeated the top-ranked Badgers 23-14 at Ohio Stadium on Oct. 11, 1952.

Punter's Delight

B.J. Sander's punting effectiveness during Ohio State's 16-13 overtime victory over Purdue in 2003 was one of the finest in school history. Sander punted 10 times for a 41.3-yard average, and seven of his punts were downed inside the Purdue 20-yard line. Sander's punting success had a major impact upon the game's outcome,

GREAT GAME REMEMBERED
No. 1 Ohio State 42 - No. 2 Michigan 39
Nov. 18, 2006 - Columbus, Ohio

It was the first No. 1-vs.-No. 2 clash in this grand series, and just the third time both teams entered the game undefeated and untied. In a contest that even exceeded its pre-game hype, both teams scored in each quarter. The combined score of 81 points is the third highest in the majestic rivalry.

Courtesy The Columbus Dispatch, Nov. 19, 2006

After taking their first lead of the afternoon at 14-7 early in the second quarter, the Buckeyes led the remainder of this historic afternoon. Quarterback Troy Smith was outstanding, completing 29 of 41 attempts for 316 yards. Smith threw touchdown passes to four separate receivers. Tailbacks Beanie Wells and Antonio Pittman dented the Wolverine defense with thrilling touchdown runs of 52 and 56 yards, respectively. The Buckeyes led in first downs, 24-17, and total offensive yards, 503-397.

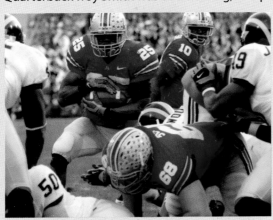

Tailback Antonio Pittman rushed for 139 yards including a third quarter 56-yard touchdown run. *Courtesy Brockway Collection at The Ohio State University Archives*

especially since Ohio State won without scoring an offensive touchdown. Sander became an All-American that season.

Longest Continuous Series Ends

Ohio State and Illinois did not meet in 2003, breaking what was (at the time) the Buckeyes' longest continuous series at 89 games. The two schools had faced each other each season beginning in 1914 (they also met in 1902 and 1904). The Ohio State-Michigan rivalry is now Ohio State's longest continuous series. The two have played each year, beginning in 1918. The Buckeyes and Wolverines also played 14 times from 1897 through 1912.

Tressel-Ball in Full Force

After capturing the 2002 national title with a record of 14-0, Ohio State finished the 2003 season with a very fine mark of 11-2. The Buckeyes were able to secure three of their 11 victories without scoring an offensive touchdown:

1. Sept. 6 - Ohio State 16, San Diego State 13
Placekicker Mike Nugent kicked three field goals and an extra point and Will Allen scored a TD with a 100-yard interception return.

2. Oct. 18 - Ohio State 19, Iowa 9
Nugent kicked a field goal and two extra points, Michael Jenkins returned a punt 54 yards for a TD, Donte Whitner recovered an Iowa fumble in the end zone for a TD, and Ohio State was awarded a safety when an errant Iowa snap from center sailed out of the end zone.

3. Nov. 15 - Ohio State 16, Purdue 13 (Overtime)
Nugent kicked three field goals and an extra point, and Mike Kudla returned a Purdue fumble a single yard for a TD.

Cutting It Close

Ohio State's 21-20 triumph at Penn State on Nov. 1, 2003, was the school's first single-point victory since a 20-19 season-opening triumph over Louisville on Sept. 5, 1992. From 2004 through 2016, the Buckeyes have had three single-point victories — all within the state of Michigan:

- 17-16 at Michigan State on Sept. 29, 2012.
- 42-41 at Michigan on Nov. 30, 2013.

Coach Jim Tressel *Courtesy Ohio State University Photo Archives*

• 17-16 at Michigan State on Nov. 19, 2016.

The Buckeyes' last single-point loss was 17-16 to Southern California in the Rose Bowl on Jan. 1, 1980.

Ginn's Versatility Sparks Triumph at Spartan Stadium

After gaining a 17-0 first quarter lead at Michigan State on Nov. 6, 2004, the Buckeyes found themselves trailing 19-17 with just 3:06 to play in the final period. Ohio State miraculously rallied for two quick touchdowns to win, 32-19.

Ted Ginn Jr. scored three of Ohio State's four touchdowns in three different manners:
• A 17-yard run with 9:43 remaining in the first quarter.
• A 60-yard punt return with 8:15 remaining in the first quarter.
• A 58-yard pass reception from quarterback Troy Smith with 1:37 left in the game.

Placekicker Mike Nugent booted a 53-yard field goal with 2:50 left in the first period, and tailback Maurice Hall raced 51 yards for the game's final score.

Talented Trio

Bobby Carpenter, Anthony Slagel and A.J. Hawk formed one of the finest linebacker trios in Ohio State history. Carpenter and Hawk played four seasons from 2002 through 2005, and Slagel played in 2004 and 2005 after transferring from the Air Force Academy. They were the team's leading tacklers in 2004 — Hawk 141, Carpenter 93, Slagel 84. Their career totals were 394, 191, 166 respectively. Hawk was a two-time All-American, who captured the Lombardi Award and the Big Ten Defensive Player of the Year Award in 2005.

Prior to the 2005 season Hawk, Carpenter and Slagel, along with center Nick Mangold, grew their hair long to honor the late Pat Tillman. Tillman in 2002 turned down a new NFL contract for more than $3 million, after playing four seasons with the Arizona Cardinals. He thought it was more important to serve his country than

From left: Bobby Carpenter, Anthony Slagel, A.J. Hawk. *Courtesy Ohio State University Photo Archives*

play football. Tillman joined the Army Rangers and served several tours of combat before losing his life in Afghanistan at age 27 on April 22, 2004.

Close to Home

Ohio State's fine record of 11-2 in 2007 included three victories over opponents from within the state of Ohio. The Buckeyes defeated Youngstown State 38-6 on Sept. 1, downed Akron 20-2 on Sept. 8, and blasted Kent State 48-3 on Oct. 13. It was the first season Ohio State had faced as many as three opponents from within Ohio since 1926.

Opponent Familiarity

In 2007, Jim Tressel became the fourth Ohio State coach to face an opponent that he had previously coached when the Buckeyes defeated Youngstown State, 38-6. Tressel had been head coach at YSU 15 seasons from 1986 through 2000.

John Cooper directed Ohio State to a 20-17 Rose Bowl triumph over Arizona State on Jan. 1, 1997. Cooper was ASU's head coach from 1985 through 1987. Ohio State faced the Pitt Panthers each of coach Wes Fesler's four seasons of 1947 through 1950, going 3-1. Fesler had been Pitt's head coach in 1946. Coach Francis Schmidt's Buckeyes defeated Texas Christian 14-0 in their 1937 season opener. Schmidt was head coach at TCU from 1929 through 1933.

GREAT GAME REMEMBERED
No. 1 Ohio State 37 - No. 24 Penn State 17
Oct. 27, 2007 - State College, Pennsylvania

This convincing performance was Ohio State's 19th consecutive conference victory, equaling the record established by Michigan from 1990 through 1992. The partisan home crowd of 110,134 was the second-highest in Beaver Stadium history. Playing their third night game away from home in the last five weeks, the Buckeyes took charge early and outscored the Nittany Lions in each of the four quarters.

Quarterback Todd Boeckman was very impressive, completing 19 of 26 passes for 253 yards and three touchdowns. Tailback Beanie Wells was the game's leading rusher with 133 yards. Ohio State converted 12 of 16 third-down attempts and did not punt all evening. Linebacker Marcus Freeman led the Buckeye defense with 14 tackles. With this victory, Ohio State edged ahead in the all-time series with Penn State, 12-11.

Repeaters

Chris "Beanie" Wells is Ohio State's most recent two-time team Most Valuable Player, receiving the honor in 2007-08. Wells is fifth in school career rushing with 3,382 yards and 30 touchdowns on 585 carries from 2006-08.

Ohio State's other two-time team MVPs are tailback Archie Griffin (1973-74), end Jim Houston (1958-59), halfback Howard "Hopalong" Cassady (1954-55), halfback Vic Janowicz (1950-51), center Ralph Wolfe (1936-37), and center Gomer Jones (1934-1935).

Tailback Beanie Wells raced 52 yards for a second-quarter touchdown against Michigan in 2006. *Courtesy Jim Davidson*

Perfection

Three Big Ten opponents were unable to defeat Ohio State during Jim Tressel's 10 seasons as head coach from 2001 through 2010. Tressel's teams were 8-0 against Indiana, 6-0 against Michigan State and 8-0 against Minnesota.

Three-Timers

Linebacker James Laurinaitis (2006-07-08) and safety Mike Doss (2000-01-02) are Ohio State's most recent three-time All-Americans. Ohio State's other three-time All-Americans are punter Tom Skladany (1974-75-76), tailback Archie Griffin (1973-74-75), end Merle Wendt (1934-35-36), halfback Lew Hinchman (1930-31-32), end Wes Fesler (1928-29-30), and halfback Chic Harley (1916-17-19).

James Laurinaitis. *Courtesy Jim Davidson*

Mike Doss. *Courtesy Ohio State University Photo Archives*

GREAT GAME REMEMBERED
Ohio State 33 - No. 15 Wisconsin 29
Oct. 29, 2011 - Columbus, Ohio

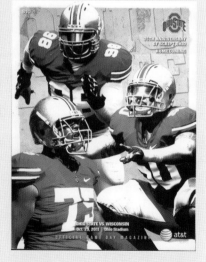

Quarterback Braxton Miller passed 40 yards to wide receiver Devon Smith for the winning touchdown with 20 seconds remaining. Smith's lone reception of the evening provided coach Luke Fickell's squad with one of the program's most memorable homecoming triumphs. The lead changed hands four times. Ohio State became the last team standing after 28 of the game's 62 points were scored in the last 4:39 of play. The Badgers had been the only team to defeat the Buckeyes the previous season.

Buckeye tailback Boom Herron was the game's leading rusher with 166 yards on 33 carries. Wisconsin quarterback Russell Wilson connected on 20 of 32 attempts for 253 yards and three of his team's four touchdowns. One week earlier the Badgers were beaten at Michigan State, 37-31, after the Spartans scored with a 44-yard desperation pass on the game's final play.

CHAPTER THIRTEEN

2012-2016

Making Ohio Proud

Urban Meyer was introduced as Ohio State's new head football coach on Monday, Nov. 28, 2011. He immediately declared that, "We're going to make the great state of Ohio proud with everything we do!" Meyer was no stranger to Ohio State fans. In 2006 he led the University of Florida to the 2006 BCS national title with an astonishing upset of the top-ranked Buckeyes, 41-14.

After graduating from the University of Cincinnati in 1986, Meyer became a graduate assistant to Ohio State coach Earle Bruce during the 1986-1987 seasons, and developed a strong connection with Bruce and second-year graduate assistant Tim Hinton. He made significant progression for 13 seasons as a respected assistant coach at Illinois State, Colorado State and Notre Dame from 1988-2000. In 1989 he married Shelley Mather, a University of Cincinnati graduate.

Meyer immediately was successful as a head coach, leading Bowling Green to a record of 17-6 in 2001-2002 and Utah to a mark of 22-2 in 2003-2004. With the Utes he continued his development of a distinctive spread formation with the quarterback in the shotgun position. Meyer next directed the Florida Gators for six seasons, with a prominent record of 65-15 that included the 2008 national championship in addition to 2006. He stepped down after the 2010 season, citing the need for more personal balance with his family.

Courtesy The Columbus Dispatch, Nov. 29, 2011

On Dec. 20, just 22 days after Meyer was named head coach, Ohio State was totally shocked when penalized by the NCAA with a bowl ban for the 2012 season. The Buckeyes also were denied the opportunity to compete in that year's Big Ten Championship game. The school voluntarily had vacated its 12 victories and Big Ten championship from the 2010 season, after six players were involved with a "tattoo scandal" that eventually led to the resignation of head coach Jim Tressel. Ohio State officials felt this self-imposed penalty was sufficient for the infractions incurred, but elected not to appeal the additional punishment.

Throughout December of 2011, Luke Fickell (who would return to defensive coordinator in 2012) and his assistants prepared the Buckeyes for their Gator Bowl encounter against Florida (which the Gators won 24-17) on Monday, Jan. 2, 2012. During December, Meyer was very busy with recruiting and hiring a new staff. In early January, the new coach became thoroughly incensed when a handful of players arrived late or did not attend his first two team meetings. Meyer immediately began the winter conditioning program (instead of a week later as originally announced), and held the first few sessions on outside practice fields instead of inside the heated Woody Hayes Athletic Center.

More than 80,000 fans attending the April 21 spring game got their first look at Meyer's up-tempo spread offense. Quarterback Braxton Miller's quickness and elusive running ability helped make him an ideal fit for Ohio State's new attack. Practices were very fast paced and more challenging than in recent years.

Even after being denied the opportunity for postseason play, Meyer's first Ohio State team more than met each challenge to finish this exceptional season at 12-0 and claim the 2012 Big Ten Leaders Division Championship. Nebraska captured the Legends Division. It was the sixth perfect record in school history, and the team finished third in the final *Associated Press* poll. Miller was selected the Big Ten Conference's Offensive Player of the Year and Most Valuable Player.

Meyer's second Ohio State team won all 12 regular season games. The winning streak ended with a 34-24 setback to Michigan State in the 2013 Big Ten Championship game. Miller repeated as the Big Ten Offensive Player of the Year and Most Valuable Player.

Ohio State finished 12-0 in 2012. *Courtesy Ohio State University Department of Athletics*

Ohio State played its 125th season of collegiate football in 2014. Redshirt freshman quarterback J.T. Barrett surprisingly became the starting quarterback just 11 days before the season opener in Baltimore against Navy. Miller was lost for the season after re-injured his throwing shoulder in practice. The Buckeyes defeated the Midshipmen, 34-17, then lost their home opener to Virginia Tech the following Saturday, 35-21. After winning its first 24 games under Meyer, Ohio State had now lost three of its last four. The Buckeyes regrouped to win their eight remaining regular-season games and advance to the Big Ten Championship game against Wisconsin. The first-ever College Football Playoff rankings became public on Tue., Oct. 28, 2014. Mississippi State at 7-0 was ranked first. Ohio State was listed 16th with a record of 6-1.

Barrett's season ended abruptly after he broke an ankle during the fourth period of his team's 42-28 victory over Michigan. Sophomore Cardale Jones, who had thrown just 14 passes all season, replaced Barrett. Jones led the Buckeyes to an astounding 59-0 victory over the favored Wisconsin Badgers in the Big Ten Championship Game. Following this prized triumph, Ohio State was awarded the fourth spot in the first College Football Playoff. The point totals were not announced, but it is almost certain that Ohio State narrowly finished ahead of fifth-place Baylor for the final playoff position.

From left: Braxton Miller, J.T. Barrett, Cardale Jones. *Photos Courtesy Jim Davidson*

Ohio State triumphed, 42-35, over top-ranked Alabama in the Sugar Bowl, then defeated No. 2 Oregon, 42-20, in the CFP National Championship game, played in Dallas. Jones was sensational in his new role as the starting quarterback. During the three postseason victories, he completed 46 of 75 passes (61.3 percent) for 742 yards and five touchdowns while Ezekiel Elliott rushed 76 times for 676 yards and eight scores.

The Buckeyes followed their 2014 national title season with impressive records of 12-1 and 11-2 in 2015 and 2016, respectively. Those two seasons Ohio State faced

Michigan State and Michigan back-to-back for the very first time. In 2016, Big Ten teams began playing nine conference games instead of eight.

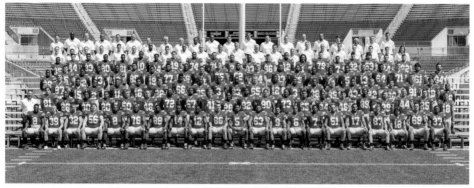

Ohio State 2014 National Champion. *Courtesy Ohio State University Department of Athletics*

GREAT GAME REMEMBERED
No. 14 Ohio State 17 – No. 20 Michigan State 16
Sept. 29, 2012 – East Lansing, Michigan

Ohio State overcame three turnovers for this exciting single-point victory, played before a packed Spartan Stadium crowd of 76,705. It was Urban Meyer's first Big Ten Conference game as head coach after four non-conference wins against less-talented opponents. With his team trailing 13-10, quarterback Braxton Miller passed 63 yards to split end Devin Smith for the winning score with 3:05 to go in the third quarter.

This victory became the turning point of the 2012 season, as the players demonstrated a noticeable belief in their new coaching staff. Miller ran for 136

Coach Urban Meyer. *Courtesy Jim Davidson*

yards and passed for another 179. The punting was exceptional on both sides — Ohio State's Ben Buchanan averaged 44.0 yards on four punts and Michigan State's Mike Sadler punted five times for a 55.4-yard average. The game marked the beginning of Ohio State's 100th season as a member of the Big Ten Conference.

Meyer Tops Among Active Coaches

Ohio State's Urban Meyer finished his 15th season as a major college head coach in 2016. His five-year record at Ohio State was 61-6 for a winning rate of 91.0 percent, the highest for any five consecutive seasons in school history. Meyer's head coaching winning rate of 85.1 percent through the end of the 2016 season is the highest among all active major college coaches with 10 or more years at a four-year school. He is third all-time among major college coaches with 10 or more seasons, behind Notre Dame's Knute Rockne and Frank Leahy.

Knute Rockne	**Frank Leahy**	**Urban Meyer**
88.1%	**86.4%**	**85.1%**
13 years	13 years	15 years
105-12-5	107-13-9	165-29
1918-1930	1939-1943, 1946-1953	2001-2010, 2012-2016
Notre Dame	Boston College	Bowling Green – Utah
	Notre Dame	Florida – Ohio State

Rockne and Leahy photos courtesy University of Notre Dame Department of Athletics
Meyer photo courtesy Jim Davidson

Arranged Breakfast

Skip Holtz was the wide receiver coach during Earle Bruce's first year as head coach at Colorado State University in 1989. Skip and Urban Meyer began a close friendship when Skip left Colorado State after one season and was replaced by Meyer in 1990. Skip departed CSU to become the wide receivers coach at Notre Dame, where his father Lou Holtz was head coach. After working with his father for four seasons, Skip advanced to head coach at Connecticut in 1994. He and Meyer talked often over those years, and they frequently called each other for suggestions and advice.

Lou needed a new wide receivers coach in 1996, and Skip strongly suggested he interview Meyer. Lou told his son he already knew who he wanted to hire, and had no interest in even interviewing Meyer — someone he knew nothing about. Skip repeated the suggestion, but Lou strongly told Skip that he had no interest in interviewing Meyer.

Skip persisted. He asked his father to meet him for breakfast on the last day of the American Football Coaches 1996 Annual Convention in New Orleans. Skip did not tell Lou that he had also invited Meyer to join them for breakfast. Lou was totally surprised. After quickly finishing his breakfast, Skip excused himself and left Meyer alone with Lou. Meyer and Lou talked for an additional hour, and Lou obviously became very impressed with Meyer. When Lou called Meyer the following week to offer him Notre Dame's wide receiver position, Meyer immediately accepted.

Since that "arranged breakfast" in 1996, Meyer frequently has acknowledged

that without Skip's persistence with Lou, He likely would never have been the wide receivers coach at Notre Dame. Meyer's five seasons with the Fighting Irish significantly helped him prepare for his first head coaching position at Bowling Green in 2001 — and the rest is history.

Versatility Plus

Senior Zach Boren began the 2012 season as Ohio State's starting fullback. When the defense needed help, Boren shifted to a starting linebacker position in the season's seventh game at Indiana on Oct. 13. Boren immediately helped improve the defense. He finished the year with a total of 50 tackles — 24 solos and 26 assists. Boren was Ohio State's sixth-leading tackler that season, while playing only the last six games on defense.

Linebacker Zach Boren in action at Indiana in 2012. *Courtesy Jim Davidson*

Poise Under Pressure

Ohio State faced Purdue at home on Oct. 20, 2012. With 29 seconds remaining in the third quarter and the Buckeyes trailing 20-14, quarterback Braxton Miller suffered a game-ending injury while being tackled at the Purdue 39. Miller was replaced by junior back-up Kenny Guiton.

Early in the final period, Ohio State incurred a team safety and now trailed 22-14. Purdue was forced to punt on its ensuing possession and Ohio State took control on its own 20 with 6:03 on the clock. It soon looked very dim for the Buckeyes after Guiton had a deep pass intercepted, allowing the Boilermakers to take over at their own 18 with 2:40 remaining. Many Ohio State fans rapidly headed for the exits.

Purdue managed the clock very poorly and soon punted. The Buckeyes grabbed control

Quarterback Kenny Guiton in action against Purdue in 2012. *Courtesy Jim Davidson*

at their own 39 with 47 seconds on the clock and no timeouts remaining. Guiton masterfully drove his team the needed 61 yards in 44 seconds to bring OSU within two points. The key plays were a 39-yard completion to Devin Smith followed by an 8-yarder to Evan Spencer. With eight seconds left, Guiton rolled left, then threw back across the grain to a racing Chris Fields for the touchdown from two yards out. He next connected with tight end Jeff Heuerman for the all-important two-point

GREAT GAME REMEMBERED
No. 4 Ohio State 42 – No. 1 Alabama 35
Jan. 1, 2015 – New Orleans, Louisiana

This Sugar Bowl triumph before a Louisiana Superdome crowd of 74,682 was a semifinal game in the first College Football Playoff. Both teams scored in all four quarters. The Buckeyes tallied 28 consecutive points to lead 34-21 late in the third period, after trailing 21-6 midway through the second quarter. A surprise 13-yard momentum building scoring pass from Evan Spencer to Michael Thomas, just 12 seconds

Coach Lou Holtz celebrates Ohio State's Sugar Bowl victory with Shelley and Urban Meyer. *Courtesy Jim Davidson*

before halftime, brought the Buckeyes within a single point of the Crimson Tide at 21-20. Spencer had lined up as a wide receiver to the right, then received a reverse lateral from Jalin Marshall before passing to Thomas.

Ohio State's fine defensive play in the second half was a major factor in the game's outcome. OSU led in total offensive yards, 537 to 407. The Buckeyes averaged 6.9 yards per play; the Crimson Tide 5.8. Ohio State tailback Ezekiel Elliott rushed for 230 yards, a Sugar

Ohio State's Ezekiel Elliott, the game's offensive MVP, and coach Urban Meyer hold up the Sugar Bowl trophy.

Courtesy The Columbus Dispatch, Jan. 2, 2015

Bowl record. The game lasted three hours and 41 minutes.

conversion to tie the score at 22. The momentum had swung, and the Buckeyes won 29-22 in overtime with a one-yard rush over left guard by Carlos Hyde. The miraculous comeback was complete

Guiton's leadership and poise in the heat of this thrilling comeback was extraordinary. He remained the back-up to Miller during his senior season of 2013. Guiton had earned the respect of the entire team and became one of the very few players in school history to be elected a team captain as a non-starter.

GREAT GAME REMEMBERED
No. 4 Ohio State 42 – No. 2 Oregon 20
Jan. 12, 2015 – Arlington, Texas

The Buckeyes outscored the Ducks 21-10 in each half to claim the first CFP National Championship, played before a high-spirited crowd of 85,788 at AT&T Stadium. Heisman Trophy winner Marcus Mariota completed 24 of 37 attempts for 333 yards and both Oregon touchdowns, but the Ohio State defense became more effective as the game progressed. The Ducks were only two of 12 on third-down conversion attempts. OSU scored the game's final 21 points.

Tailback Ezekiel Elliott scored four touchdowns and rushed for 246 yards, a record for a national

Tailback Ezekiel Elliott. *Courtesy Jim Davidson*

title game. He became the first Ohio State player to rush for more than 200 yards in three consecutive contests. Cardale Jones was good on 16 of 23 attempts for 242 yards and a touchdown. Tyvis Powell led the Buckeye defense with nine tackles, followed by Darron Lee with eight. Elliot was named the game's offensive MVP and Powell the defensive MVP. Ohio State increased its all-time record against Oregon to 9-0.

Spartan Spoilers

Ohio State won its first 24 games after Urban Meyer took charge of the program in 2012. The Buckeyes were 12-0 in 2012 and won their first 12 games of 2013. This broke the previous school winning streak of 22 games that was established from 1967 through 1969. Michigan State broke the streak with a 34-24 victory over OSU in the 2013 Big Ten Championship game, played in Indianapolis.

The Buckeyes won their first 30 Big Ten Conference games under Meyer from 2012 through 2015, establishing an NCAA record for consecutive conference victories. Florida State had held the record with 29 straight Atlantic Coast Conference wins from 1992 through 1995. Michigan State again was the spoiler, defeating Ohio State 17-14 in Columbus on Nov. 21, 2015.

Dr. Football

Jarrod Barnes may not be a well-known Ohio State football player, but he's earned the respect of his team, the school administration and much of the college sports world. Barnes is the first Ohio State football player to also be pursuing a PhD.

In 2012, Jarrod graduated from Westerville South High School where he was captain of the football team. He accepted a scholarship to play football at the University of Louisville, and earned his Bachelor's Degree in Health and Human Performance in just three years. After redshirting his freshman year, he earned two letters as an active member of the special teams.

Jarrod enrolled in graduate school at Ohio State in 2015. With two remaining years of football eligibility, he walked-on as a special teams player with the football team. In just one year he completed his Masters Degree in Sports Management with a 3.67 GPA, and was accepted by the department as a PhD candidate. He played in a total of five games during his two seasons at Ohio State, and in 2016 was honored on senior day when Ohio State defeated Michigan in a thrilling double overtime.

Jarrod's passion is to redefine what's possible for student athletes in both the classroom and the community. As part of his research, he's developed a curriculum to inspire student athletes to set goals, develop communication and leadership skills and plan what else to do outside of sports.

GREAT GAME REMEMBERED
No. 3 Ohio State 45 - No. 14 Oklahoma 24
Sept. 17, 2016 - Norman, Oklahoma

Ohio State won impressively before a record Memorial Stadium crowd of 82,979. The night contest was delayed 90 minutes because of heavy rain and lightning. The Buckeye defense played very well, applying pressure to the Sooner offense all evening. Chris Worley was OSU's leading tackler with 10, followed by Malik Hooker, Damon Webb, and Raekwon McMillan with eight each.

Quarterback J.T. Barrett completed 14 of 20 throws for 152 yards and four touchdowns — all to wide receiver Noah Brown, equaling an Ohio State single-game record. Freshman tailback Mike Weber ran for 123 yards on 18 carries. Cameron Johnston punted five times for an excellent 50.3 average, with all five being downed inside the Oklahoma 15-yard line. The victory improved the Buckeyes' all-time record against the Sooners to 2-1.

Outscoring the Opposition

During Ohio State's first 127 seasons of football from 1890 through 2016, the school has won 12 games while giving up 35 or more points. The most ever surrendered during an Ohio State victory is 49 at Indiana in 2012. Following are the 12 victories in order of points scored by the opponent:

1. Oct. 14, 2012 – at Indiana, 52-49
2. Nov. 8, 1980 – vs. Illinois, 49-42
3. Nov. 30, 2013 – at Michigan, 42-41
4. Nov. 18, 2006 – vs. Michigan, 42-39
5. Oct. 7, 2012 – vs. Nebraska, 63-38
6. Sept. 13, 2003 – vs. North Carolina State, 44-38 (3 OT)
7. Oct. 13, 1984 – vs. Illinois, 45-38
8. Oct. 28, 1989 – at Minnesota, 41-37
9. Nov. 8, 2014 – at Michigan State, 49-37
10. Oct. 28, 1995 – vs. Iowa, 56-35
11. Nov. 16, 2013 – at Illinois, 60-35
12. Jan. 1, 2015 – vs. Alabama, 42-35 (Sugar Bowl)

Biggest Comeback in 25 Seasons

Ohio State defeated Alabama, 42-35, in the Sugar Bowl of Jan. 1, 2015. With 8:07 remaining in the second quarter, the Buckeyes trailed the Crimson Tide by 15 points, 21-6. This was Ohio State's biggest comeback since 1989. That season the Buckeyes won 41-37 at Minnesota after trailing 31-0 near halftime.

"FanQuake"

In 2016 seismic activity rocked Ohio Stadium. But it wasn't an earthquake. It was "FanQuake." And it was impressive!

The FanQuake project is a collaborative effort between The Ohio State University, Miami University, and the Division of Geological Survey of the Ohio Department of Natural Resources to measure how much Ohio State fans are "Shaking the Shoe" during football games. Inspired by "BeastQuake" on Jan. 8, 2011, when thunderous fan reaction at a Seattle Seahawks game was picked up by seismograph a few miles away, a team of university students and industry experts set out to measure similar fan-induced effects at Ohio Stadium. Seismometers were installed in different parts of Ohio Stadium to record vibrations during games.

A scale similar to the Richter scale was created to compare the shaking to actual earthquake vibrations. It was dubbed "FanQuake Magnitude Scale." Three specific games produced quality data:

1. While playing Indiana on Oct. 8, 2016, Ohio State fans erupted with joy after a 91-yard kickoff return by Parris Campbell. FanQuake = 4.0.

2. On Nov. 5, 2016 against Nebraska, a 75-yard touchdown pass from J.T. Barrett to Curtis Samuel on the first play of the second half caused thunderous reaction. FanQuake = 5.2.

3. Curtis Samuel's 15-yard winning touchdown run in a double overtime victory over Michigan, on Nov. 26, 2016 was the record breaker. FanQuake = 5.79. What's most interesting is that the vibration after the touchdown was high, but it grew much stronger a few seconds later as the Ohio State Marching Band joined the celebration. The rhythmic pounding of fans in synch with the music amplified the "Shaking the Shoe."

The data is being used in the classroom to teach measurement techniques, data interpretation methods and the physics of wave propagation. Football makes physics fun. Who would have thought?

High-Scoring Machines

Ohio State played 1,273 football games during its first 127 seasons from 1890 through 2016, with a record of 898-322-53. The Buckeyes scored more than 50 points in 91 of these 1,273 games. During Urban Meyer's first five years as head coach from 2012 through 2016, Ohio State scored more than 50 points in 19 games. This is the highest for any Ohio State coach, and it was done within only five seasons. Woody Hayes is second with 17 games over 50 during his 28 years. Following is a summary of the 91 games when Ohio State scored more than 50 points.

Head Coach	Period	Years	Games
11 Different	1890-1912	23	10
John Wilce	1913-1928	16	8
Sam Willaman	1929-1933	5	4
Francis Schmidt	1934-1940	7	4
Paul Brown	1941-1943	3	2
Carroll Widdoes	1944-1945	2	2
Paul Bixler	1946	1	0
Wes Fesler	1947-1950	4	1
Woody Hayes	1951-1978	28	17
Earle Bruce	1979-1987	9	9
John Cooper	1988-2000	13	9
Jim Tressel	2001-2010	10	6
Luke Fickell	2011	1	0
Urban Meyer	2012-2016	5	19
Totals		**127**	**91**

GREAT GAME REMEMBERED
No. 2 Ohio State 30 - No. 3 Michigan 27
Nov. 26, 2016 - Columbus, Ohio

THE GAME

JOY, RELIEF

Courtesy The Columbus Dispatch, Nov. 27, 2016

With the lead changing hands six times, Ohio State outlasted Michigan in double overtime for the breathtaking triumph. It was the first overtime contest in this storied series. The Wolverines were often in position to take control of the game, but three turnovers at crucial times seriously hindered their offense. The Wolverines led 17-14 after three periods of play, but could gain only 6 yards of offense in the final quarter. Buckeye linebackers Raekwon McMillan and Jerome Baker were the game's leading tacklers with 16 and 15, respectively.

In the second overtime, quarterback J.T. Barrett kept the game alive by narrowly converting a decisive fourth-and-1. On the following play, Curtis Samuel darted 15 yards through left tackle for the winning touchdown. Played before a record Ohio Stadium crowd of 110,045, the game lasted three hours and 51 minutes. With the victory, Urban Meyer became the first Ohio State coach to win his first five games against Michigan.

Linebacker Raekwon McMillan was Ohio State's leading tackler in 2015 with 119 tackles and 2016 with 102 tackles. *Courtesy Jim Davidson*

Ohio State Fans - Happiest Fans!

In August of 2017, ESPN revealed the results of its "Happiest Fans" rankings. Ohio State was first among the 128 major college football programs. The schools being evaluated were members of the 10 major conferences plus independents Army, BYU, Massachusetts and Notre Dame.

Fan contentment is evaluated on a scale of 1-100, according to a "Fan Happiness Index" that includes criteria in six categories: Program Power, Rivalry Dominance, Coaching Stability, Recruiting Trends, Revenue Growth and Twitter Buzz. Ohio State fans scored a perfect 100 in each of the first two categories, 98 in Coaching Stability, 85 in Recruiting Trends, 27 in Revenue Growth, and 5 in Twitter Buzz. Fans are happy with Urban Meyer! Rounding out the top five were Florida State, Alabama, Louisville, and Kansas State, respectively.

Three-Time Leader

J.T. Barrett is Ohio State's only three-time captain. The fine quarterback from Wichita Falls, Texas, was elected one of the Buckeyes' leaders in 2015, 2016, and 2017.

Through the 2017 season, Ohio State has had 10 two-time captains:

> 2016-2017 – C Billy Price
> 2016-2017 – DE Tyquan Lewis
> 2014-2015 – QB Braxton Miller
> 2011-2012 – DE John Simon
> 2007-2008 – LB James Laurinaitis
> 2000-2001 – LB Joe Cooper
> 2000-2001 – QB Steve Bellisari
> 1981-1982 – LB Glenn Cobb
> 1974-1975 – TB Archie Griffin
> 1891-1892 – E Richard T. Ellis

Quarterback J.T. Barrett. *Courtesy Jim Davidson*

CHAPTER FOURTEEN

The Fifth Quarter

Ohio State football extends far beyond the championship players and coaches who have fashioned this vast legacy. Many individuals, groups and organizations have become vibrant elements of the great Buckeye tradition. Here are the stories of only a fraction of these dedicated people.

The Griffin Family Legacy

James and Margaret Griffin wanted college educations for their seven sons and daughter. Knowing that athletic scholarships would help immensely, they immersed their children in sports from an early age. Archie Griffin, middle brother of the eight siblings, recalls that his love for Ohio State football started in early childhood. "On Saturday afternoons we would all listen to the Ohio State games on WVKO Radio. Burt Charles and color analyst Vic Janowicz called the action. When my family moved to Duxberry Avenue, down the street from Linden-McKinley High School (Columbus), my buddies and I would walk to Ohio Stadium and sit

Duncan, Archie and Ray Griffin at Eastmoor Academy Griffin Field. *Courtesy Jim Davidson*

outside and listen to the announcers. Sometimes we even got in — without tickets! It became my dream to play at Ohio State, but I never really thought it would happen," Archie remembers.

Archie and younger brothers Ray and Duncan all played football at Eastmoor High School in Columbus (now Eastmoor Academy High School). Archie was contacted by Ohio State fairly late in the recruiting process. Years later he served on the Board of Directors of the National Football Foundation with Bo Schembechler, legendary head coach of "That Team Up North." Schembechler told Archie, "You know, Woody wouldn't have recruited you if I hadn't tried to recruit you first!"

Serendipitously, Archie enrolled at Ohio State in the fall of 1972, the year freshmen became eligible for varsity competition. Had he been a year older, he wouldn't have played as a freshman, and Ohio State history would be quite different. Archie was thrilled. "I really wanted to be part of the varsity, to suit up, travel, and play. But we freshmen didn't really think we'd get much playing time," he recalls. In the Sept. 16 season opener against Iowa, the Buckeyes were ahead 21-0 in the final quarter. Coach Woody Hayes decided to play some of the freshmen and sent Archie in at tailback. His first carry ended in a fumble that was recovered by Iowa. Knowing Hayes' strong dislike for turnovers, Archie wondered if he would ever play again.

The second game was home against North Carolina on Sept. 30. Archie recalls that Hayes allowed everyone to dress for the game, because the coach believed that you should dress for the home games if you practiced during the week. Archie was listed on the fifth team and really didn't expect to play.

Ohio State's offense started slowly and the Tar Heels led 7-0 midway through the first quarter after blocking an OSU punt. Hayes was very unhappy! With strong advice from assistant coaches Rudy Hubbard and Ed Ferkany, Hayes sent Archie in at tailback. Archie was so surprised that he started onto the field without his helmet. By the end of the afternoon, he had rushed for a then school single-game record 239 yards to help the Buckeyes defeat the Tar Heels, 29-14. Isn't it a good thing the NCAA changed the freshmen eligibility rule?

In 1974, Archie's younger brother, Ray, joined the team, followed by brother Duncan in 1975. The 1975 season was very special for Ohio State with three brothers all earning letters and playing key roles to help the Buckeyes claim the outright Big Ten title. It is the only season Ohio State has had three brothers all lettering together. The Griffins are the only three brothers in Ohio State football to each earn four letters — a very special chapter in school history.

Nebraska was Ray's top choice during his recruiting process. He admired the Huskers' Johnny Rogers, who won the Heisman Trophy in 1972, and Ray wanted to go to Nebraska and play wingback. Nebraska coach Tom Osborne had a strong interest in Ray, and made a recruiting visit to the Griffin home. Ray's father told Osborne, "I enjoy watching my kids play. We have Daryle at Kent State, Archie at Ohio State, and Larry at Louisville. My best opportunity to see them all play is if they are all close. I'd like to see Ray at Ohio State because it would be much easier to see him and Archie play at the same time."

Ray was the backup tailback to Archie in 1974. He scored the game's last two touchdowns during that season's 51-10 home-opening victory over Oregon State — his first TD was a 9-yard run on his very first carry for the Scarlet and Gray. Ray shifted to defensive safety his last three seasons and was named an All-American and team co-captain his senior season.

Super Bowl footballs on display at Eastmoor Academy honoring Ray, Archie and Keith Griffin. *Courtesy Jim Davidson*

Duncan wanted to play linebacker at Northwestern. His wakeup call came his junior year when Northwestern rejected his application because of his grades. This experience helped him understand the importance of academics, and he focused on his grades much more at Ohio State. Duncan considered Woody Hayes' wife, Anne, as the school's best recruiter. "She would talk with my mother and dad first, and by the time Coach Hayes talked with the recruits it was a done deal," he remembers.

Duncan recalls preparing for a major accounting examination one afternoon during his senior season. He felt it was more important to continue his studying than go to football practice. The course was Accounting 523, a Cost Accounting class. He told assistant coach Gary Tranquill, "If coach Hayes has a concern about me missing practice, I'll talk to him about it, but right now graduation is in my sight and I need this time to study." Hayes never mentioned the skipped practice to Duncan, who passed the accounting examination. Hayes was passionate about education and talked openly about the importance of getting a degree.

Duncan's first game was the season opener at Michigan State on Sept. 13, 1975. This was a major game with the Buckeyes ranked No. 3 and the Spartans ranked No. 11. Duncan remembers Coach Hayes sitting at the Friday evening dinner with all the freshman and telling them that the assistant coaches had said that the freshmen were all ready for the game. Ohio State won, 21-0.

Columbus Eastmoor Academy High School is home to many fine football legends, but none as unique as the Griffins. A display case inside the high school contains three Super Bowl footballs honoring graduates who have played in Super Bowls. Archie and Ray both played for the Cincinnati Bengals in Super Bowl XVI (1981 season), held in Detroit. Younger brother Keith, who played college football at Miami (Fla.), played for the Washington Redskins in Super Bowl XXII (1987 season), held in San Diego.

How the Second and Seven Foundation is Tackling Illiteracy

Ryan Miller was an excellent linebacker at Ohio State during the 1993-96 seasons when the Buckeyes captured two Big Ten titles. He is now the successful co-owner of m2 Marketing, a Columbus-based graphic design and marketing firm that he operates with his business partner and fellow Ohio State alumnus/athlete Megan McCabe. Miller is also very proud to be one of three co-founders of the Second and Sev-

Mike Vrabel, Luke Fickell and Ryan Miller at University of Cincinnati Nippert Stadium. *Courtesy Ryan Miller*

en Foundation, a non-profit organization with student athletes volunteering to read to second graders. Miller says, "While I was at Ohio State, the athletic department had community outreach opportunities for athletes, such as volunteering to read to local grade-school children. I did it, although somewhat reluctantly at the beginning. But when I first walked into the classroom and saw the look on the students' faces, and how they were hanging on my leg, treating me like a rock star and soaking up every minute of someone taking interest in them, I was changed."

After graduation, Miller and teammates Luke Fickell and Mike Vrabel thought the experience of reading to second graders was so rewarding they wanted to replicate it with the added benefit of providing a free book for every child in the class. To raise money to purchase the books, the three held a football camp for players from 7 to 14 years of age. The first camp was in 1999, and featured Vrabel (who was playing for the Pittsburgh Steelers) and former OSU quarterback Kirk Herbstreit as special speakers. The camp hosted 48 children at $50 each and produced a profit of nearly $800 that was immediately used to purchase books. West Broad Elementary School in Columbus was the first of seven schools that year to accept their offer to provide books and read to second graders.

The following year, the trio of friends formed the Second and Seven Foundation. The down and distance reference is cleverly convenient for football players, but the name has its roots in the foundation's history. That first year they reached out to second graders in seven schools, thus "Second and Seven."

More than 150 youngsters attended their second summer camp, and a corporate sponsor was secured. Each year the camp grew, allowing them to reach more and more classrooms. Another fundraiser was initiated in 2004, the Celebrity 8-Ball Shootout Pool Tournament. Miller recalls that, "After the shootout, schools started

telling other schools and we were getting more and more calls. But there were still just the three of us reading, and we were so busy. I was working at Sports Radio 97.1 The Fan, Vrabel was now with the New England Patriots, and Fickell was coaching at Akron and then Ohio State. We needed help."

The trio approached Ohio State Athletic Director Gene Smith to seek collaboration with the student athletes for the reading activities. Smith loved the idea and made it a department community service initiative, giving all Ohio State student athletes an opportunity to be involved. Their meeting with Smith not only opened the door for student athletes to volunteer, it solidified the Second and Seven mission, which is "to **promote reading** by **providing free books and positive role models** to kids in need while encouraging young athletes of the community to **pay it forward**." Miller, Fickell and Vrabel took a small community service project and turned it into a large-scale program called, "Tackling Illiteracy."

Since purchasing books was a huge budget item, they decided to write and publish their own book series. "The Hog Mollies (Duke, Hoppy, Harley and Sprout) and the Pickle Pie Party," which teaches the value of teamwork, was published in 2008 as the first in the series. Each year a new Hog Mollies book is published that teaches a character quality lesson, such as "do your best" and "kindness is contagious."

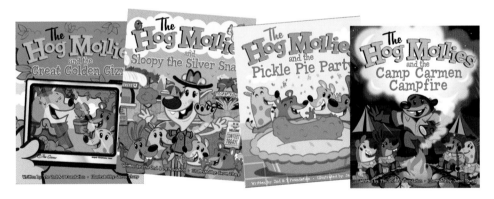

The Second and Seven Foundation has exploded, reaching far beyond the borders of Columbus. As Ohio State athletes graduated and moved to other locations, they took the foundation and the Hog Mollies with them. As of 2017, the Tackling Illiteracy program is in 21 different states, drawing volunteers from dozens of colleges and reaching 126 grade schools. During the 2015-16 school year, over 35,000 books were given to second graders across the country. More than 200,000 books have been distributed since the program's inception.

Miller is blown away with the growth of the organization. "We want every kid to be excited about reading. It's in our heart to do this for the kids, but this wasn't on our dream map. This is way bigger than we ever anticipated — way bigger," Miller expresses. Indeed it is. What started with the kind gesture of a linebacker reading to a grade school class has ballooned into something beyond reading, beyond football and beyond the vision of three Ohio State teammates. It gives kids hope and teaches them to dream and aspire.

The football camp has now become more of a leadership camp, with extraordinary results. Miller tells one particularly inspiring story of a youngster who attended one of the first football camps. He wanted to be a quarterback, but simply lacked the talent. The camp coaches encouraged him to keep trying, and if quarterback didn't work out he could try another position. Years later it still wasn't working and he kept getting cut from his school teams.

As the boy got older he thought, "There are other ways to get onto the field. I'll learn to play an instrument." He enrolled at Ohio State, made the marching band, and realized his dream of playing in Ohio Stadium. He invited the people from Second and Seven to watch him play at a home game. Miller related, "He did great, and we were excited. He's a great kid. There are a lot of reasons why he turned out like he did, but we like to think we were at least a tiny part of that. His story is inspiring. In fact, we invited him to speak at a camp to encourage the kids with his 'When I was your age...' story. It's cool to see how this story perpetuates itself."

The Second and Seven Foundation is thriving, both locally and nationally. Fundraising continues with the football camps, the Celebrity 8-Ball Shootout, a golf outing, a horserace derby and donations. Miller says, "We're excited. Each year we exceed our projections, so we'll keep on doing what we're doing." Additional information can be found at www.secondandseven.com.

Life After Ohio State

Jim Tressel became President of Youngstown State University on May 9, 2014. Tressel believes the similarities and differences between coaching Big Ten football and serving as President of a large state university are not related to the size or status of the entity. "The key is building the relationships to get different groups of people going in the same direction. It's a little bit harder at a university because there's a broader scope and more groups," Tressel said.

"On a football team, you all have similar interests, and the goal is pretty clear — win games. At a university, each college or department is focused on its own issues," Tressel related. "Everyone agrees that higher education is important, funding is tight, and we need to make changes — but not in my department. In fact, my area should be emphasized more!" At Youngstown State University there are four different bargaining units, six different colleges and a graduate school. It's more difficult to get everyone on the same page, but Tressel loves the challenge.

Tressel's passion for helping students is clear. One of his biggest concerns is the amount of student debt and the impact it has, not only on the students but on the nation as a whole. Youngstown is a city still bouncing back after the closing of many steel mills decimated the local economy in 1977. Four decades later, the struggle still continues and YSU, under Tressel's leadership, is repurposing itself. Students are being recruited from all across Ohio and neighboring states instead of just the Youngstown area. He believes that a culture of success for students and football players alike begins with caring for them and having respect for everyone.

Tressel's parents, Lee and Eloise Tressel, were strong role models who poured themselves into others. They lived on the Baldwin Wallace University campus where Lee was the head football coach, and players were always at their home. Ironically, Tressel is now living on campus and helping students himself.

Lee and Eloise were gracious hosts when recruiting for the football program. Tressel recalls that, "The recruits would come to the house for dinner. We didn't have a lot of money, so mom would cook spaghetti and tell her children to not eat anything until the recruits were done. When there were a lot of big linemen being recruited, I often wondered if there would be any spaghetti left since linemen are normally very big eaters!"

President Jim Tressel, Youngstown State University. *Courtesy Youngstown State University*

Tressel and wife Ellen are very active in the faith-based organizations Fellowship of Christian Athletes and Athletes in Action. His faith has been a part of his life since his childhood, although it's grown much stronger as an adult. He says, "Growing up, we were church members, but not really active. My high school football coach suggested I go to a Fellowship of Christian Athletes camp. I didn't know much about faith, but at the camp I had a desire to learn more, to see if it made sense, and be around people who could teach me about it. From that point on, to this day, it's been very important for me. Its been helpful, calming, something to turn to when things aren't going well. With the things in life that I've done, some good and some not so good, I don't know how my life would have gone without my faith."

After Ohio State, Tressel didn't really know what he wanted to do next, so he made a commitment to read 100 books before doing anything else. He received a call from the NFL's Indianapolis Colts in 2011, and agreed to work on the football weekends as a consultant — but nothing more because of his personal reading commitment. He also received inquiries from Wittenberg University and Baldwin Wallace University about applying for their President positions. Tressel soon decided to accept a position as Vice President of Strategic Engagement at the University of Akron. Looking back he reflects that, "It was a good decision. There's no way I could have been a college president without that Akron experience."

Tressel has been a very good fit at Youngstown State, where his efforts at recruiting and fundraising have made a noticeable difference. A December 2016 press release from the university reads:

"Under Tressel's leadership, YSU's enrollment is up for the first time in six years, and incoming freshmen have the highest standardized

test scores and grade-point averages in the university's history. Residence halls are at capacity, and the university spearheaded a private development plan for the construction of a 382-bed apartment complex and a new Barnes & Noble student bookstore on the West Side of campus. In addition, YSU approved its first operating budget in five years without a structural deficit and froze tuition to maintain its position as the most affordable public university in Ohio."

Being Buckeyeman

There is quite a Buckeye heritage in the family of Larry Lokai, better known as Buckeyeman. In 2017, Larry could count 22 Ohio State degrees in the extended Lokai family, plus six young Lokais in school on the Ohio State campuses.

Larry grew up on a farm in a tiny rural Ohio community. He recalls that, "a school field trip for us was going to church on Sunday!" In high school he was active in the Future Farmers of America, and while attending an FFA competition in Columbus he visited the Ohio State campus for the spring football game. Larry saw a world much larger than his farm, and after graduating from high school in 1961 he earned both a bachelor's degree in agriculture and master's of science from Ohio State. He taught high school agriculture classes for more than 30 years.

Larry's alter-ego, Buckeyeman, debuted in 1998. He landed front-row tickets to the Ohio State-Michigan game at Ohio Stadium and wanted to do something visually different. Enter the wild wig, face paint and animated antics. In 2000,

Maureen Zappala and Buckeyeman Larry Lokai
Courtesy Larry Lokai

he won a local "The Loudest Fan" contest sponsored by Halls cough drops. That win sent him to the national "Yell-Off" contest at the College Football Hall of Fame, located at that time in South Bend, Indiana. After placing third, his celebrity status with Buckeye fans catapulted. He has since become a mainstay at every Ohio State game.

His trademark face paint, hair and bulky buckeye necklaces are more than just fan props — they're symbolic. There are 13 stripes on his face for the 13 original colonies. His eight buckeye necklaces represent each of OSU's national titles. In 2016, his necklaces contained a total of 113 buckeyes, representing the 113 Ohio State-Michigan games to date. He adds a new one each year at the time of this great rivalry game.

The necklaces weigh a total of 7 pounds, representing Ohio State's seven Heisman Trophies. Each year he provides Ohio State with tens of thousands of buckeyes for freshman orientation.

Outside of being Buckeyeman, Larry has served as a poultry judge at 82 of Ohio's 88 county fairs, and provides 30 buckeye necklaces for poultry winners at each fair. He spends approximately 90 days a year with Buckeyeman-related activities that include visits to nursing homes, Ohio State student sendoffs, alumni club meetings and other community events. Larry is a robust 75 years old and thoroughly enjoys the pleasant expression on people's faces when he hands them a necklace. He plans to continue as Buckeyeman as long as his energy holds and it continues to be fun.

Caroline and Megan Piatt enjoy talking with Buckeyeman Larry Lokai. *Courtesy Jack Park*

Urban Meyer Was a Mascot!

When Emily (Moor) Williams, former OSU Brutus Buckeye mascot, heard Urban Meyer himself say that he had past mascot experience, she looked at him unsure of what she just heard, and said "Yah right, sure you did." Then she looked at his wife, Shelley, and said, "That can't be true, right?" Shelley nodded her head and said, "Yep! He was Swoop The Hawk (University of Utah's mascot) for part of a game back in 2003 when he coached there.

"The real Swoop was to have the traditional yearly unveiling of the student behind the costume at a Utah basketball game. Instead, the person who took off the mascot head in front of the large crowd was Urban!" Shelley continued on and said, "That was quite an undertaking to coordinate when you think about just convincing Urban to do it! He was such a good sport, though, and we're glad it all worked out! The crowd was entertained, and we developed a new appreciation for mascots."

Urban and Shelley

Urban Meyer as Utah's Swoop the Hawk. *Courtesy Shelley Meyer*

have pictures to prove it. Emily said, "You guys just made my day, possibly my year with this story! Who would have ever known?"

"Rudy"— The Inside Story

Daniel "Rudy" Ruettiger played high school football at Joliet Catholic High School in Joliet, Ill. Four years later he attended Holy Cross College for two years before transferring to Notre Dame in 1974 at age 26.

Ruettiger always had dreamed of playing football for the Fighting Irish, even though he was only 5'6" and 165 pounds. Notre Dame coach Ara Parseghian encouraged walk-ons from the student body. Through hard work and determination, Ruettiger became a member of the scout team in 1974.

Parseghian retired after the 1974 season and was replaced by Dan Devine. Ruettiger stayed on as a member of the 1975 scout team and was especially encouraged by assistant coach Merv Johnson.

Notre Dame defensive end Gene Smith. *Courtesy University of Notre Dame Athletic Department*

The Fighting Irish faced Georgia Tech on Nov. 8 in their last home game of 1975. With Notre Dame leading 24-3 and only 28 seconds remaining, defensive ends Gene Smith and Jay Case were replaced by two reserves. Veteran defensive line coach Joe Yonto had wanted all of his players to see the playing field. One of those two reserves entering play in the game's last 28 seconds was Ruettiger, who was experiencing his very first game action for the Fighting Irish.

Ruettiger was in for the final three plays of the afternoon. The first was a kickoff and the second an incomplete pass. On the last play, Ruettiger fittingly helped sack Georgia Tech quarterback Rudy Allen. As a tribute to Ruettiger's effort and dedication, his teammates joyfully carried him off the field. Ruettinger's story was later told in the 1993 film, *Rudy*, starring actor Sean Astin.

Gene Smith graduated from Notre Dame in 1977, and that year was an assistant coach on the school's national championship team. Smith entered athletic administration and served as Director of Athletics at Eastern Michigan, Iowa State, and Arizona State before being named to the same position at Ohio State in 2005. He was elevated to Senior Vice President and Wolfe Foundation Endowed Athletics Director in 2016. Smith has been recognized as "one of the most powerful people in collegiate sport." Ohio State sponsors 36 fully-funded varsity sports with more than 1,000 student athletes competing for Big Ten Conference and NCAA championships.

But one of Smith's biggest claims to fame remains the fact that he was once teammates with "Rudy."

THE Tailgate Spot

What started in 2005 as a few different groups of friends looking for a place to tailgate has taken on a life of its own. THE Tailgate Spot continues to grow since finding a permanent home at the corner of Lane and Neil avenues behind Tommy's Pizza. They host over 150 fans for some of the Buckeyes' biggest games. The Tailgate officially starts with the 'Joe Coyle Toast' in remembrance of a longtime Buckeye fan and father of one of the tailgate's organizers, Mike Coyle. Football, food, and fun are what THE Tailgate Spot is all about. Tailgate On!

Courtesy Mike Coyle

Appreciating the Military

Jim Tressel's support for the United States military is well known. While serving as Ohio State's head coach, he often found ways to honor the men and women who defended our country. He created a staff position of "Director of Military Appreciation" and spearheaded many events and privileges extended to the armed forces. In 2009, as part of the USO Coaches Tour, Tressel visited military troops in Germany, Turkey, Iraq, Kuwait, Djibouti and Spain.

In 2010, Tressel was recognized with the Patrick Henry Award, an honor bestowed by the National Guard to a civilian who has shown extended and extraordinary support for the United States military. The 2011 Ohio State Spring Football Game was dubbed the Military Appreciation game, and Tressel replaced his trademark sweater vest with a military-issue camo hat, tan desert boots and camo pants. The coaching staff followed his lead, and all players wore camouflage helmets.

Columbus resident Beth Siracuse is the daughter of retired Air Force Colonel George Siracuse. In 2011, she was an Associate Vice President of Nationwide Better Health. One of her co-workers was Jennifer Romanoff Critchfield, daughter of Larry Romanoff, Director of External Affairs for Ohio State Football, and then-wife of Buckeye All-American tackle Kirk Barton. Beth is not an Ohio State graduate. She earned an MBA at the University of Southern California, which can make for a lonely football cheering season in Ohio. However, she admits you can't help but be absorbed into the Buckeye world while living in Columbus. She relates this wonderful story:

Retired Air Force Colonel George Siracuse with Jim Tressel
Courtesy Beth Siracuse

> *"In May, 2011, my dad came to visit. He's a former college football player, decorated veteran, Distinguished Flying Cross recipient, and was sporting his USAF Vet hat. While in a restaurant, we ran into Kirk Barton, who at the time was on the OSU coaching staff. Kirk commented on my dad's hat and then invited us to the Woody Hayes Center for a little tour. I knew my dad would love all the trophies, the chalkboard of Woody's handwriting, the equipment and the military wing.*
>
> *We arrived at the center, and Kirk led us down the recruiting hall with all the trophies, player profiles, golden pants and the *ichigan countdown clock. As Kirk and my dad swapped stories, we arrived at the military wing. They talked about Coach Tressel's affinity for the military, and his father's (Lee Tressel) Naval service. I watched the colliding of two worlds, military and sports, the commitment and pride. It was moving.*
>
> *We continue the tour into the team meeting room, marveling at how cool it was to be in this room. Kirk then weaves us around and through a door … BAM — we're in the middle of Jim Tressel's office! Jim walked from behind his desk, reached to shake my dad's hand and thanked him. I froze in awe. I noticed Jim slipped a shiny silver object into my dad's hand. They talked about my dad's military service, and Jim's coaches' tour to visit the troops overseas.*
>
> *The mutual admiration could be felt throughout the room. Jim's phone buzzed a few times, and he would look down, stating that it was recruiting time. But for that moment, Tressel's admiration for the military trumped football. As we left, my dad said, 'Bethie, that's why he is so respected. He takes a genuine interest in people. He respects you and you feel honored to have his respect.'*

The shiny object Tressel handed to Siracuse was a medallion, about two inches across, that he gives to veterans as a sign of his respect. One side shows the Ohio State emblem and the other says "It's a privilege to be a member of this Ohio State Football Family. Practice Like a Champion." Beth said, "It may be small, but to my dad, it was a huge gift."

Just a short time later, on Monday, May 30, 2011, Tressel would tender his resignation after 10 years as Ohio State's head coach. That day also happened to be

Memorial Day, the day we remember the members of the U.S. Armed Forces who died serving our country. The irony may be lost on Tressel. He went on to become the President of Youngstown State University, which is recognized as a Military Friendly® school, a place where veterans and military are welcomed to pursue their educational goals. YSU's commitment to honoring the military clearly is in line with Tressel's. It's a perfect match.

Brutus — Was He Ever a Female?

Emily (Moor) Williams with mother Marilyn. *Courtesy Emily (Moor) Williams*

Emily (Moor) Williams is the only female to be Brutus Buckeye since 1983, a sport she relished for more than two years before graduating from Ohio State in 2003. Her mascot career started as a Bulldog at Elida High School in Lima, Ohio. She recalls how Brutus candidates go through a rigorous tryout process, competing on strength, endurance, creativity, and professionalism.

Emily's most exciting moment as Brutus was cheering on the crowd in the Fiesta Bowl when the Buckeyes captured the 2002 national title. She vividly remembers rolling around in confetti on the field after the win. She also has fond memories of the "Holy Buckeye" Krenzel-to-Jenkins game-winning touchdown pass at Purdue earlier that season. Emily's mother, Marilyn Moor, a registered nurse at Ohio State, was her biggest fan and never missed a game.

Brutus doesn't have a particular season — it's nonstop and involves many other sports and active community service. Emily often shares her story about Sam DeLong, a complete stranger who passed away from cancer in the early 2000s. Sam was a young Buckeye fan, and Emily recalls giving him the wristbands from her Brutus uniform. "It was heart-breaking, and I'm just glad I could put a smile on his face in his final days by showing up to his house as Brutus," she recalls. Emily has continued to remain in contact with DeLong's siblings.

Realizing there was an unmet need for helping young people who aspire to become high school and college mascots, Emily and her brother, Jeff Moor, initiated Brutus Mascot Camp — a single-day summer program that reveals the elements of being a mascot. Proceeds from the camp support "The Brutus Fund" at Ohio State, which was started by Emily and Jeff to benefit Ohio State mascot scholarships.

Emily works in healthcare management in Columbus. Her husband, Jerry Williams, enjoys the "Brutus afterlife" with her and strongly supports the program. Jerry believes that, "Brutus is the top ambassador for the university, so it's perfect to support the Buckeyes through Brutus."

One of Ohio State's Highest Honors

Script Ohio celebrated its 80th anniversary in October of 2016. This "most memorable tradition in college band history" culminates in the ceremonial dotting of the "i" by a senior sousaphone player. Additionally, as Buckeye fans know, an invitation to be an honorary i dotter is the highest honor bestowed by the band. Only 15 times since 1971 has this privilege been extended. Richard Heine and Paul Droste are the only former members of the band to receive this honor.

1971: OSU President Novice Fawcett (1956-1972) and his wife, Marjorie, in recognition of his impending retirement.

1974: Longtime Marching Band composer and arranger Richard Heine.

1978: Comedian and Ohio native Bob Hope.

1979: Former Band Director Jack Evans and his wife Carol.

1983: Former coach Woody Hayes.

1984: Former Band Director Paul Droste and his wife Anne.

1985: Former Ohio State Ticket Director Robert Ries.

1990: Former Heavyweight Boxing Champion James "Buster" Douglas.

1995: OSU President E. Gordon Gee and his wife Constance.

2003: The 13 seniors of the 2002 Ohio State national title team, during a postseason championship celebration in Ohio Stadium on Jan. 18.

Coach Earle Bruce with family before dotting the i in Script Ohio on October 1, 2016. *Courtesy Jim Davidson*

2006: Golfer Jack Nicklaus.

2009: Senator John Glenn and wife Annie, appropriately during the 2009 OSU-Navy game.

2011: Les Wexner, Ohio State alumnus, donor, and CEO of Limited Brands.

2011: Band Director Jon Woods upon his impending retirement after 38 seasons with the band.

2016: Former coach Earle Bruce.

Government Intervention

In 2013, the rivalry between Ohio State and Michigan reached to the highest level of state government. On Friday, Nov. 29, 2013, the day before the much-anticipated game at Michigan Stadium (OSU was ranked No. 3), Ohio Governor John Kasich intensified the rivalry in a fun way. Kasich posted a resolution on his twitter account declaring Nov. 30 as "Scarlet Letter Saturday," and asked fans to boycott the letter M.

The response was immediate and dramatic, as students used red tape to cover up nearly every letter M on campus. Building signs, historical plaques, road signs, and even social media posts all sported the letter M X'ed out. The game was closer than expected. The Buckeyes won, 42-41, after stopping a Michigan two-point conversion attempt with 32 seconds left in the game.

Each year since 2013, the governor's office issues a similar resolution and fans rally to support the resolution.

STATE OF OHIO

Executive Department

OFFICE OF THE GOVERNOR

Columbus

RESOLUTION

WHEREAS, since 2013 the State of Ohio has proclaimed the day of The Game "Scarlet Letter Saturday" and urged Ohioans to avoid using the 13th letter of the alphabet on that day; and

WHEREAS, this year's game marks the ten year anniversary of Heisman Trophy winning quarterback Troy Smith leading the number one ranked Buckeyes over their number two ranked opponents by a score of 42-39 in the "Game of the Century"; and

WHEREAS, by virtue of their high rankings in the College Football Playoff standings, impressive strengths of schedule, and the superior play of the B1G conference, the 2016 matchup between Ohio-born coaches Urban Meyer and Jim Harbaugh is a virtual playoff game; and

WHEREAS, Meyer is seeking to win his second national championship at Ohio State and Harbaugh is hoping to win that school's first since winning ½ of the 1997 title; and

WHEREAS, many Ohio State fans will celebrate by going out to dinner Saturday night, though none will drink milk with their steak like the coach of the visiting team does; and

WHEREAS, when the outcome is decided on Saturday, it will be more decisive than a ruling by Judge Judy, who the visiting coach believes should be on the Supreme Court.

NOW, THEREFORE, We, John R. Kasich and Mary **Taylor, Governor and Lieutenant Governor of the State of Ohio,** do hereby recognize November 26, 2016 as

SCARLET LETTER SATURDAY

throughout the state of Ohio and encourage all Ohioans to avoid using the letter M, and to cheer on The Ohio State University Buckeyes to victory in the 113th edition of The Game.

On this 25th day of November 2016;

John R. Kasich
Governor

Mary Taylor
Lieutenant Governor

Football is a Family Affair

James and Margaret Griffin raised seven sons and a daughter. All seven sons played college football: James, Jr. at Muskingum College; Larry at the University of Louisville; Daryle at Kent State University; Archie, Ray and Duncan at The Ohio State University; and Keith at Miami (Fla.). Daughter Krystal ran track at Drake University and Wayne State College in Nebraska. The accompanying picture was taken in July of 2017 when more than 60 relatives attended the Griffin family reunion.

Left to right: Ray, Daryle, Keith, Larry, Krystal, Duncan and Archie. *Courtesy Duncan Griffin*

"Big Nut" Pays Forward

At an athletic booster fundraiser contest sponsored by Ross High School in Freemont, Ohio, and just before the 1995 Ohio State-Michigan game, Jon Peters entered a best-dressed fan contest with his eye on winning the grand prize — a three-and-a-half-foot high Buckeye snowman, an item he thought would be perfect for his man cave. He really wanted to win it, but remembered that the competition was tough. Many of the older women were wearing fancy stitched cardigan sweaters and matching stitched pants and he wanted to beat them. That's when he decided to paint his face. It worked, and he was lucky enough to win the snowman! In fact, he won it two years in a row.

It seemed fitting. Jon has been a Buckeye fan nearly his whole life. As a young boy living on a farm with his grandfather, who was a 1932 Ohio State graduate, Jon listened to the games on the radio while doing chores. His attended his first game in 1976 — the game of all games against "that team up north." Unfortunately the Buckeyes lost, 22-0, but he still felt the magic and power of the Buckeye Nation.

Jon's first appearance as Big Nut was at the Fiesta Bowl national title game on Jan. 3, 2003 — a magical night for Buckeye fans. Originally, he had planned to paint up for the previous evening's pep rally but not the game. Jon recalls that, "People at the pep rally wanted their picture taken with me. I couldn't understand it because I'm just a fat guy with face paint! I then decided to also paint up for the game. I was so blessed and honored to be included on the championship DVD. That's how it all started."

After a few years of appearing at Ohio State events, Jon found that people wanted to pay him for the buckeye nut necklaces he gave them. He preferred giving them for free and didn't feel right pocketing the money. Jon considered giving the money to cancer or Alzheimer's research, and a friend suggested starting a scholarship program. It took a year to get the non-profit organization running. Through 2016, his organization has awarded 30 separate $500 scholarships for a total of $15,000. His Big Nut activities have become the engine for funding the scholarships. Jon was raised in a church-going family that taught him to do the right thing. What started as a way to make people laugh and smile has become so much more — a way for him to pay forward — and he hopes to build it into an endowment that will benefit children long after he is gone. The 500-word application stresses both academic achievement and the need for community involvement.

Big Nut is not a one-man operation. He partners with his wife, Terese, who he affectionately calls "First Lady Nut." First Lady is Jon's rock and he couldn't do this without her. She does his makeup, which takes about 90 minutes. They live in Fremont, two hours from Columbus, and need to get up at 4:30 a.m. for a game with a noon start. Behind the scenes, Terese orders the supplies and keeps things running smoothly.

Jon is a blue-collar factory worker without a college education. Terese and their son and daughter are all college educated, but

Big Nut Jon Peters and Maureen Zappala. *Courtesy Jack Park*

Jon is the one who most stresses education. He always wanted a degree from Ohio State but just could not make it happen. Helping make a college education become a reality for others is a big driver behind what he does. Jon models his philosophy after Woody Hayes who always stressed the importance of "paying forward." He looks up to Archie Griffin who had raised a lot of funds for his own scholarship programs. Jon believes that being a Buckeye is about helping others, and he just wants to do the right thing.

The-Ozone, a Pioneer in Journalism

The-Ozone was founded on Oct. 31, 1996, with the sole purpose of providing information on Ohio State athletics through the Internet. The founders were John Porentas, Robert C. Bradlee and Theodore R. Saker. Porentas had a strong passion for Ohio State athletics and Bradlee brought technical expertise. Saker was a practicing attorney and provided administrative skills. The founders hoped to attract at least 100 visitors when the site went operational. To their astonishment, the number of visitors was in the tens of thousands in the first month of operation.

While the public immediately accepted the site, things were very different with Ohio State, the Big Ten Conference and the NCAA. Internet coverage at that time was virtually non-existent and it was difficult to gain acceptance as a legitimate part of the media. The-Ozone persisted and eventually became the first website to be credentialed as media at Ohio State.

As the internet was becoming an established medium for sports news, The-Ozone was invited to become a part of both the Rivals Sports Network and the Scout Sports Network. Despite the overtures, The-Ozone remained independent because its underlying philosophy of remaining free to all Buckeye fans conflicted with the subscription model of the networks. It was during this period that Porentas purchased the shares of Bradlee and Saker and became the sole owner of The-Ozone.

As The-Ozone grew, so did internet competition. All traditional media outlets established an internet presence and other independent sites emerged to cover Ohio State athletics. Newspapers, television stations, radio stations and magazines all became internet competitors. After more than 20 years of service, The-Ozone remains free of charge to all visitors as it continues to grow and provide fans with daily coverage of Ohio State sports. It can be accessed at http://theozone.net.

Ohio State Benefits from the Dover-New Philadelphia Rivalry

Dover and New Philadelphia are two neighboring Ohio cities in Tuscarawas County east of Columbus. The two share a border and their combined population is approximately 30,000. Their high school football rivalry is one of the longest and strongest in any state across the county. It was selected the "best small town football rivalry" by *USA Today*. Since their first meeting in 1896, the two have faced off 113 times through the 2016 season. Dover holds a slight edge at 55-49-9.

In 1949, New Philadelphia defeated Dover 27-6. The New Philadelphia quarterback was junior Dave Leggett, while Dover was quarterbacked by freshman Frank Ellwood. New Philadelphia won again in 1950, 19-12. Leggett again directed his team but Ellwood was unable to play because of injury.

After high school, both Leggett and Ellwood were recruited by Woody Hayes to play at Ohio State. During his senior season of 1954, Leggett quarterbacked Ohio State to an outright Big Ten title as well as the national championship. The following season of 1955, Ellwood (a junior) quarterbacked the Buckeyes to a second-consecutive outright Big Ten title. It was the first time the Buckeyes were able to claim back-to-back outright league championships since the 1916-17 seasons.

Dave Leggett and Frank Ellwood. *Courtesy Ohio State University Photo Archives*

Ellwood wore jersey No. 24 because his older brother, Dick, had worn that number as a member of Ohio State's 1949 Rose Bowl championship team. The 1955 season was also special for OSU fans with halfback Howard "Hopalong" Cassady winning the Heisman Trophy.

Shelley Graf. *Courtesy Shelley Graf*

A Marching Band First

In 1981, Shelley Graf became the first female Drum Major to lead the Ohio State University Marching Band, and the first female Drum Major in the Big Ten Conference.

Born and raised in Sugar Grove, Ohio, Graf began twirling a rubber-tipped baton at age 7. In her teenage years, she participated in baton competitions and ultimately became the head majorette at Berne Union High School for three years. Shelley entered Ohio State in 1978, majoring in physical therapy. She knew Dwight Hudson, who was one of Ohio State's most highly respected drum majors, and she often sought guidance from Hudson about the drum major position.

In 1979, Shelley became a member of the drum major squad and was able to learn the responsibilities of the position. She was named assistant drum major in 1980, another first for The Ohio State University Marching Band before being named drum major in 1981.

Shelley's time as drum major provided many fascinating, unique and outstanding memories for her. The mayor of her hometown of Sugar Grove proclaimed a "Shelley Graf Day." Festivities included a parade and an awards banquet. The village also placed signs at the entrance to the town stating its claim to fame — Shelley Graf. She was honored by the Ohio Legislature, where Senator Marigene Valiquette presented a resolution in honor of being the first female drum major at The Ohio State University. One of Shelley's proudest accomplishments is having a photo of her leading the band that hangs in the College Football Hall of Fame band section in Atlanta.

Shelley graduated from The Ohio State University in 1983 with a bachelor's degree in physical therapy. She continues to perform each year at the alumni reunion game. One of Shelley's most memorable honors was leading Dr. Paul Droste (director of OSUMB when she was drum major) and his wife, Anne, out to dot the "i" in Script Ohio after he retired from the band in 1984. Shelley is a physical therapist and manager of the Acute Care Rehabilitation at The Ohio State University Wexner Medical Center. She lives in Columbus with her fiancée, Craig Campbell, and her two dogs, Seamus and Daphne.

Like Father Like Son

Dick and Jeff Logan are one of many father-son duos who played football at Ohio State. Dick was from Mansfield and played tackle from 1949 through 1951. Wes Fesler was his coach his first two years and his senior season of 1951 was Woody Hayes's first year as head coach. The 1949 Buckeyes were the first Ohio State team to win the Rose Bowl and

Dick and Jeff Logan. *Courtesy Ohio State University Photo Archives*

the 1950 team concluded its season with the noted "Snow Bowl" against Michigan.

Son Jeff was from Canton and played tailback and fullback four seasons from 1974 through 1977. Ohio State won outright or shared the Big Ten title each of those four years. Jeff was Ohio State's leading rusher in 1976 with 1,248 yards on 218 carries with six touchdowns. His career totals are 2,026 yards on 349 carries with 12 TDs. His senior year he was chosen All-Big Ten and was an Academic All-American.

Some of the other father-son dues who played for the Buckeyes include Burke and Bill Wentz, Howard and Craig Cassady, Jim Houston and Jim Houston, Jr., Jim and Kirk Herbstreit, Archie and Andre and Adam Griffin, Pepper and Dionte Johnson, and Stan White and Stan White, Jr.

Explaining the Rivalry

Bruce Madej enjoyed a fine career with the University of Michigan Department of Athletics that spanned nearly 36 years from 1978 through 2014. Madej was highly respected as one of the finest Directors of Athletic Communications throughout the country.

John U. Bacon and Jack Park. *Courtesy Jack Park*

Madej is now a Lecturer at the University of Michigan School of Education, and teaches a 3-credit class titled The History of Intercollegiate Athletics. On the Monday prior to the 2016 Ohio State-Michigan game, Madej invited good friends John U. Bacon and Jack Park to conduct a class on the history of this great rivalry. The two shared stories of trends in the series, great games that had an impact on national titles, and of course the "Ten Year War" between coaches Woody Hayes and Bo Schembechler. The class was live streamed and archived for later viewings.

The class was highly rated by the students. Bacon and Park have accepted an invitation to repeat the class in 2017.

On the Air

Radio has played a major role in bringing the enjoyment of college football to fans of all ages. The very first game to be broadcast was the University of Pittsburgh's 21-13 victory over West Virginia University on Oct. 8, 1921. The contest was played at old Forbes Field near the Pitt campus, and was carried by station KDKA with Harold W. Arlin doing the announcing. The first game to be nationally aired was Princeton's 21-18 win at Chicago on Oct. 28, 1922. Chicago station KYW fed the broadcast to station WEAF in New York city, and from there to the remainder of the nation.

The first Ohio State game to be broadcast was the first game played in newly constructed Ohio Stadium on Oct. 7, 1922. Station WEAO carried the play-by-play of OSU's 5-0 win over Ohio Wesleyan.

Authors Jack Park and Maureen Zappala on the Sports Radio 97.1 The Fan set prior to the 2016 Ohio State-Michigan game. Left to right, Emily Everett, Beanie Wells, Bobby Carpenter, Anthony Rothman, and Jay Taylor. *Courtesy Jim Davidson*

The station's call letters were changed to WOSU in 1931. For many decades through the 1983 season, many Columbus radio stations all did their own individual broadcasts of Ohio State football, as did some stations in Cleveland and Cincinnati.

Beginning with the 1984 season, WBNS Radio in Columbus (now Sports Radio 97.1 The Fan) was awarded the exclusive right to broadcast the games and

Big Ten Football Media Days 2016 in Chicago. Executive Producer Skip Mosic, Play-By-Play Announcer Paul Keels and Color Analyst Jim Lachey interview Iowa Head Coach Kirk Ferentz. *Courtesy Jack Park*

syndicate the action to approximately 75 affiliated stations throughout the state on The Ohio State Football Radio Network. Pregame and postgame shows provide additional information and enjoyment for the fans.

Gate Crasher Extraordinaire

Jerry Marlowe developed quite a reputation as a creative gate-crasher during home games against Michigan. He began his outrageous stunts in the 1970s and continued through the 1990s. His inventive disguises included imitating a marching band director, referee, TV cameraman, team doctor, Boy Scout, nun, and pizza delivery man. It was all in fun, and the Ohio Stadium ushers took it as a challenge

Jerry Marlowe. *Courtesy Jack Park*

to identify him before he was able to gain entrance to the stadium. After the games Marlowe always made a cash contribution to the athletic department that exceeded the value of a ticket.

Marlowe graduated from Ohio State in 1961. He retired in 2017 after 56 years of operating the Marlowe family pharmacy in Dover, Ohio.

Candidate No. 26 Meets Quarterback No. 26

In the early 1960s, Homecoming Queen candidates performed musical skits and passed out their photos at the mens' dormatories and fraternities before the elections. In 1962, Canfield Hall candidate Linda Nelson always had wanted to meet Buckeye quarterback Bill Mrukowski. When she performed her skit at the Kappa Sigma fraternity house, Bill was sitting in the front row. Linda sang her last song and gave Bill her picture.

Bill kept Linda's photo, and after that year's Ohio State-Michigan game — which the Buckeyes won 28-0 — he called her for a date. Bill later learned that Linda had been queen candidate #26, which was Bill's football jersey number. They both had July birthdays; Bill's was on the 26th. After they dated and married in 1965, they always considered 26 to be their lucky number.

To this day, Linda continues to drive her car with license plate: MRUK 26. Though Linda did not become the Homecoming queen, she won something far more lasting — the love of her favorite quarterback.

Top: Homecoming queen candidate Linda Nelson. Above: Bill and Linda attended games home and away through their 47 years of marriage. Bill passed away in 2012. Linda still attends all the games. *Courtesy Linda Mrukowski*

Humorous Moments from TBDBITL

Dr. Paul E. Droste was director of The Ohio State Marching Band from 1970 through early 1984 and marched with the band during his undergraduate days of 1954-57. Paul shares some of his favorite band stories that have evolved over the years:

1. Eugene Weigel was director from 1929 through 1938. Rather than use paper charts to illustrate the halftime formations, Weigel would pace off every position for each of the 120 band members. This was very time consuming, and on cold afternoons band members would often build small fires on the practice field to keep warm.

2. Band rehearsals under director Jack Evans (1952-1963) ended promptly at 6 p.m. One evening Evans called for a run through of the ramp entrance at 5:55 p.m., a very unpopular directive since this would mean overtime and the ramp entrance had been rehearsed earlier that afternoon. The band was slow to line up, making Evans upset. It was already dark and Evans was running

Paul and Anne Droste dot the i in Script Ohio on Sept. 8, 1984. *Courtesy Ohio State University Photo Archives*

the practice from the stadium's B deck. The entire sousaphone section reversed their bells and marched backwards down the field with the bells pointed forward. Evans never noticed!

3. Charles Spohn was an Assistant Director when rehearsals were held at Rehearsal Hall on the corner of 19th and Neil avenues. The facility was an old barn with a door large enough to allow a tractor to unload inside. Several band members carried Spohn's Isanti (a microcar) through the door and angled it so that he could not drive it out. After the rehearsal Spohn had to beg/threaten/bribe some band members to carry out his car so that he could drive home.

4. Droste had a fool-proof system to prevent him from dropping his conductor's baton while in uniform. Spohn would cut a small hole in the right hand first finger of his band glove, then insert the baton into the glove. However, he had to be especially careful any time he tried to shake someone's hand or render a salute. The baton almost became a lethal weapon.

Woody Controls the Weather

Duncan Griffin remembers a practice on a cold and rainy afternoon during the 1975 season. The team had taken a bus from the nearby athletic facility to practice inside Ohio Stadium. Because of the pouring rain, Coach Woody Hayes had all the players remain on the bus. Hayes walked out to the center of the stadium field, put his hands together above his head and then pulled them apart. Suddenly the rain stopped! After the completion of a two-hour practice, the rain returned. People often said Hayes could even control the weather! Duncan and his teammates saw it happen.

Beating the Traffic

The Schiermeier Olentangy River Wetland (ORW) Research Park is located by Dodridge Street north of the Ohio State campus. Dr. Jerry Pausch was Chairman of the ORW advisory committee for several years, beginning in 1995. Jerry and wife, Lenora, in 2007 donated a pontoon boat named the ORW Natalie, in memory of their daughter.

Dr. Jerry Pausch and friends attend OSU's opener by boat in 2010. *Courtesy Dr. Jerry Pausch*

One of Ohio State's most dedicated longtime followers, Jerry decided it would be fun to go to an Ohio State football game by boat. Jerry, Professor Bill Mitsch and a couple of friends rode the ORW Natalie approximately 1 mile from the wetlands to attend the 2010 season opener against Marshall on Thursday evening, Sept. 2.

The ride down the Olentangy River was covered on local live news television. They landed close to a large sycamore tree adjacent to the 50-yard line. It is believed to be the first time fans ever attended a game at Ohio Stadium by boat. *The Columbus Dispatch* called it a good way to beat the traffic!

Alumni Support from Far and Wide

The Ohio State University Alumni Association is one of the very largest and most active in the country. Chapter events often include "TV watch parties" of football and basketball in their cities, and chapter excursions to Columbus to attend an Ohio State football game.

Left to right, former Ohio State linebacker Jim Laughlin, Coach Bob Tucker, Coach Bill Conley, Coach Earle Bruce, Jack Park, Buckeye Sports Bulletin Publisher Frank Moskowitz and Bill Gue. *Courtesy Jack Park*

Many members of the Atlanta Chapter travel to Columbus for several games each season. The group is led by Ohio State alum Bill Gue, past president of the club and one of Ohio State's most supportive alums. Their football weekend in Columbus begins with Friday evening dinner at a fine Columbus restaurant. Some Columbus area alums and past coaches who are close to the Ohio State football program are often invited. The photo on the previous page was taken at an Atlanta Chapter dinner in Columbus the evening prior to the Michigan State game on Nov. 20, 2015.

Left to right, James Warvel, Schlegel, Byers Vice President George Kauffman, Scott Basinger and Ben Neidenthal. *Courtesy Jack Park*

Fan Favorites

Ohio State fans always enjoy reminiscing with former Buckeye coaches and players. One very popular fan experience is an autograph and photo opportunity with a different former player prior to each home game. The activity takes place on the south side of St. John Arena and is sponsored by the Byers Auto Group. The accompanying picture was taken prior to the UNLV game on Sept. 23, 2017, when former linebacker Anthony Schlegel met and talked with fans attending the game.

Football Boosts the Banquets

Most Ohio State Alumni Association Chapters hold an annual banquet to celebrate the year's activities and raise money for student scholarships. Former football players and coaches often are requested as keynote speakers for these dinners, partly to help encourage chapter members to attend. There likely is not a chapter in the country that would not like to have Urban Meyer or Archie Griffin as its keynote speaker.

Authors Jack Park and Maureen Zappala enjoyed attending the Cleveland Chapter's 2016 banquet, held at the popular Windows on the River. The Ohio State Alumni Band played during the social hour. Following dinner, the

Left to right, former players John Conroy, Mike Kudla, Rob Sims, Adrien Clarke and T.J. Downing. *Courtesy Jack Park*

members were thoroughly entertained as five former players shared many of their memories and experiences while playing for the Scarlet and Gray.

Quarterback Club

The Columbus Dispatch Quarterback Club was founded in 1984 as a support group for Ohio State football and head coach Earle Bruce. The club meets for lunch weekly during the football season to hear the head coach and selected assistant coaches analyze the past week's game and preview the upcoming opponent. Coaches John Cooper, Jim Tressel, Luke Fickell and Urban Meyer have continued their support of the club's loyal members, who celebrated the organization's 33th year in 2016.

Left to right, Bobby Joseph, Archie Griffin, Coach Urban Meyer, Bill Cairnes, President Bruce Peterson, Coach Earle Bruce, Patrick Smith, Pete Johnson and Ron Rotaru. *Courtesy Bruce Peterson*

The club was founded by the late Samuel Farb, the late David Thompson, Patrick Smith and Robert (Bobby) Joseph. It is a proud donor each year to the Urban and Shelley Meyer Cancer Research Fund. The club is proud of its diverse membership and welcomes new members who want to support Ohio State football. Inquiries about membership can be addressed to Patrick Smith at (614)794-9955.

Coming Home

Over the years, no fewer than 15 Ohio State assistants have returned to face the Buckeyes as the opposing team's head coach.

One of the best remembered is Bo Schembechler, who had been a five-year assistant to Woody Hayes from 1958 through 1962. Bo guided the Michigan Wolverines 21 seasons from 1969 through 1989, achieving an 11-9-1 record against the Buckeyes.

Schembechler's first 10 seasons at Michigan were Hayes' last 10 at Ohio State, and those contests (known as the Ten-Year War) were some of the most electrifying and intense ever played. Schembechler attained a slight edge over his old mentor at 5-4-1.

Mark Dantonio, former OSU defensive coordinator under Jim Tressel from 2001-03, became head coach at Michigan State in 2007. Since taking charge of the Spartan program his teams are 3-5 against OSU through 2016. As head coach at Cincinnati from 2004 through 2006, Dantonio lost twice to the Buckeyes.

Bill Mallory, a three-year Hayes assistant from 1966-68, led Colorado against Ohio State in the Jan. 1, 1977 Orange Bowl (won by OSU 27-10). He also faced the Buckeyes 13 times as head coach at Indiana. In 1998, Nick Saban's Michigan State

Spartans handed OSU one of its most painful setbacks, 28-24. It was the Buckeyes' only loss that season, and it prevented OSU from playing in the national championship game. Saban had been a member of Earle Bruce's coaching staff in 1980-81.

Coach Lou Holtz, defensive backfield assistant for Ohio State's 1968 national champions, directed three different schools against the Scarlet and Gray. Holtz's South Carolina Gamecocks recorded consecutive victories over the Buckeyes in the Outback Bowl at the end of the 2000 and 2001 seasons. OSU twice defeated Holtz's Notre Dame teams in 1995-96, and also recorded victories over his Minnesota Golden Gopher squads in 1984-85.

Other Ohio State assistants who have returned to face the Buckeyes as the opposing team's head coach include Tim Beckman at both Toledo and Illinois, Gary Blackney at Bowling Green, Jim Colletto and Darrell Hazel at Purdue, Minnesota's Glen Mason, Dave McClain at Wisconsin, Ron Zook at Illinois, Larry Coker at Miami (Fla.), Chris Ash at Rutgers, and Akron's Lee Owens. Jim Tressel's first game at Ohio State was a 28-14 victory over Owen's Akron squad on Sept. 8, 2001.

Seven Ohio State head coaches had been OSU assistants prior to being named to the top position — Luke Fickell (2011), Tressel (2001-2010), Bruce (1979-87), Wes Fesler (1947-50), Paul Bixler (1946), Carroll Widdoes (1944-45), and Sam Willaman (1929-1933). Urban Meyer was a graduate assistant to Bruce in 1986-87.

Fesler, Willaman, and Meyer also faced Ohio State as opposing head coaches. In 1946, Fesler's Pitt Panthers lost to OSU 20-13. Willaman's Western Reserve team was humiliated 76-0 by the Buckeyes in 1934 at old League Park in Cleveland. Meyer's second-rated Florida Gators denied the top-ranked Buckeyes the 2006 national title with a stunning 41-14 victory in the BCS Championship Game.

Buckeye Boosters

An Ohio State support group was created in 1955 to provide fans with an organized way of attending the 1955 Rose Bowl between the Buckeyes and Southern California. Bill Wickes founded the group as a way to support the Ohio State football teams at the Rose Bowl. Led by Wickes and then President John Otto, the organization officially became the Buckeye Boosters in 1960. The Ohio State Athletic Department needed a group that would both support the football program and generate revenue through various activities and events.

President Butch Moore, Mike Schoedinger, Coach Urban Meyer, Paul Ballinger, Pete Fingerhut, Jim Smith. *Courtesy Butch Moore*

Buckeye Boosters

travel to all away football games and bowl games, hold an annual golf outing and support a football kickoff dinner each season. Throughout the years the organization has averaged nearly 1,000 members a year, and has generated more than $5 million for the Ohio State Athletic Department.

Richard "Dick" Smith became President in 1984 and directed the organization with much success until his passing in 2013. The baton was then handed to Butch Moore, who as President presides over an 11-member Board of Directors. Donations have both benefitted the football program and the entire athletic department in a variety of ways. A $200,000 donation helped renovate and update the football team meeting room at the Woody Hayes Athletic Center, and the organization donated $250,000 to assist the baseball program with the construction of Bill Davis Stadium.

Master of Memorabilia

Brian Fogle is not only one of Ohio State's most avid memorabilia collectors, he owns one of college football's most extensive collections. Brian has been hooked on the Buckeyes since he was a child. His grandfather took him to his first game in 1975, when he had the unforgettable experience of meeting both Woody Hayes and Archie Griffin.

Because of his love and passion for Ohio State, Brian has been collecting memorabilia for more than 25 years. He owns an Ohio State jacket that has been autographed by nearly 300 of the Buckeyes' greatest players. Among his many other

Brian Fogle. *Courtesy Brian Fogle*

prized possessions is a program and ticket stub from Chic Harley's last Ohio State game against Illinois on Nov. 22, 1919.

Confessions of an OSU Usher

Ushers play major roles at Ohio Stadium, helping fans find their seats and enjoy a safe and fun environment. Trevor Zahara, who has been an Ohio Stadium usher since 1997, wrote a most interesting book titled *Confessions of an OSU Usher* that was published in 2014. The book describes many humorous, heartwarming and amazing stories from inside Ohio Stadium. Trevor reveals some of the most unusual and captivating experiences of this very dedicated group of ushers and redcoats. He has also learned many interesting stories from season ticket holders, boy scout ushers, coaches, band members and many dedicated fans. One of his favorite stories describes six students dressed in gorilla suits doing a pyramid in the end zone during a game.

Trevor is a proud 1971 graduate of The Ohio State University and an Army

Author and Usher/Redcoat Trevor Zahara is a frequent speaker for Ohio State Alumni Association chapters. *Courtesy Trevor Zahara*

Dennis Parks is one of many ushers/redcoats who have served the Ohio State football program with distinction. Dennis began in 2001. *Courtesy Jack Park*

veteran. He was one of the ushers honored on military appreciation day during a game against Illinois on Nov. 10, 2007. He considers himself a novice compared with 12 peers who were honored during the Wisconsin game on Nov. 3, 2007, for their 50-plus years of service as ushers.

Trevor has missed only one game since 1997 — and that was to attend his daughter's wedding on Saturday, Oct. 7, 2006 while the Buckeyes were defeating Bowling Green, 35-7. He was shadowed by WBNS-10TV's Bryant Sommerville during the 2017 spring game for an interview describing his and other ushers' experiences at Ohio Stadium.

Corso's Admiration for Woody

Ohio State's game at Indiana in 1978 was one of the most competitive and evenly played between the two schools. Woody Hayes' Buckeyes entered the game at 6-2-1, while coach Lee Corso's Hoosiers were a better team than suggested by their 4-5 record. Corso had practiced his squad behind closed doors all week in an attempt to register IU's first victory over the Buckeyes since 1951 — the Hoosiers were 0-21-1 in their last 22 meetings with Ohio State.

Indiana Coach Lee Corso.
Courtesy Indiana University Department of Athletics

A Memorial Stadium crowd of 47,450 saw Ohio State come from behind for a narrow victory, 21-18, after trailing 10-7 at halftime. The Hoosiers had one last opportunity for the upset late in the final quarter. Pulling out all the stops, Corso called a pass play off of an end-around-reverse, with split end Mike Friede throwing deep into Ohio State territory. But Ohio State's Mike Guess wasn't fooled — he intercepted at the OSU 27-yard line to end IU's final threat with just 1:37 remaining.

Even though his team was defeated, Corso has fond memories of that particular afternoon and his relationship with Hayes. Corso's good friend and avid Hoosier fan, Al Carpenter, attended all the games and most of IU's practices. Carpenter, a teenager with cerebral palsy, watched most of the games from the IU bench.

As the Ohio State squad warmed up that afternoon, Carpenter asked Corso if it might be possible for Carpenter to meet Hayes. When the two head coaches met at midfield, Corso told Hayes about Carpenter and recalls how Hayes gladly went out of his way to talk with him. "It was heart-warming," Corso remembers. "He autographed Al's program and took such a sincere interest in speaking with him. Al could not have felt greater."

After Hayes finished, Carpenter graciously thanked Corso, who in turn kidded Carpenter by saying, "Al, I've known you for several years, and you've never asked me for *my* autograph." "That's right, coach," a joyous Carpenter replied, "but then, you're not Woody Hayes!"

Corso recalls when longtime Indiana assistant coach Howard Brown passed away in 1974, Hayes was the only other Big Ten coach to attend his funeral. Brown, a guard, had been selected the Hoosier's MVP in '45 and '47. A plaque recognizing Brown's dedication to Indiana football is proudly displayed in IU's Memorial Stadium.

Corso also vividly remembers the morning in 1982 when he was fired following his 10th season with the Hoosiers. "Mrs. Anne Hayes was the very first person to call my wife, Betsy," he said. "Mrs. Hayes offered a lot of warmth and encouragement, and wanted us to know it wasn't the end of the world. In our book, Woody and Anne Hayes were two very special people."

As the teams left the Indiana playing field late that afternoon of Nov. 18, 1978, no one could have realized that Woody Hayes had just coached his final victory. The Buckeyes would play two more games, and Hayes' outstanding 28-year career as their head coach would end abruptly following the Gator Bowl. Hayes finished with an Ohio State record of 205-61-10.

A Record Like No Other

John Crawford attended a remarkable 455 consecutive games in Ohio Stadium. His 74-year streak is strongly believed to be an all-time record among Ohio State fans. Crawford's string started at age 12 with OSU's 26-23 victory over Illinois on Nov. 13, 1943, and concluded with the Buckeyes' 30-27 double-overtime triumph over Michigan on Nov. 26, 2016.

Crawford was an Ohio State varsity cheerleader in 1953-54, and cheered the 1954 national champion Buckeyes to a 20-7 Rose Bowl victory over Southern California. Some of his favorite games included a 31-14 triumph over Wisconsin in 1954, a 13-0 shutout of No. 1 Purdue in 1968, and the Buckeyes' classic 14-9 victory over Michigan in 2002. In 1973, he married Harriet Romanoff who had four beautiful daughters — Karin, Julie, Laurie, and Lynn. Crawford often stated he married a whole family and considered his marriage the luckiest thing in his life. He worked in local television and theater at a young age, and later taught radio and television production classes at the Fort Hayes Career Academy in Columbus. Crawford passed away from a blood disorder at age 86 on Aug. 30, 2017.

John Crawford, Ohio State's all-time top fan at Ohio State-Indiana game Oct. 8, 2016. *Courtesy Jack Park*

BUCKEYE
REFLECTIONS

THE AUTHORS

Jack Park has presented his award-winning leadership development program, *The Leadership Secrets of Football's Master Coaches*, to clients in 47 different states. He has delivered more than 100 keynote addresses for Ohio State University Alumni Clubs in 19 different states. His Certified Speaking Professional designation, the CSP, has been granted to fewer than 19% of the 3,700 members of the National Speakers Association.

Jack is an Ohio State Football radio commentator each season for Sports Radio 97.1 The Fan. He is the author of *The Ohio State University Football Vault* and *The Official Ohio State Football Encyclopedia*.

Jack played football and basketball at New Lexington High School and has been honored with membership in the school's Athletic Hall of Fame. He writes a weekly football column for *The Columbus Dispatch*, and is featured frequently in football programming on ESPN, The Big Ten Network, and TWC.

Jack is a CPA. He received his MBA from The University of Pittsburgh and his BS from The Ohio State University. He is a member of The Football Writers Association of America and lives in Columbus, Ohio.

Maureen Zappala, a New York City native, is an award winning speaker, author and presentation skills coach. She has a BS in Mechanical Engineering from the University of Notre Dame and spent 13 years conducting jet propulsion research at the NASA Lewis Research Center (now the NASA Glenn Research Center) in Cleveland, Ohio. She became the youngest and first female manager of NASA's Propulsion Systems Laboratory.

She's the founder of High Altitude Strategies, a speaking and coaching organization where she works with high-performers who struggle with the "Impostor Syndrome," the internal voice that says "I'm not as smart as everyone thinks I am!"

In 2009, Maureen was in the top 10 of 30,000 contestants in the Toastmasters International World Champion of Public Speaking contest. She's the author of "Great Speakers are Not Born, They're Built" and "Over-Achiever, Under-Believer: How to Match Your Confidence to Your Competence" (to be released in 2018). She's a member of the National Speakers Association (NSA), and is the 2017-18 President of the NSA-Ohio chapter. Maureen lives in Medina, Ohio.

Other Resources by Jack Park

Keynote Presentations and Workshops

In this unique and entertaining presentation, Jack uses case studies of the greatest coaches such as Vince Lombardi, Bo Shembechler, Woody Hayes and Knute Rockne, to show how to develop leadership talent at every level.

Jack also speaks about the history of Ohio State football, the rivalry between OSU and Michigan, and other football related talks. For Jack's other programs, visit his website at www.jackpark.com

Books by Jack

The Ohio State University Football Vault is a distinctive scrapbook of Buckeye photos and memorabilia including program covers, tickets, and playbooks. This exceptional publication comes in a collector's box and is signed by the author. Foreword by Head Coach Jim Tressel and Afterword by two-time Heisman Trophy winner Archie Griffin.

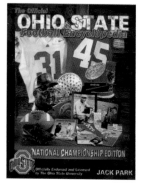

The Official Ohio State Football Encyclopedia describes the tradition and rich history of Ohio State football, and the coaches and players who made it happen. Includes the schedule and scores for each season, beginning with 1890. Foreword by ESPN's Kirk Herbstreit and Reflection by College Hall of Fame member Jim Houston.

Ohio State Football... The Great Tradition examines the tradition and storied history of Ohio State Football against each of the other Big Ten teams. Includes chapters highlighting non-conference and bowl games. Foreword by two-time Heisman Trophy winner Archie Griffin.

To inquire about these resources, or to hire Jack to speak at your event, contact him at 614-481-0214 or visit his website at www.jackpark.com

Other Resources by Maureen Zappala

Keynote Presentations and Workshops

Over-Achiever, Under-Believer:
How to Match Your Confidence to Your Competence

If you're a really successful professional, you may be familiar with the Impostor Syndrome. It's the chronic feeling you're not as talented as people think you are, and you feel like a fake. This presentation can set you free from that haunting fear.

Leadership is NOT Rocket Science

Discover a unique twist on leadership that can transform a technical expert into a managerial superstar. Learn to lead with authority, passion and confidence, so your teams will begin to explode with loyalty and camaraderie.

How to Add S.P.I.C.E. to Your Speeches!

In this workshop, you will learn the *Five Non-Negotiable-Must-Have-But-Often-Omitted-Game-Changing-And-Astoundingly-Simple Ingredients* that make every presentation an awesome experience.

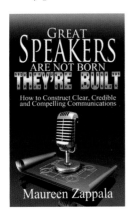

Great Speakers are Not Born. They're Built. How to Construct Clear, Credible and Compelling Communications. This book uncovers a simple systematic process to put you on the path to becoming an amazing presenter...no matter what presentations you make.

Maureen is also available for presentation skills coaching. To hire Maureen to speak at your event, contact her at 330-441-0722. To learn about her other resources visit her website at www.maureenz.com.

BUCKEYE
REFLECTIONS

LEGENDARY MOMENTS FROM
OHIO STATE FOOTBALL

Jack Park and Maureen Zappala

Introduction by Archie, Ray and Duncan Griffin
Foreword by Luke Fickell, Ryan Miller and Mike Vrabel

**Additional copies of Buckeye Reflections
can be obtained at:
BuckeyeReflectionsBook.com**